Blood from the Sky

Jeffersonian America

JAN ELLEN LEWIS, PETER S. ONUF,
AND ANDREW O'SHAUGHNESSY, EDITORS

Blood from the Sky

Miracles and Politics in the Early American Republic

ADAM JORTNER

University of Virginia Press

CHARLOTTESVILLE AND LONDON

University of Virginia Press
© 2017 by the Rector and Visitors of the University of Virginia
Printed in the United States of America on acid-free paper

First published 2017

ISBN 978-0-8139-3958-2 (cloth)
ISBN 978-0-8139-3959-9 (e-book)

9 8 7 6 5 4 3 2 1

Library of Congress Cataloging-in-Publication Data
is available from the Library of Congress.

Cover art: Engraving from *New Illustration of the Celestial Science of Astrology* by
Ebenezer Sibly, 1795. (L. Tom Perry Special Collections, Harold B. Lee Library,
Brigham Young University)

MONTICELLO

Publication of this volume has been supported
by the Thomas Jefferson Foundation

For Emily

The truth is, that the sense of the miraculous
has not declined, and never can.
—CHARLES UPHAM, *Salem Witchcraft*

John said to him, "Teacher, we saw someone
casting out demons in your name, and we tried to
stop him, because he was not following us."
—MARK 9:38

Contents

Preface

When *The City of God* spilled into its twenty-second book, Augustine realized he was running out of space. "What am I to do?" he asked. "I am constrained by my promise to complete this work, a promise which must be fulfilled; and that means that I cannot relate all the stories of miracles that I know." I know how he feels. I suspect most of us are grateful that *City of God* is no longer than it already is. I hope readers will feel similarly about this book.

I first began thinking about American miracles while reading the *Autobiography* of Charles Finney. Charles Finney met Jesus Christ on October 11, 1821. After a day of weeping and self-debasement, he stumbled upon his savior in the counsel room of his office. "I met Him face to face," Finney later recalled, "and saw Him as I would any other man." His friends found Finney hours later, weeping on the floor. "I am so happy," he said, "that I cannot live." Finney abandoned law for the ministry and became America's leading revivalist.

By coincidence (or providence, if you like), I came across Finney's conversion narrative a few hours after I had finished reading John Thayer's. Thayer—a Congregationalist minister traveling in Italy—experienced no such marvel as Finney but heard others confess their experience of the cures wrought through the Venerable Labre (whose miracles were just then abroad in Rome). Thayer investigated the witnesses and the evidence and became "fully convinced that the reality of each one of these miracles was at least as well proved as the most authentic facts." Thayer left his ancestral religion for Catholicism.

If America's paramount Protestant and a Roman Catholic convert both based their conversion on supernatural events, then it seemed to me that American historians needed to know more about the supernatural. I soon found out that Americanists know woefully little about this topic, perhaps because it sits uncomfortably with our notions of what Americans care about. ("Yankee supernaturalism, forsooth!" wrote John Greenleaf Whittier, imagining a New Englander's response to magic and miracles.) Yet there was a world of miracles and wonders in the early republic, perhaps not as wide as among the Puritans, but far broader and more intense than historians had previously imagined, and those miracles were caught up in ideas about fact, knowledge, liberty, and masculinity. It is this world I have tried to capture in this book, covering the first sixty years of American independence and conveniently bracketed by two major events regarding the supernatural: the Dark Day of 1780, which among other things brought the Shakers into public prominence, and the ejection of Mormons from Missouri in 1838, in part because of their presumed "supernaturalism." The disparate threads of the supernatural did not start or stop on those dates, so where necessary I have moved forward and backward for relevant evidence. What I have tried to capture, however, is how the late Enlightenment challenges to epistemology increased the theological and religious importance of miracles, and the subsequent effects this manner of thinking had on the origins of the American state, from the Revolution until the incarnation of the Second Party System. The book is not a complete account of these miracles, but it is an effort to sketch their history and suggest how we might profitably integrate this world into our current thinking about the early United States, its politics, and its religion—and especially the combination thereof.

As the project grew dizzyingly broad, my understanding of miracles and the supernatural became much more nuanced and extensive—so much so that, like Augustine, I was unable to fit in all the miracles I met in the course of my research. In the end, I needed to make some fine distinctions about the "miraculous" and the merely "marvelous," or between a "wonder-worker" and an "orthodox" Christian. I have tried to hew as closely as possible to the language of the time, although given the changing definition of the supernatural, a clear distinction was not always possible. As I discuss in the introduction and chapter 1, however, early republicans understood a difference between an interior and exterior supernatural. Misty mentalisms, prophesying, and dreams might *come* from God, but they were of a different order than angel visitations, the blind made to see, or golden plates dug out of the earth.

Excising the merely mental (for the most part) also means that many mystical experiences of the evangelical Christians—primarily Baptist, Methodist, and Presbyterian revivalists—do not appear in this volume. Such Christians claimed to be Spirit-filled and to have communications from heaven. When Finney met Christ, he noted that this experience was a "wholly *mental* state." Unusual or fantastic things that took place in the mind were different from those that could be physically proved—at least in the arguments of the day— and evangelicals overwhelmingly kept to this distinction. The distinction can be seen as somewhat arbitrary, and I have little doubt that the supernatural (and its political consequences) existed as a spectrum. I have here chosen to examine one part of that spectrum: the case for the physical supernatural—the miraculous in this world—that reshaped lives and upset the political order of republicanism, forcing legal and military solutions to theological conflicts. This end of the spectrum best demonstrates the problem of the supernatural in the early republic, and the quiet religious assumptions inherent to republicanism that nevertheless pervaded the early American state. And so Finney, for the most part, appears only as a cameo.

I have also largely avoided a few other beliefs and practices often labeled supernatural or "occult," but that I feel properly belong elsewhere. I do not here consider millennialism and prophecy (related fields of religious revolt in the early republic) or providentialism (Protestant ancestor of American religion). Prophecy certainly had supernatural origins but derived once again from thoughts and interpretation. Fulfillment of prophecy rarely broke natural laws. Millennialism—the effort to situate Christian thought and practice on the Second Coming and efforts to definitively date or explain that event—also did not involve the supernatural. Indeed, millennialism was a cornerstone of Christian practice, and classifying it as "occult" belief misrepresents Protestant theology.

Some readers asked pointed questions about this enterprise. One asked whether we could ever get away from truth claims—whether we can simply take an antirealist stance (as I do) and refuse to bother with any referential reality of particular claims. He mentioned Mormonism in particular, but he could have brought up any Western religion. In 2002, Gordon B. Hinckley, then-president of the LDS Church, elucidated the central status of historicity to Mormon faith: "We declare without equivocation that God the Father and His Son, the Lord Jesus Christ, appeared in person to the boy Joseph Smith. . . . It either occurred or it did not occur. If it did not, then this work is a fraud. If it did, then it is the most important and wonderful work under the heavens." Faithful Mormons—then and now—could be forgiven for a lack of patience regarding my attempt to discuss their miracles as part of a "debate." The physicality of the miracles—the referent, as I discuss in the introduction—is what matters.

Yet this work is a history of beliefs, and not a believing history. If a history of religion must account for what different people believe—and if we must reject the notion that "correct" ideas rise and "wrong" ideas fade—then the theological or ontological status of any particular miracle claim becomes irrelevant, from the broader standpoint of historiography. This book is about the defense of miracles; it is not in itself a defense of miracles.

Another reader had a more prosaic question: Was this project just an attempt to cash in on the endless fad for vampires, zombies, and all things magical? The current vogue for supernatural films and other media makes the question valid, though I suspect that fad will have begun to fade by the time this work sees print. I contend that what people believe about the invisible world tells us a great deal about what they do. The transformation of supernatural monsters into mass entertainment in the last decade (and the recurrent apocalypticism of much of that entertainment) reflects pervasive ideas in our own times about order, secrecy, and power—to say nothing of the political desire to cast the world into easily identifiable categories of good and evil. The ubiquity of vampire and zombie films is not mere entertainment but a significant piece of modern American life. So, too, with the misadventures of Moll Pitcher and treasure hunters, the witchcraft of Ann Charity, and the exorcisms of Shakers and Mormons in the Age of Jefferson. We have much to learn by reconstructing the invisible world.

In the course of my research I have logged many hours in the archives and accrued many debts both personal and scholarly. This project began under the guidance of Peter S. Onuf, whose endless patience and encouragement are legendary—as in, once you see them, you will be telling stories of awe about them for the rest of your life. I cannot overstate my debt to Peter, who was always willing to give me a little more rope, and then turned my noose into a net to catch worthwhile ideas. H. C. Erik Midelfort introduced me to the world of the Reformation and witchcraft, weathering hundreds of queries about historiography, witches, and wonders in the European context over the years. Without Peter and Erik, I would never have completed this work. (After reading the book, some of you may regret that. Be assured everything good here is to their credit; everything ill is my fault.)

In the ten years I have been working on this volume, numerous people read chapters or the complete draft. I am particularly grateful for the chance to present my work at the McNeil Center for Early American Studies, Southern Historical Association, Society for Historians of the Early American Republic, Early American Seminar at the University of Virginia, University of Tennessee Center for the Study of War, and Alabama Seminar on Early America. Colleagues who read chapters or drafts include Monica Black, Kathryn Braund, Owen Davies, Spencer Fluhman, Patrick Griffin, Laura Keenan-Spero, Roger D. Launius, Carol Medlicott, Ben Park, Daniel Richter, Christina Snyder, Patrick Spero, and Glendyne Wergland. Dick Holway and the entire staff at the University of Virginia Press endured many versions of this text and numerous missed deadlines on my part. Dick is a wonderful and very patient editor. Susan Murray's copyediting saved me from many errors for which, in a more just world, I would have been held accountable. I am grateful to my colleagues on the history faculty at Auburn University. It is possible, I suppose, to find another department in America as amiable, brilliant, and supportive, but such things are about as rare as a rain of frogs.

Financial support for the project was provided by the Charlotte Newcombe Dissertation Fellowship and the McNeil Center for Early American Studies, where I spent the 2007–8 academic year—an intellectual experience I treasure. I also received funding from the American Antiquarian Society, Massachusetts Historical Society, Maine Historical Society, Kentucky Historical Society, Lilly Library of Indiana University, and Charles Redd Center for Western Studies at Brigham Young University. I am grateful to the tireless and thoughtful staffs at the Ralph Brown Draughon Library at Auburn, the Alderman Library at the University of Virginia, the Rush Rhees Library at the University of Rochester, the Quaker and Special Collections Department at Haverford College, the Marriott Library at the University of Utah, the New Hampshire Historical Society, the Alabama Department of Archives and History, the Family History Library of the Church of Jesus Christ of Latter-day Saints, the Winterthur Library and Gardens, and the Sabbathday Lake Shaker Library.

My greatest thanks go to my family. Charles and Sam are not yet old enough to read this book, but Charles has occasionally taken books down from shelf and run over to me, saying, "Let's play going to work!" Then he sits and flips through the book, intoning words only he knows to let us know he is hard at work. I am utterly in love with the two of them, and their mother, too. This book would not have been possible without Emily's continual support, encouragement, and love. This book is dedicated to her; she is something of a miracle herself.

Blood from the Sky

Introduction

History, Reality, and Miracles

It rained blood in Ohio in 1804. A few miles from the Turtle Creek Meeting House where Richard McNemar nursed the northern edge of the Cane Ridge revivals, there came one summer day "an extraordinary shower of blood . . . traces of which are preserved to this day." Writing several years later, Mc-Nemar likened the event to the biblical prophecy of Joel: "I will show wonders in heaven above, and signs in the earth beneath, blood and fire and vapors of smoke." Combined with the astonishing worship exercises of the revival ("shouting, jerking, barking, or rolling"), McNemar believed the blood was meant "to show where God was about to open his everlasting kingdom of righteousness."[1]

Americans of the early republic lived in a world of miraculous reports and supernatural adventures, backed with the language of facticity and sense evidence. Those miracles and reports helped create the political, ideological, and religious world of the Age of Jefferson. The most prominent of these events are well known: the return of the Christ Spirit in Ann Lee and her Shakers; the divine protection and miracles of Tenskwatawa, Hillis Hadjo, and other Native American prophets; the resurrection of Jemima Wilkinson as the genderless Public Universal Friend; the presence of the "necromancer" Gullah Jack Pritchard in the 1822 Denmark Vesey conspiracy; the golden bible of Joseph Smith Jr.

These infamous events, however, coexisted with a host of lesser-known visitations—miracles, wonders, magic—which John Greenleaf Whittier dubbed *supernaturalism:* "the unearthly and the superhuman bursting up through the thin crust of convention and common-place existence."[2] Solomon Bayley escaped from slavery when a supernatural flock of birds made him invisible to slave catchers.[3] A Carolina mob rounded up a handful of suspected witches and tortured them to break their spells.[4] In 1816, Jacob Cochran claimed to have all the powers of the apostles. Ann Mattingly, of Washington, DC, was twice healed when she appealed in prayer to the mysterious Prince Hohenlohe, an ocean and a continent away. In 1782, William Plumer encountered a woman who "began to shake and tremble astonishingly. She told me this was not a voluntary motion, but that she was acted upon by a supernatural impulse." When he asked if anyone might hold her while she trembled, "She said it would be a blasphemy against God to attempt such a thing."[5] Thomas Tawlman was Maine's greatest preacher—but only when he was asleep. "When the Lord first called him to preach, he could not read," wrote his fellow minister John Colby, "and on that account, he refused." God apparently had other ideas: "Upon his refusal, he immediately began to preach in his sleep, in the dead of night; and often talked so loud, as to waken all the people in the house. He said he continued in this way, about six months; and then consented to obey the Lord."[6] Another rain of blood drenched South Carolina in 1841, this time complete with physical debris, "the appearance of flesh . . . very red, and some what transparent when held up toward the light."[7] A mystical turnip—covered in occult sigils—appeared in Stratford, Connecticut, in 1850.[8]

This book is about miracles, wonders, and other supernatural events in the early republic: what people believed, how they discussed, debated, and shared those beliefs, and most importantly, what they did about them as a result. It is not a book about whether such things were or were not literally true. My concern is with McNemar's claims and interpretations of the rain of blood, not with the nature or plausibility of the "traces . . . preserved to this day."

The subject matter is voluminous, pertaining to (in the early republic) the expected realms of theology, ecclesiology, and philosophy but also to the more surprising realms of law, literature, music, manners, folklore, and— most ominously—politics and the military. It is a comparative history, with investigation directed both at general beliefs in the supernatural as well as specific sectarian groups that emerged based on modern miracles. Such an approach better captures the nature of the debate and the contours of miracle belief than a study limited to one particular denomination or region.[9]

The problem with writing a history of miracles and the supernatural, as Stuart Clark put it, is that the primary sources "appear to have been radically incorrect about what could happen in the real world." Clark wrote in the field of witchcraft historiography, wherein strange events—diabolical festivals with the devil, birds' nests filled with human genitals, blue-tinted flatulence, etc.—appear with unsettling regularity in the treatises and court records of the great European witch hunts, 1400–1800. The long-standing response of historiography, as Clark pointed out, was to assume that those Europeans who reported witchcraft had somehow managed to get the world objectively wrong. If people reported flying on broomsticks or having sex with demons, and if, by all accounts, people cannot actually fly on broomsticks or copulate with demons, then those who recorded such experiences must have been making a category mistake. Explaining witchcraft, therefore, became a task of explaining *why* people made that mistake. Clark contended that witchcraft beliefs have therefore "either been dismissed out of hand as mistaken and, hence, irrational, or . . . explained away as the secondary consequences of some genuinely real and determining condition . . . some set of circumstances (social, political, economic, biological, psychic, or whatever) that was objectively real in itself but gave rise to objectively false beliefs." Something *else*, often something measurable, was the real engine of change.[10]

Clark (and others) took the linguistic turn as a way out. If the language of historical subjects appears not to match reality, that is not an indication of madness or error on the part of the subject—particularly if language constructs reality rather than reflects it. If language is at all times a coherent system unto itself, then what historians are looking for is the presence or absence of categories by which people constructed their world and lived in it. Social, political, economic, and other factors then become aspects of beliefs about witchcraft—or miracles, or angels, or ghosts—rather than the determinants of those beliefs.[11]

Clark advocated an antirealist approach to counteract the realist assumptions of witchcraft historiography; rather than spill more ink in search of finer definitions of these well-worn terms, I will simply borrow Clark's. Realist approaches assume that "a mistaken belief cries out for an account of why it continued to be held despite its falseness, other than because it was believed in; while explaining a belief away depends, logically if not actually, on a prior decision that it was incapable of self-support in terms of its reference to something real."[12] Antirealism prefers to avoid the "referential truth or falsity" of beliefs in the supernatural, "other than as, themselves, subjects of debate" in a particular time and place. The historian's task regarding witchcraft is to understand its meaning in context and its capacity to inspire actions.[13]

These are not novel observations, nor is the corresponding caution that assuming language to be solely constitutive of larger forces reduces all intellectual discourse to "mere power plays," in the words of one scholar. Yet historians of early national religion have tended to treat skepticism and rationality as transhistorical terms rather than seeing all of these ideas as embedded in a single debate in the Age of Jefferson.[14] Historiography remains haunted by earlier social science models that saw the rise of industrialization and the end of witchcraft trials in western Europe as a coordinated social process rather than a historicized development.[15]

Yet such an apparently secular approach ironically leads us out of history and into theology. If we assume that exorcisms cannot happen because demons do not exist, then we must also assume that any reported exorcism in the historical record *did not* happen, because exorcism *cannot* happen. Yet such thinking amounts to a theological argument: an explanation of historical events by way of an assertion about the invisible world. We are compelled to assent to a theological argument as the price of historical explanation. Even worse, we are compelled to assume that our subjects either lied or made an enormous epistemological error, and the process of historical reconstruction becomes one of explaining that error, either as insanity, delusion, false consciousness, or some other notion that assures modern readers that *we* know what they were doing even if they did not.

This work, therefore, is intended as a gesture toward an antirealist history of American miracles. Despite calls to "take religion seriously," the field is still concerned with referents and not thought. Useful protests have been raised; when David Holland notes that American religious history tends to be sociological rather than ideational, he is in some ways making an antirealist plea.[16] Whatever sympathy it may bring to its subjects, American historiography still generally treats the supernatural as something that must be argued around or explained in naturalistic terms. Supernatural events are "ethnographic oddities," in Monica Black's critique, "things you might see in a museum, not valid historical artifacts." Black summarizes the prevailing historiographical suspicion that demon possession, visitation by gods, or conversations with the dead seem "not just anomalous or flamboyant, or deeply at odds with a certain normative conception of modernity—though they are indeed all of these things. They are also somehow wrong."[17] If language itself does not necessarily refer to exterior realities, as Clark argues, then we do not have to concern ourselves with the ultimate truth or falsehood of those beliefs—whether or not Tenskwatawa really caused an eclipse or whether Joseph Smith Jr. truly cast out a demon.[18] Rather, the historical focus should be on what kinds of decisions about reality people made, and the effects of their decisions to believe or disbelieve in certain supernatural phenomena. At some level, we must believe that our subjects meant what they said. "The process of conversion," as Ramsey MacMullen has written about the primitive Christian church, "took place in people's minds on the basis of what they knew, or thought they knew. It is useless in the process to consider all the things that we know."[19]

The realist predilection takes many forms in the historiography of the early republic. Often economic concerns explain supernatural events. The poor have the supernatural because they are poor; the wealthy have education instead. The supernatural requires a reason—a referent—and so poverty causes people to believe in miracles; they do not believe because they find the case compelling. One study assigns the hundreds of angel visitations reported by Elizabeth Babcock to "a process of accommodation by which traditional religious beliefs and practices were reconciled to the new, competitive social and economic climate of postrevolutionary America."[20] In the eighteenth century, one historian concludes, "Humbler folk were largely unaffected by these new intellectual currents and continued to see the world as an enchanted place."[21] Jon Butler contends that the supernatural did not decline so much as it "became confined to poorer, more marginal segments of early American society."[22] Alternatively, Butler suggests that magic and "the occult" became "folklorized," which again suggests a division between knowledge possessed by "the people" and the elites.[23] John Demos argues that eighteenth-century "persons of more than average education and wealth composed an advance guard of skeptics," while the poor failed to catch on because they possessed less "access to the advanced learning of the day." If they had possessed the learning, they would have been skeptics. Skepticism in this formulation occurs automatically once certain books have been read. Yet as Wolfgang Behringer points out, it is not the presence or absence of skepticism that creates a culture of skepticism.[24]

Then there is the attempt to explain the upwelling of supernatural beliefs by assigning them to specific sects or ethnic groups. Realist logic explains that group by reference to its supernaturalism, providing reasons why Mormons or Shakers or Native American prophets would see angels or report healings, when (in theory) no one else did or could. This particularist strain defines miracles as bizarre, irrational, or otherwise beyond a purported mainstream; belief in such miracles or supernaturalism is then taken as the defining characteristic of the group. They are outside the mainstream because they are participants in a broad epistemological error (or vice versa), and the group—

rather than their belief—is explained.[25] In this way, Catholic historiography explains Catholic miracle claims as a means to crafting American Catholic identity. Native American prophets and angel visitations in the early republic have long been explained as an effort by which Indians "established their boundaries and strengthened their cultural reintegration" rather than as the playing out of divergent ideas about supernatural power. Similar efforts have been made to explain Shaker and Mormon identity through Shaker and Mormon miracles.[26]

Writing separate historiographies of the supernatural for separate American communities prompted Douglas Winiarski's criticism that American historiography has only taken magic seriously when it is practiced by minority populations.[27] Magic (and by extension, the supernatural) becomes a means of resistance ("at odds with a certain normative conception of modernity") which once again makes Enlightenment rationalism that normative (white) experience. This formulation leads to a distressing tendency to read African American or Native American witchcraft as culture, but to interpret white American witchcraft as ignorance.[28] Dividing up magic by groups also obscures the broader concepts of the supernatural that crossed communities and shaped the American idea of the invisible world. It also risks isolating "skepticism" to white communities. Some of the most stinging antebellum criticisms about magic came from African American narratives. Henry Bibb "fully tested" the magical roots and powders he received from conjure doctors and found to his sorrow "there is no virtue at all in it"; magic existed only as "vain imagination."[29] In My Bondage and My Freedom, Frederick Douglass referred to magical notions as "very absurd and ridiculous, if not positively sinful. . . . I had a positive aversion to all pretenders to 'divination.'"[30] Jacob Stroyer, enslaved at the Kensington Plantation in South Carolina, saw a witch who rode human beings like horses at night. But when he told his father, Stroyer got a whipping, for "father having been born in Africa, did not believe in such things."[31]

The pervasiveness of American supernatural claims undermines this particularist argument, which relies on an exclusivity of miracles to one group and implicitly seeks real referents to explain apparently nonsensical claims. Take the case of angels. Leigh Eric Schmidt writes that in the early republic, "talking to angels carried a steep price." From this assumption, Schmidt dismisses both the importance and continuation of the supernatural. Other scholars have written that "speaking with angels" was deeply abnormal, "pathologized" by medical opinion. Such comments impart a dominance to the rationalist critique of angel visitations and imply that angelic visitations were both unheard of and unconvincing in the early republic.[32]

Neither is true. There were at least six well-known angelic visitations in the United States between 1776 and 1830, when the more fecund Mormon angels gained public notoriety. Each visitation has received scholarly treatment as an individual case, abstracted as it were from its fellow angels. Of course, the problem might have been that the angels were denominational; in each case, the angelic appearances provided a supernatural confirmation of religious belief—several different religious beliefs, as it turned out.[33]

Caleb Rich encountered "a person, or the likeness of one . . . with a bible in his hand" in April 1778. This angel sermonized on the biblical truth of universal salvation, then vanished. Rich joined the Universalists.[34] In Appalachia, Adam Livingston applied to a Catholic priest to exorcise his haunted house, and once the ritual was completed, an angel appeared, "and staid with them three days and nights, & instructed them in all points of Religion."[35] Livingston became a Catholic. The Seneca Prophet and the Delaware holy woman Beata each encountered angelic beings between 1799 and 1806. The Prophet referred to angels who invested him with supernatural powers when he met with President Jefferson in 1802.[36] Elizabeth Babcock received 235 angelic visitations between 1806 and 1811. She and her husband broke with the Freewill Baptists, forming a new church based on the primacy and authority of direct contact with God through angels. Similarly blessed with manifold angelic visits were the Shakers, whose sojourn in America quickly turned biblical: when the sect settled in Ashfield, Massachusetts, the town became the battleground where "Michael and his angels fought against the dragon and his angels." The battle could be heard for seven miles, according to the 1816 *Testimonies of the Ever Blessed Mother Ann Lee.*[37]

Thus, by the time Joseph Smith had his first visit from the angel Moroni (traditionally dated to 1823), angels had already visited Universalists, Catholics, Native American prophets, Freewill Baptists, and Shakers—and those are simply the angelic visits whose subjects did not claim to be dreaming. If we include all those who saw angels in a mental state only, the list gets much longer: Jemima Wilkinson visited heaven in 1776; John Colby took the same trip in 1815. Polly Davis was instantly healed when an angel appeared to her in 1792. Angels guided Sarah Alley from heaven into hell in 1798. A Vermonter named Bullard dreamed an angel warned him of the approach of bears. Julia Foote saw an angel with a scroll who commanded her to become a preacher. Abel Sarjent built his Halcyon Church in Ohio in part based on angelic communication. Angelic power was proclaimed in the printed works of American magic; in Johann Georg Hohman's *Long-Lost Friend* (German version 1820, English version 1844), angels gave their power to treasure diggers and water witchers. Chloe Russel's *Complete Fortune Teller and Dream Book* (1824) advised that when an angel appeared in a dream, "the rest of your dreams shall prove true."[38] This supernatural ubiquity, more than anything else, suggests an underexplored aspect in American historiography.

And, of course, angels continued to visit America after 1830. They frequented Mormon meetings, preachings, and temple endowments, sometimes with and sometimes without the approval of official church authorities. Upon the death of Joseph Smith in 1844, an angel came to James Jesse Strang and anointed him with oil; Strang used this visitation (in part) as the basis of his own church. The angel Al'sign te're Jah' appeared at the Shaker community in New Lebanon, New York, in 1842, part of a surfeit of angels crisscrossing the Shaker villages from the 1830s to the 1850s. The Spiritualists who materialized in the 1840s received word about the activities of celestial beings in heaven from dead souls reporting from the undiscovered country. As with angels, so, too, with the profusion of healings, exorcisms, magic, and other miraculous and supernatural events that occurred throughout the early republican period: they kept breaking through the thin crust of commonplace existence.

Questions of miracle, magic, and the supernatural are not questions with which Americanists typically deal. American historians have relied almost solely on Keith Thomas's *Religion and the Decline of Magic* and its correlation between the decline of magic and the dawn of modernity to establish the supernatural context of the early republic, favoring Thomas's work often to the literal exclusion of others.[39] Yet in the last fifteen years, the study of the so-called "decline" of witchcraft across the West has received much more attention in European historiography. Séances in London, miraculous cures at Lourdes, and angels in Sweden suggest that supernaturalism remained a going concern in the later Enlightenment and early Industrial Age.[40] Recent studies on this period in England, Scotland, France, Sweden, and elsewhere, taking folklore and newspapers as source materials in lieu of trial records, now speak of a "transformation" of supernatural beliefs rather than a decline.[41] As Owen Davies has written, supernatural beliefs may decline, but they do not all decline simultaneously. After all, in 1795 Maine, Paul Coffin worried about "witchcraft in plenty" but laughed off belief in ghosts.[42]

Thinking about transformation rather than decline may help explain why supernatural religious beliefs functioned perfectly well in revolutionary Jeffersonian America, and how, despite a vigorous campaign waged against them through culture, law, and force, these beliefs survived and even thrived. Some Americans found the supernatural—and miracles in particular—convincing for the same reason that other Americans found them to be foolish: the arguments through which they were presented were consonant with what was broadly accepted as reasonable at that time and in that place. The notion that skepticism itself brought about a decline of magic is as insupportable as the notion that tradition is the opposite of skepticism. Indeed, the language of skepticism, in the early republic, could be turned to the defense of supernatural events themselves. In his essay on the Cane Ridge revivals, Adam Rankin used David Hume (by name) to argue for a real diabolism in Kentucky. Rankin agreed with Hume that no miraculous account could be credited unless its falsehood would be more miraculous than its veracity. Rankin assumed that only Christ and the apostles met this criteria, and therefore, when other unusual events occurred, they must be lying wonders and "of Satanical influence."[43]

American historians also seem to have mistaken the *decline* of magic for the *cessation* of magic. There is no doubt that the "world of wonders," as David Hall described colonial New England, was not the same world encountered by revolutionary Americans. Yet rarity does not imply marginality. Indeed, miracles and other supernatural events in some ways became more important in the early republic precisely *because* they were comparatively uncommon. Supernatural events that occurred once in a lifetime might seem more momentous than those that occurred yearly or fortnightly. A decline of magic may have made the supernatural *more* significant in the early republic—so it should be a critical topic for scholarly discussion.[44]

Therefore, this book is to some extent an effort at historical reclamation. Our knowledge of the early republican supernatural is incomplete. My intention is to bring into focus the strange and the heteroclite in order to demonstrate that, when strung together, they possessed a coherency that shaped American experience, religion, and politics. The supernatural was not mundane or common, but its continued presence amid the theological and political debates over its real or unreal existence would have been familiar in Jeffersonian America—an enigma familiar then but of which only vestiges survive today. It was not a world of wonders, but it was a world that wondered about wonders, and that wondering was pasted onto the theological and political crises that shook American religious structures as miracles emerged again and again in the new republic.[45]

Those wonderings were firmly grounded in the same Enlightenment discourses that gave rise to American revolutionary ideology. Those who performed and those who denied miracles both borrowed the language of natural philosophy and appealed to similar forms of authority. When wonder-workers called themselves rational and discussed the nature and persuasiveness of miracles, they inserted themselves into a Common-Sense Enlightenment dialogue and expected to be taken seriously at all levels of discourse, from high to low. *They* saw themselves as gathering evidence, thinking through interpretative schemes, and challenging a too-rigid orthodoxy overly committed to tradition. The idea of a straightforward progression that continually increased the difficulty for proving miracles from the New Testament era to modern times is an illusion. As R. M. Burns notes, the idea that skepticism about miracles grows in relation to scientific attitudes "is not confirmed by the actual facts about the debate."[46]

Indeed, the debate on miracles turned on "facts" and the nature of facticity as a means of establishing proof. The cultural cachet of the "fact" as an idea—separated from theory and pre-extant in the world—had long been germinating in Anglo-American culture.[47] American miracles took up the language of facticity. Stephen Post arrived in the Mormon enclave of Kirtland, Ohio, in November 1835: "I had not been here long before I heard the gift of tongues manifested," and though "many had told me that the gifts were not in the church . . . now it was confirmed to me by testimony that would not be resisted without going in the face of intelligence."[48] Post became a faithful Mormon. The Congregationalist minister John Thayer traveled to Rome in the 1790s with "a formal disbelief of the miraculous facts which are said to have happened" in the city, which had recently seen a rash of miracles attributed to the deceased mendicant Benedict Joseph Labre. Thayer "thought that it was my duty to examine the matter myself." Upon conducting interviews and investigations, he found these miracles were as "well proved as the most authentic facts." He returned to Boston and publicly "declared that I had more proofs of the truth of his [Labre's] miracles, than I would require for any fact whatsoever."[49] Thayer became a Catholic, and his account of his conversion based on miraculous testimony went through twenty-two printings.

So ingrained was the requirement for sensory evidence that numerous wonder-workers could only express their experience through the figure of Doubting Thomas. In the New Testament, the apostle Thomas would not believe in Christ's resurrection until he actually touched the savior's wounds.

So, too, when Isaac Post wrote in 1848 about his experience with the Spiritualists: "I suppose I went with as much unbelief as Thomas felt when he was introduced to Jesus after he had ascended."[50] Post later became a medium. Abigail Crosman felt "like Thomas" and "could not believe without evidence palpable to the physical senses." When she received such signs from the Shakers, her faith in them was confirmed.[51] In the Book of Mormon's 3 Nephi, Thomas's experience was extended to every single person in the New World: "And it came to pass that the multitude went forth, and thrust their hands into his sides, and did feel the prints of the nails in his hands and feet . . . going forth one by one, until they all had gone forth, and did see with their eyes, and did feel with their hands, and did know of a surety, and did bear record, that it was he."[52] Wonder-workers made their case in keeping with the general intellectual climate of the early United States; given the increased confidence in the reliability of the senses and the American reliance on individual experience, it was probably *easier* to prove a miracle in 1830 than in 1430. Thus it may well have been—as H. C. Erik Midelfort wrote of Germany in the same period—that the "best arguments were on the side of the exorcists."[53]

The persistence and success of the exorcists should obviate any lingering doubts that the supernatural is antithetical to modernity because modernity has no supernatural. If we also reject the notion that the exorcists and miracle workers merely committed category mistakes that must be explained by something other than belief, what we are left with is a diachronic debate about the nature of nature, supernature, and rationality. Concepts such as "miracle," "supernatural," "credulity," and "superstition" were themselves terms in that debate. And once that debate is analyzed as a debate, some very interesting political implications emerge. Cries of imposture and credulity—when denuded of any requirement to have a real referent—suggest the troubled intellectual relationship of rationality, belief, and democracy. This language in turn reflects back on the ongoing debates about the role of religion in early American political life, and the place of "coercion" and toleration within it. In this way, thinking about miracles as beliefs clarifies important political and historical questions about the "religious" nature of the American Founding and the American republic.[54]

Here again Clark's work on early modern Europe presages the political underpinnings of magic and the supernatural in the early republic. The demonologies that formed the bulk of the printed discourse on witchcraft in the early modern era almost invariably included a plea for action by the state.

Supernatural witchcraft *required* state action because it represented a threat to order and to the public, argued the theorists. Demonologies were therefore concerned not just with witches and their actions but also with the broader idea of *communitas*. "In addressing magistrates," Clark writes, "they committed themselves to views about authority and about the general desirability of certain forms of rulership." Demonologies reinforced the emerging divine right monarchies, and for good reason: those ordained by God to establish order and the true church were the logical choice to eliminate the persistent satanic conspiracies at work in the world. Witches and demons "became the perfect antagonists of those who claimed power by divine right, since their defeat could result only from supernatural, not physical authority." If the duly constituted authority could prosecute and execute witches, and thereby vanquish satanic plots within their borders—a task in which witch trials invariably succeeded—then that authority proved itself to be of God and, hence, justified in its claim to the adherence of the people. Other supernatural acts accompanied divine right kingship; the Stuart kings, especially Charles II, repeatedly invoked the power of the king's touch—the divine gift that allowed the rightful monarch to cure scrofula. Charles's repeated touches (and the subsequent cures reported) supernaturally confirmed him the rightful monarch. Witch trials were not a by-product of divine right theories, but a central premise. The politics of early modern Europe possessed an inherent supernatural dimension.[55]

If divine right monarchs required witchcraft as their sinister antithesis, then undermining witchcraft also undermined divine right. English royalists certainly conflated opposition to the rightful king with skepticism about witchcraft; Nathaniel Bernard in 1644 was one of several royalist divines to attack those who "maintaine, That there are no Witches in the World," and, citing 1 Samuel 15:23, urged his listeners to "take heed of Rebellion, *which is as the sinne of witch-craft.*"[56] At the same time, as Brian Levack notes, "royalist professions of hatred for revolution and rebellion created a public mood, at least in some communities, that was especially conducive to witch hunting."[57]

Thus it fell to the Whigs, the *philosophes,* and other opponents of the monarchy to undermine witchcraft, demonology, and, more broadly, supernaturalism. The English Whig Francis Hutchinson wrote his 1718 *Historical Essay Concerning Witchcraft* in part to suggest that "these Doctrines have often been made Party-Causes both in our own and other Nations. One side lays hold of them as Arguments of greater *Faith* and *Orthodoxy*," and "sometimes Governments are shaken, if they oppose their Notions."[58]

Across the Channel, Bernard le Bovier de Fontenelle rejected demonism as an explanation for ancient oracles and instead suggested the oracles were the tools of impostors out for mere power. The parallel to his own France was clear. The American Revolutionaries became heirs to this intellectual tradition regarding the supernatural.[59]

Dispossession was a republican activity as well as a monarchical one, the difference being that republicans needed to dispossess the state (and populace) of the idea of the supernatural itself. God certainly existed, of course, but he did not interfere in the natural world or human affairs beyond a mild sort of providence. It was *fear* of magic, witchcraft, and divine visitation that represented a threat to order and a danger to the citizenry. State and society needed to be cleansed of such notions—and of those who proclaimed and practiced them. When New York's Frederick Quitman, author of the 1810 *Treatise on Magic*, purchased a purported magical charm and found it to be nothing more than an scrap of paper with the Latin endings for pluperfect verbs, he sternly declared that "Government ought to stop such fatal practices, whereby the lives of many are put in jeopardy." After all, it was "the sacred duty of those, who are appointed guardians and teachers of the people . . . to deliver those that were entrusted to my care, from the shameful yoke of superstition, and to help them to the enjoyment of rational liberty." The Congregationalist divine Joseph Lathrop agreed: "Hearkening to diviners tends, not only to destroy religion, but to dissolve our mutual confidence and subvert our social security. . . . On social, therefore, as well as on religious principles, these diviners ought to be prosecuted rather than encouraged—to be punished rather than patronized." Demonology *itself* was the problem.[60]

Early republican invective against the supernatural did not merely hold that those who claimed wonders were *mistaken;* instead, they argued that all such efforts were deliberate lies, intended as a gaff to hook the credulous and simple-minded. David Hudson attacked Jemima Wilkinson's "impositions which she attempted to practice in working miracles, healing the sick, and raising the dead." Hudson went on to explain that once such miracles—and the Wilkinsonianism they implied—were accepted, autocracy followed: "So strong [was] the delusion which she had already fastened upon her too credulous people, that few of her devoted followers dared to disobey her unhallowed mandates."[61] One of the first extended reports on the Nat Turner rebellion insisted that "*General Nat* . . . like a Roman Sybil, he traced his divination in characters of blood, on leaves alone in the woods; he would arrange them in some conspicuous place, have a dream telling him of the circumstance," and by such measures, "acquired an immense influence" over "some ignorant black[s]."[62] Numerous such allegations stuck to Joseph Smith Jr., and to Mormonism—"a deep laid scheme . . . designed to allure the credulous and the unsuspecting, into a state of unqualified vassalage," according to one newspaper.[63]

The concept of "civilization" occupied a critical place in the case against supernaturalism. Antisupernatural writings assumed that women, African Americans, and Indians were all more prone to the corrupting influence of supernatural belief. Quitman's *Treatise* mocked superstition as a characteristic of "toothless old women, that vegitate rather than breathe" and "Laplanders, who have scarcely as much sense as the reindeer," not to mention "gypsies, strollers, jugglers, quacks, and ragamuffins."[64] William Bentley's 1799 assessment of the 1692 Salem witch trials was a typical rationalist Jeffersonian critique of the supernatural. Salem fell, Bentley explained, because judges listened to people who were not white men: "Children, below twelve years of age, obtained a hearing before magistrates. Indians came and related their own knowledge of invisible beings. Tender females told of every fright, but not one man of reputation ventured to offer a single report."[65] Ideas about rationalism were bound to ideas about race, gender, citizenship—and superstition.

There was, therefore, a kind of religious cast to the statecraft of the early republic. A republican people needed to ground their choices on reason; anyone who could not base decisions on that ground was dangerous. Republicans also believed in a class of "impostors" who deliberately attempted to defraud or mislead the public into making bad decisions. In supernatural matters, the unwitting accomplices of the impostor were the "superstitious" and the "credulous"—those who believed or could be persuaded to believe in the powers beyond the natural operating in the world. "The superstitious man is to the rogue what the slave is to the tyrant," Voltaire wrote.[66] And so, in an ideal republic, Voltaire explained, "the magistrates will stop the superstition of the people from being dangerous. These magistrates' example will not enlighten the mob, but the principal persons of the middle-classes will hold the mob in check." In the United States, the minister and politician Charles Upham insisted, a republican citizen must "do what he may to enlighten, rectify, and control public sentiment . . . to accelerate the decay of superstition, to prevent an unrestrained exercise of imagination."[67] The mystical element of American politics lived in the effort to rid the state of the supernatural.

This religious aspect of the early republic was therefore of a very different order and complexity than is captured in popular twenty-first-century debates over whether America was founded as a "Christian nation."[68] Republicanism assumed that Americans (or at least American citizens, that is, white men) would possess a religious perspective that would not countenance superstition and credulity and would assume a rationalized (Christian) attitude toward the state. These notions were a critical component of the concept of civic virtue so often discussed in the early republic. Questions of religious coercion in the early republic need to be read in light of these considerations; there were religious beliefs—that is, beliefs about the supernatural world and humanity's obligations and powers therein—that were beyond the ken of republicanism as it was understood in the eighteenth and early nineteenth centuries. Those views had to be opposed at best and silenced at worst.[69]

These ideas about liberty and rationality explain the persistent violence that followed wonder-workers. Mobs and militias chased Mormons, Shakers, and Native American prophets across (and in some cases, out of) the new nation. Such efforts change supernaturalism from mere "ethnographic oddities" into a persistent part of the early American experience, as individuals, civic groups, churches, and governments in republican states sought to expose and expel religious practice that they dubbed "superstitious," "fanatical," or "credulous." Indeed, the United States twice went to war with wonder-workers—the followers of Tenskwatawa and the Red Sticks—between 1811 and 1814.[70] Secularism was not denuded of religious concerns, after all.

These attitudes about power, miracles, and magic explain why, for example, Luman Walter of New Hampshire was imprisoned in 1818 for "imposing himself on the credulity of the people in this vicinity, by pretended knowledge of magic, palmistry, conjuration, &c." Walter escaped from his cell to practice conjuration in New York—which likewise banned "all jugglers [conjurers], and all persons pretending to have skill in physiognomy, palmistry, or like crafty science, or pretending to tell fortunes." Similar laws existed in Connecticut, Massachusetts, New Jersey, and Maryland.[71]

But why should New Hampshire care about fortune-telling? What interest did the state have in policing a service exchanged for money in a free capitalist marketplace? The answer lies in the question of supernatural legitimacy; a state that had divested itself of a church needed to demonstrate that supernatural powers could not exist, because of course the state itself could not offer any. The republican state was supernaturally powerless, and hence anyone who claimed direct divine interference (and hence preference) in human affairs was in some way challenging the state. Relegating religion to the private sphere (in most respects) meant that the state could tolerate a great many kinds of religious belief—but not those that hearkened back to monarchism. An enormous swath of treatises, sermons, histories, tracts, and plays emerged in the early republic claiming that any form of supernaturalism—even divination and treasure digging—had the touch of autocracy, and needed correction.

When miracle-mongers established their own towns and polities or raised arms to defend their claims, the rhetoric of antisupernaturalism often translated into violence. If supernaturalism threatened republicanism, then republicans needed to get rid of it. James Smith incited a mob against the Ohio Shakers, claiming that the United Believers intended to "destroy marriage and also our present free government" because "theirs is a despotic monarchy."[72] When the Gentile residents of Jackson County demanded an end to Mormon settlement there, they justified their demand by noting that if Mormons "continue to increase they would soon have all the offices in the county in their hands; and that the lives and property of the other citizens would be insecure, under the administration of men who are so ignorant and superstitious as to believe that they have been the subjects of miraculous and supernatural cures." Liberty and supernaturalism were incompatible.[73]

Miracles wielded authority amid a crisis in authority in the early United States. If new miracles demanded obedience, then the supposedly wise vox populi would *lose* that obedience. The threat of miracles was the threat of an independent faction, a state within a state, an *imperium in imperio*—and that prompted a political crisis, again and again. Miracles were not just a matter of personal belief; they could be parlayed into a different form of *communitas* and a variation on republicanism. Supernatural belief poisoned republican minds; and some worried that such excess "threatens to drown this commonwealth in a deluge of anarchy and confusion."[74]

So the state acted to eradicate them. Militia forces sacked Prophetstown in 1811 and again in 1812. Holy Ground was destroyed soon after, and Andrew Jackson told his men that by killing Creeks, they would "undeceive" the prophets. "They must be made to know that their prophets are impostors," he wrote.[75] Laws specifically targeting Shakers passed in several states. Legal action scuttled Jacob Cochran's incipient wonder-working church in Maine. South Carolina courts singled out Jack Pritchard—who crafted magical charms for the 1822 Denmark Vesey conspiracy—for special opprobrium in sentencing; Pritchard "endeavored to enlist on your behalf, all the powers of darkness, and employed for that purpose, the most disgusting mummery and superstition." South Carolina executed Pritchard.[76] As the Mormons surrendered to the Missouri militia in 1839, Gen. John B. Clark claimed his intent was "to break that chain of superstition, and liberate you from the fetters of fanaticism."[77]

This long-term war over religion and the supernatural formed a fundamental piece of the American religious firmament and represented a working out of the ideas of liberty and representative government rarely explored in American historiography. It suggests that the place of religion in the political structure of the early U.S. state was far more subtle and diffuse—but perhaps more abiding—than the usual church-state questions asked about the Founding (which tend to focus on questions of the personal faith of individual Founders, the suppression of fast days, and the presumed Jeffersonianism of Connecticut Baptists). Religious notions were not merely affected by political order in the United States; they were in some respects constitutive of it—not in the form of any particular religion or confession but as a presumption of how the natural and the supernatural world worked.

This political disposition did not stop the wonder-workers, of course; nor did the belief in wonders and miracles easily break down into categories where antirepublicans believed in miracles and republicans did not—except, of course, in the texts of the antisupernatural writers of the time. Indeed, the conflict about miracles seeped into numerous and diverse areas of early republican life precisely because it was a struggle over ideas. Reconstructing that debate is possible only through a broadly comparative and antirealist approach, seeking parallels over multiple traditions. We must also assume that terms like "superstitious" and "credulous" did not require referents in the real world; they, too, were terms in a debate. Only then can we read magic and miracle back into the early republic, and therefore—without the necessity of explaining it away as a mistake—understand its role in the American Founding and, perhaps, the American Founding's role in magic and miracle.

The approach therefore is twofold: an analysis of the structure of the antebellum supernatural, and a study of its most prominent practitioners. Chapter 1 examines the theological, philosophical, and scientific shifts in the concepts of nature and the supernatural in the seventeenth and eighteenth centuries. It is an attempt, following Jane Shaw's and Alexandra Walsham's work on British history, to jettison the Americanist historiographical assumption of a "cessation" of miracles as the traditional Protestant approach. Chapter 2 reconstructs the practice of magic, witchcraft, and treasure seeking in the early republic—taking these beliefs as case studies for the host of early republican supernatural beliefs (in angels, demons, curses, etc.) that did not rise to the level of organized religions. Chapter 3 examines the broad case against the supernatural—the "demonologies" of the early republic—in both the formal treatises as well as in literature, theater, sermons, and broadsides.

The second section examines the sectarian results of American miracles by looking at several cases in which supernatural claims blossomed into new religious movements. These chapters investigate these beliefs in the context of religious and political debate: How did believers justify their miracles, what did those miracles require of them, and what did nonbelievers try to do about it? It focuses on the denominations for whom extensive documentation has survived: Shakers, Native American prophets, and Mormons. Several smaller supernaturalist sects that never developed a sustained following—Wilkinsonians, Cochranites, Osgoodites, and Babcockists—get a chapter as well. In context, each of these "sects that weren't" must be considered as a potential Latter-day Saint movement—one that could have, given different circumstances, survived into a worldwide church of millions.

Focusing on the wonder-working sects may prompt the question, "Were these people not just peculiar outliers in an otherwise 'normal' society?"—the same one posed to Monica Black in her study of faith healings and exorcisms in the divided Germany of the 1950s. Black sympathizes with the scholarly impulse to bypass supernatural events, to "exile them because they do not fit within a secular or rationalist frame." But Black has a better question: "What indeed was normal in the context of post-1945 West Germany?"[78]

The same should be asked of the early republic. The early republic re-worked, rethought, and resurrected all manner of social and political structures: constitutions, family structures, slavery, law, economics. "The world that is on the rise remains half buried beneath the debris of the world that is in collapse," wrote Alexis de Tocqueville, and "no one can say what will remain of old institutions and ancient mores and what will ultimately disappear."[79] As the world turned upside down around the newly independent Americans, some of them began to believe that God had once again begun to speak to them, and validated his presence with tongues, angels, and exorcisms. Others heard those arguments and sought to silence them for the good of the republic. The early republic was a world on fire with wonders and searching for answers, some of which fell from the skies and "traces of which are preserved to this day."

PART I

The Supernatural World

ONE

The Language of the Supernatural

"In every point of view in which those things called miracles can be placed and considered," wrote Thomas Paine, "the reality of them is improbable, and their existence unnecessary." A moral principle, to Paine, was true whether it came with miracles or not; indeed, since miracles were harder to accept than moral principles, adding the former to the latter made it *less* likely that hearers would become believers. But it was no mere moral system that Ezra Stiles and other clerics defended through recourse to godly intervention: "Jesus X and his apostles spoke Infallibility. This is proved by their Miracles."[1]

It is not surprising that Paine and Stiles took opposite views of religion; the shared assumption in their arguments, however, is more significant. Stiles took miracles as an uncomplicated proof of the supernatural origin of Christianity. Paine pulled at the thread of miracles for the same reason: if miracles could be disproved, religion would vanish with them—and good riddance, in his mind. The orthodox sage and the goading atheist both agreed that miracles made Christianity.

Miracles and the supernatural had become an incontrovertible test in the early republic—an all-or-nothing proposition about the truth of any particular religious claim. By 1858, Horace Bushnell classified three distinct schools of thought concerning the miraculous, namely, the parties of discontinuance, restoration, and denial: those who claimed that miracles had ended with the closing of the canon, those who claimed they still occurred, and those who claimed they had never occurred.[2] For all three, however, the question of miracles was central to the question of religion itself.

Miracles had not always been so crucial to Christian theology; like all aspects of Christian belief, the place of miracles changed over the centuries. By the end of the eighteenth century, miracles shone brightly in the

Protestant firmament. The same Baconianism and Scottish Common-Sense philosophy in vogue in early America (a consequence of a long Anglophone debate and new American realities) made the "facts" of Christianity central to religious interpretation in the early republic. Miracles became the ultimate facts—obvious violations in the natural world that justified supernatural claims. Christianity was true because of its evidences—documented miracles and other supernatural events. Many American apologists limited miracles to the apostolic age—where biblical texts provided sure warrant for Christ's miracles. Yet in making evidences central to Christianity, Anglo-American theologians provided the ideological origins of a new age of miracles. This move toward moderate empiricism—informed by the rise of legal skepticism, the end of state-sponsored witch trials, and the shift of natural philosophy away from the preternatural—inadvertently opened the door for new miracle reports to receive a thorough consideration in Jeffersonian America. The evidentialist turn—itself a historical development—made validating new miracles *easier*.

Miracles, as Paine observed, were easy to recognize: "Mankind has conceived to themselves certain laws, by which what they call nature is supposed to act; and that a miracle is something contrary to the operation and effect of those laws." Paine took this definition as a starting point: the supernatural took place in this world but did not obey the known laws of this world. That notion was held alike by the party of discontinuance, the party of restoration, and the party of denial: if it was supernatural, it had a physical existence. Things that could take place in the mind alone, even when placed there by God, fell outside this definition. To be supernatural, the world and not the mind had to change.

Orthodox divines like Timothy Dwight told parishioners that *only* in the apostolic age had such things happened, and modern "pretensions to miraculous powers" could only provoke "in most men of sober thought, indignation and contempt." Nevertheless, miracles *had* been given to the apostles, "to prove them inspired with a knowledge of the divine will."[3] Even if they had only occurred in ancient Judea, they gave the divine stamp to Jesus's teachings. The miracles of Christ moved to become the validating proofs of Christ's mission. Christianity was true because of its miracles.

That had not always been the case. Questions as to the purpose of and penchant for miracles in Christian theology and practice began within the Christian scriptures themselves. Early Christian writings suggest that distinguishing between true and false miracles—and assessing the authority of the miracle worker—caused headaches even for the apostles. In the Book of Acts, Simon Magus performs wonders and miracles through pagan gods. Simon earns Peter's censure by offering to pay for the power to work healing miracles.[4] In the apocryphal Acts of Peter, Simon and Peter produce dueling miracles; Simon's magics slay several children, whom Peter then miraculously raises from the dead.[5] The differences between true miracles and delusive magic were serious matters for the early Christian church. Peter needed to remind his listeners at Pentecost that the miracles of the disciples were not alcohol-induced hazes: "These are not drunk, as you suppose, for it is only nine o'clock in the morning."[6]

Similar questions dogged the Church Fathers and their successors; even Augustine was of two minds on miracles. The bishop of Hippo recorded more than seventy miracles in two years after the bones of St. Stephen were moved to his North African diocese, and argued in *City of God* that the presence of miracles among Christian communities proved that God remained with them even though Rome had fallen.[7] In an exposition on Jonah (and elsewhere), he had more cautious words, for "the pagans spread word of many of their miracles without any reliable source, even though demons, do some things like what angels do, not in reality, but in appearance."[8] Critics of the miraculous accounts of St. Martin of Tours wondered why, if he could repulse flames and raise the dead, had he also gotten a bad burn? Adam, biographer of Hugh of Lincoln, believed the holy intestines of the saint's corpse were miraculously free of wastes, a trait other observers ascribed to dysentery. Nevertheless, miracles were commonly cited as proofs of God's presence and employed as agents in the evangelization of pagan regions.[9]

Over the course of the Middle Ages, church officials developed increasingly rigorous standards of judgment for miracles. In the thirteenth century, Innocent III, Thomas Aquinas, and Caesarius of Heisterbach crafted ecclesiastical warnings about accepting reports of miracles at face value. The problem was again one of invisible agents; Christian thinkers knew angels and demons could affect the physical world, and mistaking a diabolical act for a divine one worried the theologians. Innocent III warned that "evidence of miracles . . . is on occasions misleading and deceptive, as in the case of magicians." By the end of the thirteenth century, under rules inspired by Aquinas and Caesarius, miracles alone could not prove the case for a saint's canonization, and a vigorous inquisition was established to test claims of saintly miracles.[10] Proving a miracle in 1300 was no matter of mere popular belief; doubt was not an invention of the Enlightenment.

The Protestant Reformation is usually credited with ending miracles for at least part of Christendom. Historiography has often interpreted the Reformation as a kind of ironic doorway to secular modernity. With the end of a wonder-working church, Protestants could in theory begin to cull other forms of supernaturalism. Most works on the Anglophone supernatural begin with the Protestant doctrine of the cessation of miracles. Yet this doctrine, to paraphrase the historian Jane Shaw, is both overemphasized and understudied. As a Reformation Protestant ideal, the cessation of miracles served an important rhetorical purpose. Reformers insisted that miracles were necessary proofs of God's mission only in biblical times—unnecessary after the establishment of the church. This interpretation possessed a confessional advantage: if miracles had ceased, Catholic supernaturalism was a sign their church was false.

That doctrine, however, was not a static prologue or unchanging "tradition" from which American religion emerged; even if the white-hot Calvinists of the sixteenth century passionately believed that miracles had ended centuries beforehand, their descendants had their doubts. As Alexandra Walsham points out, English Calvinists did not look for miracles, but they were perfectly happy to accept wonders and prodigies as evidence of God's direct interference on behalf of his chosen church. Wonders were explicable events—the collapse of a floor, defeat in battle—which could be tied to the desires of God. Prodigies, on the other hand, were unusual happenings in the natural world—apparitions in the sky, monstrous births, multiple suns. Wonders and prodigies could be interpreted as portents: divine warnings or messages for the mortal world. God would no longer violate the laws of nature that he himself created, but he would allow extremely unusual things to happen that could indicate his will.

Protestants in England and the colonies sometimes missed the distinction; they still saw miracles even when their pastors told them not to. Jane Shaw points to the increase of "perfectly Protestant" miracle claims in late seventeenth- and early eighteenth-century Britain. English Baptists made claims to divine healings, adhering to a literal reading of James 5 and other texts. Quakerism—at home and in the colonies—famously based its religious appeal on the "inner light," and followers often fell into visionary trances and reported miraculous healings. The Quaker founder, George Fox, had numerous forays into the supernatural—so much so that he was once accused of being enchanted.[11] In New England, leaders sometimes had to remind the rank-and-file that miracles had ceased; John Richardson assured his militia in

1679 that "God works now by men and means, not by miracles." Nevertheless, Increase Mather explained that some events in New England were indeed "of a miraculous nature." He had seen wondrous cures and understood angels to have visited the earth. His son Cotton even *saw* an angel in 1693.[12]

The Mathers' best-known encounter with the supernatural came in 1692, and it points to another region of the supernatural that remained a going concern even among the supposedly disenchanted Protestants of the seventeenth century—witchcraft. The doctrine of cessation of miracles said nothing about the power of witches. Major witch hunts broke out in England in 1612 and 1645, and in Scotland in 1590, 1649, and 1661. Meanwhile, in the New England colonies, more than 150 accusations led to more than twenty executions—*before* the excesses of Salem 1692 added many more. In the wake of Salem, legal caution and reform ended many of the trials—but not belief. Ten years after being accused of witchcraft in Salem, Abigail Faulkner was still trying to remove the stigma of witchcraft from her name. Grace Sherwood was sentenced (though not executed) for witchcraft in 1706 Virginia; witchcraft was suspected but not prosecuted in Pennsylvania in 1701 and Massachusetts in 1720.[13]

Many scholars now suggest that legal skepticism, rather than theological doubts about the supernatural powers of demons, brought the witch trials to their slow end. "The men responsible for stopping the trials took action . . . because the crime could not be proved in law, not because the crime was impossible to perform," according to the historian Brian Levack. In the Basque territories of Spain, for example, the inquisitor Alonso de Salazar Frías could not understand why, if so many witnesses confessed to witchcraft, he could not find a shred of physical evidence.[14] Salazar believed in witchcraft but not in hearsay. He proposed a new series of evidentiary rules to govern witch trials, and his recommendations became law in 1614. In New England, the minister John Higginson (and others) claimed that witchcraft was a real phenomenon, "one of the most awful and tremendous Judgments of God that can be visited on the Societies of men," but nevertheless questioned "whether some of the Laws, Customs, and Principles used by the Judges and the Juries in the Trials of Witches . . . were not insufficient and unsafe."[15] In Scotland, George Mackenzie's theories about the inadmissibility of accusations by other accused witches found codification in the proclamation of April 1662, a legal reform that increased the number of dismissals and acquittals in witchcraft cases while reducing the incidence of legal torture. A similar correspondence between legal reform and the reduction of witch trials occurred in northern France (1624), Italy (1655), Sweden (1676), England (1736), and Hungary (1750).[16]

Legal rather than intellectual skepticism as the end of the witchcraft trials suggests a profound problem for assuming a generalized decline in supernatural belief in the West. In Scotland, England, and the colonies, ending witchcraft prosecutions did not end belief in supernatural activities. Neither the Reformation nor the end of the trials had banished the supernatural; they had only altered the kind of supernatural beliefs operating in the Anglophone world. Assumptions of secularization may be misplaced; even if other supernatural beliefs had atrophied, miracles remained a going concern in Christian theology during the Enlightenment.

In a sense, it was not the supernatural that was in trouble in the seventeenth and eighteenth centuries; it was the preternatural. Early modern Christianity followed Aristotelian classifications in creating a tripartite division of worldly events, rather than bifurcating between natural and supernatural. *Natural* events could occur always or most of the time. *Supernatural* events violated natural laws and were performed directly by God. *Preternatural* events consisted of "unusual occurrences that nonetheless depended on secondary causes alone and required no suspension of God's ordinary providence," as the historians Lorraine Daston and Katherine Park phrase it.[17] The supernatural had direct messages from God, but the preternatural was less dogmatic; it might come "to rouze and awaken the Reason of Men . . . and wind up their Reasons a little higher," as one seventeenth-century writer put it.[18] The term derived from Aquinas's concept of *prater naturae ordinem,* objects and events "above the order of nature." These were astonishing events in the natural world that did not quite qualify as a miraculous suspension of the natural order. Prodigies fell under this category, and if a miraculous event was "nature conquer'd," wrote the Cambridge scholar John Spencer in 1663, then a prodigy was "nature disturb'd and hinder'd."[19] Rains of blood, monstrous births, and armies in the sky were often classified as preternatural. Determining what was preternatural in late medieval and early modern Christendom could be tricky, for as Aquinas noted, an observer who knew more about how the natural world functioned would see fewer *preter*natural occurrences, while an ignorant observer would see more. Yet the preternatural proved useful for theologians and philosophers; theologians did not need to show that *every* aberration in nature came from heaven itself, and natural philosophers did not have to show that every aberration subscribed to regular laws.[20]

Then came the Protestants and their supposed "cessation" of miracles, and the preternatural quickly provided the signs Protestants so coveted to match Catholic miracle claims. Protestant thinkers quickly annexed Roman Catholic classifications developed from Aquinas. If, as post-Reformation theology taught, "nothing could happen in this world without God's permission," then every event had some divine purpose.[21] The more unusual the event, the more dire the message—and some events were quite unusual. In 1597, a "straunge and wonderfull herring" covered in glowing hieroglyphs was pulled from the Norwegian Sea; in 1600, a Marian judge who had condemned Protestants to death fell from his horse, "his braines straingely coming forth" from his mouth and nose. It rained wheat in Brotherton in 1648.[22] This surfeit of seventeenth-century prodigies may have emerged to take the place of miracles.

For English Protestants, preternatural events made for a nebulous theoretical territory; despite the Protestant ban on divination, they were still divined. In New England, the Mathers made ample use of such wonders; Cotton and Increase both compiled lists of wonders "above and beyond the Constituted order of nature" that proved God's watchfulness over New England, but that were, of course, not godless Catholic miracles.[23] Cotton Mather cited events such as a woman's tongue "drawn out of her mouth to an extraordinary length," stones thrown by invisible demons, and "a beast, which brought forth a creature, which might pretend to something of a human shape." (Interpretation of this marvel led to Mather's obtaining a man's confession of bestiality.)[24]

Yet most Protestants also understood that preternatural wonders could be caused by spirits or demons. Caution was paramount, for the merely preternatural might not come from God. In 1684, Increase Mather noted "things lately happening in New-England, which were undoubtedly praeternatural, and not without Diabolical operation." A man from Hartford, Mather wrote, was walloped by clods of earth and cobs of corn falling from the sky, chimney, and windows. Meanwhile in Newbery, Massachusetts, William Morse faced similar falling objects, as well as dancing furniture, self-locking doors, and "a great Hog in the house," who appeared one night while all the doors were shut. "It is sport to the Devils," Mather explained, "when they see silly Men thus deluded and made fools of by them."[25] Mather also claimed the preternatural could reverse diabolic power, as in a story related about a Frenchman who had bartered his soul to the devil and, upon regretting the transaction, appealed to Huguenot ministers for aid. The ministers fasted and prayed in the field where the bargain was signed, until a cloud appeared "and out of it the very contract signed with the poor creatures Blood dropped down amongst them." They tore up the contract, and God's grace was glorified.[26]

As interpretations of portents increased, of course, so did the need to distinguish true portents from false—to avoid the false miracles of witches, demons, and magicians (or simple human error). Protestant theologians also had to step carefully—asserting the facts and reliable witnesses of the Bible as self-evident truths (and therefore needing no Catholic magisterium). At the same, Protestants had to avoid taking every modern witness to the fantastical as doctrinaire. (Therefore, no "prodigy monger," wrote Spencer, could be relied on.)[27] Spencer and other English writers began to interpret preternatural wonders as merely natural, so as to protect themselves simultaneously from diabolism and Catholicism. Theologians began to "discredit preternatural phenomena as true signs from on high; they were rather to be rejected as forgeries from below."[28] Meanwhile, searching for a means to shatter Aristotelian syllogism, Francis Bacon alighted on wonders. These "errors" of nature broadened the range of experiences he felt it was necessary for science to explain; they were counterexamples to foil Aristotle's love for example followed by generalization. Monstrous births and groaning trees were "handpicked for their recalcitrance." In Bacon's logic, "the bizarre, the heteroclite, and the singular" disproved all conclusions based on everyday experiences; they were, in short, pieces of information without a theory.[29] To avoid a false wonder, Anglophone thinkers subjoined the preternatural to the natural.

This turn of events did not herald the rise of materialism or scientific thinking but of British probabilism. Unlike their Cartesian opponents—who claimed that real knowledge needed to be proven beyond all doubt—the probabilists preferred knowledge that was only quite likely proven.[30] This tactic made for shaky epistemology but solid theology; Joseph Glanvill, Robert Boyle, and others wrote works in the late 1600s that established a "moderate empiricist" view of miracles and the supernatural. If enough evidence could be marshaled, a miracle could be accepted.[31] Locke's *Discourse on Miracles* (1701) took a similar route, claiming that the religion with the most impressive miracles was the true religion: "Whenever there is an opposition, and two pretending to be sent from heaven clash, the signs, which carry with them the evident marks of a greater power, will always be certain and unquestionable evidence."[32] God would not, Locke argued, allow a lying wonder to appear more marvelous than a true one.[33] Signs and natural facts could be examined and compared, and the more wonderful, the more true.

In theory, Locke's work (and others like it) attempted to bulwark Protestant Christianity against an impossibility of miracles on the one hand and too many miracles on the other. Theorizing on witchcraft, angelic visitations, and resurrection was not merely an effort to work out epistemology; it had concrete religious concerns. As Thomas Sherlock wrote in his faux courtroom drama *The Tryal of the Witnesses of the Resurrection of Jesus* (1729, American editions 1754, 1788, 1800, 1804, 1808, and 1809), "every Imposter" could offer "ridiculous Pretensions" as signs of divine warrant; if so, then the danger existed that observers might accept such actions (enthusiasm) or reject all claims to supernatural warrant (atheism). Sherlock set his debate up as a legal battle and had the proponent of the resurrection prove the miracle as solidly "as a Fact which happened but last year." Insisting on the reality of miracles but requiring "more evidence in these than in other cases" was the middle way of Sherlock and many others.[34] By forcing miracle-mongers to prove their cases with clear sense evidence, natural philosophers and orthodox divines thought they had created a strong case. Jesus Christ, with his public miracles performed and attested to by reliable witnesses, had sure supernatural miracles. Modern wonder-workers had only preternatural suppositions and wonders—not real miracles at all.[35]

But it all began to go wrong: naturalizing the preternatural opened a door to those who would ask whether Christ himself had such evidences for his own miracles. And if Jesus Christ could not muster the evidence, who could? Rev. Thomas Woolston wrote his *Discourses* between 1727 and 1729 to argue against a supernatural justification for Christianity: "The literal history of many of the miracles of Jesus, as recorded by the Evangelists, does imply Absurdities, Improbabilities, and Incredibilities." A reader might mistake Christ for a mere "*Conjuror,* a *Sorcerer,* and a *Wizard.*" David Hume's "On Miracles" in 1748 admitted that witnesses *could* report phenomena accurately but also assumed the basic supposition that better evidence was needed for stranger phenomena. By extension, the amount of evidence needed to prove something as strange as an outright violation of the common course of nature was so great as to be impossible: "No testimony for any kind of miracle can ever possibly amount to a probability." Hume's arguments were only a little more radical than those of a forgotten phalanx of like-minded writers who more formally embraced deism in the face of orthodoxy. Thomas Chubb's 1741 treatise pointed out that most miracles did not come with the testimony of witnesses, but only of witnesses of witnesses, and hence were not valid. Woolston thought the true character of Christ needed no such capricious miracles. A symbolic reading of the gospels, for Woolston and other thinkers, made for better sense and a better religion. Woolston's *Discourses* sold in the thousands, prompting numerous responses by evidentialists.[36]

The empiricist cause was further damaged when some of the eighteenth-century miracle claims of Britain were unmasked as forgeries—such as the Cock Lane ghost and Mary Toft's claim to have given birth to rabbits. Moderate empiricists clumsily had to deny that Toft's miracles were faked but Christ's were real. Indeed, at the time Hume was writing, reports filtered in concerning the Jansenist miracles in eighteenth-century France—better attested and verified, Hume argued, than the miracles of the New Testament. By Hume's logic, if evidence proved miracles, the Jansenists had miracles. Since the Jansenists did not have miracles, neither did Christ. Thus, as the historian Roy Porter writes, the Jansenists became "a free gift to Enlightenment critics in their challenge to the supernatural."[37] Though a multiplicity of voices sounded in Britain, it appeared that the evidentiary proof of miracles had faded as the preferred theological and intellectual general line.[38]

In America, however, the response followed a different trajectory. Hume failed to catch on, and the arguments of Hume's fellow countryman Thomas Reid took root. Reid's bailiwick was Scottish Common-Sense philosophy (also called the Realist school), for which the problem of miracles depended not on the *amount* of evidence but on its *kind*. Reid's philosophy rejected the separation between belief and knowledge. Hume had maintained that beliefs were developed from knowledge; sense data provided the knowledge, and at some point, the observer needed to assent to the belief that the data had been provided accurately. That belief, Hume argued, could never truly be justified. Reid, on the other hand, claimed that beliefs about sense data were an inherent part of the sensory experience; to see something *was* to believe that one sees something: "*judgment* or *belief* is not got by comparing ideas, it is included in the very nature of perception." A human being perceiving a thing in the world (Reid's example was a tree) believes the tree to be real by the act of seeing rather than as a separate cognitive act. Since the connection between feeling and perceiving was common to all humanity, it was "common sense."[39]

Reid's argument returned the problem of natural evidences to the thing observed rather than questioning the observer. In so doing, it restored the thought and methodology of Francis Bacon. Indeed, Reid and his fellows intensified Baconianism—turning the preference of Bacon for facts and observations into a single-minded insistence on facts and a corresponding

disdain for interpretations not based on sense evidence and experimentation.[40] Since observation *must* be trusted, Reid and his descendants would
put trust in observers.[41]

It was this notion of cognition, epistemology, and science that would come
to dominate the American scene; the early United States was an intellectual
redoubt for Scottish Common-Sense and its nouveau Baconian fanaticism.
Scottish Common-Sense formed the basis of the curriculum at Harvard, Yale,
and Princeton.[42] In U.S. colleges of the 1820s, American-made texts of the
Scottish Realist school replaced eighteenth-century works more critical of
human faculties. Edward Hitchcock of Amherst College explained in 1845
that "the inductive principle, as developed by Bacon, forms the basis on
which to build the whole fabric of natural religion."[43] Edward Everett's *North
American Review* proclaimed in 1823, "At the present day, as is well known,
the Baconian philosophy has become synonymous with the *true* philosophy."[44]

Hume, by contrast, fared poorly. He was the object of ridicule at Yale's 1797
commencement; at William and Mary, Thomas Dew informed students that
"the Humes and Voltaires have been vanquished from the field."[45] In 1843, a
North Carolina newspaper blamed the Scotsman for turning his mother into
an infidel and then letting her die alone.[46] A Massachusetts country doctor
expressed his disapproval in longhand: "Hume contradicts himself. Back-
wards and forwards."[47] Indeed, Hume had taken so much abuse at American
hands that another *North American Review* article opened by explaining that
there was little point in reviewing "Hume's famous argument against the
credibility of miracles" since it had been "so often exposed and confuted . . .
by all persons, in fact, whose skeptical ingenuity does not transcend their
sober judgment."[48]

The rejection of Hume's variant of skepticism and the wholesale adoption
of Reid's vogue for Baconianism remade American natural philosophy into a
search for *facts* as discrete, reliable units from which tentative decisions might
be drawn.[49] Theories and hypotheses became less creditable; facts drawn
from firsthand experience (carefully tested, of course) served as a basis for
religious and protoscientific thinking. Such data would then compete against
one another in what Benjamin Smith Barton called a "democracy of facts,"
and the truth would out accordingly. Barton himself "fought for facts" in
his 1796 investigation of rattlesnake fascination, gathering firsthand reports
and interviewing men who had put snakes' head in their mouths to sense
noxious vapors. As far as Barton was concerned, these kinds of "new and
interesting facts" disproved the notion; "mere force of argument," he wrote,

"never compelled me to believe.[50] The *fact* became the culturally accepted form of truth—unproblematic and trustworthy. In postrevolutionary America, *facts* ruled all. Indeed, Noah Webster defined *fact* as "Reality; truth; as, *in fact*," and by writing that "witnesses are introduced into a court to prove a *fact*."[51]

Those witnesses also rose in the estimation of thinkers seeking to establish the groundwork for religious and philosophical conclusions. Samuel Stanhope Smith (one of Princeton's Common-Sense men), like others before, sought to refute Hume through the allegory of "the king of Siam"; the tropical monarch supposedly refused to believe a Dutch traveler who reported that at cold temperatures, water became solid and held "horses and carriages upon its surface." Therefore, "Miracles, then, as well as other extraordinary facts in nature, are susceptible of proof from testimony." Smith got in an extra dig: "No experiment," he wrote, "could possibly be applied" to such circumstances.[52]

Witnesses therefore mattered, but they had to be trustworthy. Thus, the moral character of the witness became part of the debate over what the witness had reported. John Neal, for example, gave credence to his mother's encounter with a ghost, for "she was quite remarkable for downright commonsense, without a glimmer of imagination." Her "cautiousness and conscientiousness, and her calm, cool judgment" made her a believable witness.[53] American Methodists defended John Wesley's ghost-belief by emphasizing the reliability of witnesses. The *Methodist Magazine and Quarterly Review* responded to an attack on Wesley's ghost belief by stressing Wesley's proofs: "He gathered up facts from the lips of others" and "submitted it to the decision of fact."[54] Similar tests of witnesses confirmed the presence of ghosts for the émigré Russian priest Dmitri Gallitzin, who investigated a haunting and exorcism in western Virginia. "No lawyer in a court of justice," Gallitzin wrote, "did ever examine or cross examine witnesses more strictly than I did all those I could procure," and though he arrived in 1797 "to investigate these extraordinary facts" with a skeptical attitude, "I WAS SOON CONVERTED TO A FULL BELIEF of them."[55]

Testimony, not tests, proved facts. Archibald Alexander of Princeton argued that "any fact which would be believed on the evidence of the senses, may be reasonably believed on sufficient testimony." James Carnahan preached that a miracle "would be as capable of being proved by testimony, as that the French conquered the Russians in the battle of Austerlitz."[56] A. H. Lawrence argued that natural causes and the ordinary course of nature could not be used as a basis for judging singularities—which, after all, was what miracles were.

Paine wanted to know whether it was "more probable that nature should go out of her course, or that a man should tell a lie?" But this supposition was sometimes reversed in the early American republic, with proponents of the supernatural claiming that if a credible witness of good character did not lie, then whatever he attested to—even a miracle—must be the truth. John Leland proved biblical miracles in just such a way: "The gospel was written by good men; if so, they spake the truth, for a liar is not a good man."[57]

Americans argued that skepticism had gone too far; if no amount of testimony could prove a miracle, Neal wrote, then observers' skepticism could even deny things that truly do exist. Neal asked whether his readers should not equally condemn "the poor child who thinks a juggler eats fire when he does not, as of the grown-up sage who thinks a juggler does *not* swallow a sword when he *does?*"[58] (Fire-eating is a stage illusion, but sword-swallowing is literal—it is *possible,* though not recommended, to shove a piece of metal down the esophagus without harm.) Here the absence of a preternatural pushed the debate into a dualism that meant that *when* something unusual did occur—a rain of blood, or the shudders and shakes of a man in a revival, or the discovery of golden plates within the earth—the debate could turn on whether or not the witness was reliable. And if the witness was not lying, then there was no alternative but to embrace the event as a miracle. In this sense, it may have actually been intellectually *easier* to accept a miracle in the nineteenth-century United States than in sixteenth-century Europe.

John Greenleaf Whittier, for example, did not believe the dead could return, but as he wrote: "What will that avail with the man who has actually seen a ghost? Fact before philosophy always. If a man is *certain* he has seen the thing, there is an end of the matter."[59] When the ex-slave William Grimes explained his belief in ghosts, he applied exactly that logic in determining that his master's house "is what people in general would call haunted." He had seen a staring set of yellow eyes in the dark, confirming similar sightings by other slaves on the plantation. "These stories, combined with what I myself saw, warranted me in my opinion to make this assertion," he wrote.[60] The New England folklorist and an ex-slave reflecting on the same ideas about evidence, proof, and the supernatural suggests how widely such ideas about what could be reasonably believed circulated in the early republic.

By making miracles the central validation of religious truth and trusting witnesses to report phenomena accurately, the American religious imagination had arrived at a place where many new miracles (and other supernatural activity) could establish themselves, therefore appearing to be a renewal of sacred power after a long gap of divine disinterest. If "the New Testament is true, because miracles were wrought," claimed the Mormon apologist Parley Pratt, then Mormons could claim "more than *sixty thousand* who have seen miracles wrought with their own eyes."[61] When Ann Mattingly was miraculously cured of cancer, a series of depositions was printed to confirm that she had truly been healed. These testimonies lingered on details such as the size and hardness of the tumor, Mattingly's invalid state, her "constant spitting and puking of blood, and fetid matter," and the fact that immediately after "her recovery she ate a hearty breakfast." Chief Justice John Marshall was even called in to take the deposition.[62] Yet *The Washington Miracle Refuted* tried to debunk Mattingly's claims by contesting those same facts and asserting that sense evidence did *not* show the cure to be miraculous. The "Friend to Truth" wondered why it took Catholics two months to gather those affidavits if the event was "strangely *evident to the senses*"? And of course facticity was also the mainstay of those still investigating peculiar phenomena; D. M. Dewey reported on the Hydesville rappings in 1850 by writing, "Whether proved to be the work of human agency or of disembodied spirits, it is . . . important to spread the facts before the community."[63]

Clear witnesses and sense evidence needed something else, too: a violation of natural laws. Though some thinkers insisted that regular natural laws were miraculous in themselves (Emerson, for example, called the regular working of natural laws "the miracles such as I know, such as my eyes and ears daily show me"), most American intellectuals expected something spectacular. "What is a miracle?" asked Samuel Stanhope Smith. "It is such an inversion, or suspension of the ordinary laws of nature as can be reasonably ascribed only to him by whom those laws were originally ordained. And whenever he condescends to work a miracle, the operation of his almighty power must be regarded, by every rational mind, as the sanction and seal of truth." Carnahan preached that "a miracle is a suspension or alteration of some established law of nature." Charles Finney defined "miracle" as "divine interference, setting aside or suspending the laws of nature." Tunis Wortman in 1800 defined the Genesis flood ("an extraordinary miracle") as "one of those stupendous acts of power which the Deity upon peculiar occasions performs for the wisest purposes. . . . Could it have been accounted for from universal laws, it would no longer have been miraculous." Adam Rankin concurred in a long treatise regarding angels and demons; he defined miracle as "a sensible deviation from the known laws of nature," and ipso facto, "every contradiction to this constitution of the natural system, and the correspondent course of events in it, is called a *miracle*."[64]

But what constituted a law of nature? The vanishing preternatural had in theory made the natural world observable and regular. If so, then things that appeared to violate that regularity (what might once have been preternatural) could be promoted to the supernatural—indeed, to a miracle. Moreover, given that the preternatural might cover the simply unusual (a rain of frogs, for example, or a monstrous birth), then items that had once been merely unusual now became supernatural. Numerous events that might have been dubbed preternatural (spontaneous healings, tongues-speaking, and visions, for example) came to be called "miracles" by the language of the time.[65] Ethan Allen's deist opus, *Reason the Only Oracle of Man*, explained that everything must be either "natural or supernatural, as there is no third way or medium between these two," and consequently Allen pointed to and ridiculed those who "thought . . . miraculous" such things as "Comets, earthquakes, volcanoes and northern lights."[66] Allen's mere complaint, however, suggests that such things really were "thought . . . miraculous" by some in the early republic—or at least, that the merely unusual might be callously classed with the supernatural to make a theological point. Similarly, Charles Finney had to remind a collection of ministers that a revival "is not a miracle. . . . All the laws of matter and mind remain in force. They are neither suspended nor set aside in a revival"; apparently some in the Finneyite camp termed their revivals miracles.[67] When Rachel Lucas recovered from years of illness in 1806, she felt herself grow cold, then experienced "a believing view of the angelic throng." Rev. Ebenezer Washburn confirmed this "miracle of healing," although no natural laws had theoretically been broken.[68] The Baptist minister Elias Lee had similar difficulties in determining what to call the healing of Martha Howel in 1808 but eventually decided to "let it be considered a miracle."[69] Horace Bushnell, writing in 1858, also worried that too many merely strange things had been promoted to miracles; such "glittering fire-work round us . . . really governs nothing" and could not produce true religious knowledge or repentance.[70]

This definitional slipperiness became more acute when observers merely hinted at the miraculous nature of an event. Barton Warren Stone wrote a taxonomy of the strange events at the Cane Ridge revivals—shakes, shudders, visions, and the mysterious "singing exercise," wherein subjects would "sing most melodiously," but sound came "not from the mouth or noise, but entirely in the breast, the sounds issuing thence. Such music silenced everything, and attracted the attention of all."[71] McNemar stressed the holy *smells* of Cane Ridge that accompanied the religious visions there; because they did not smell like anything on earth, skeptics could be sure the visions came from God.[72] Stone described such events as "so like miracles, that if they were not, they had the same effects as miracles on infidels and unbelievers."[73] Revivalist John Lyle similarly confided to his diary that the exercises "might answer instead of ancient miracles to arouse the attention of a sleeping world."[74] Drury Lacy compared the scenes to Sinai, and the pro-revival tract *Signs of the Times* declared, "In order to confound Infidels and Atheists, God has acted in some places and cases in a manner somewhat analogous to the Age of Miracles."[75] Thinkers were treating the merely strange—the preternatural—as though it were fully miraculous.

The eighteenth and nineteenth centuries therefore created a supernatural that was not only easier to prove but conceptually larger; more things that once could have been considered merely preternatural, or wonderful, or strange, were now fully supernatural—and much of that supernatural could be deemed miraculous. And where there were more miracles, there were more commands. "Real miracles," wrote Carnahan, "are an evidence of a commission from God, and consequently of the truth of the doctrines taught by the person who performs them."[76] If miracles stood as divine requirements—orders—then a proliferation of miracles had heady ecclesiastical consequences. And with the relative decline of ecclesiastical authority in America, anyone who *experienced* or *accepted* a miracle could simply initiate their own church—as, for example, did the Cochranites and the Cane Ridge schismatics. It was the ecclesiastical consequence of the reduction of potential categories to two—natural or miraculous.

Some established Christian traditions had prepared for such a definitional onslaught. In the wake of the Thirty Years' War, theologians both Catholic and Protestant began looking for ways to tamp down religious excess and build up institutional churches; though miracles still mattered, both Protestants and Catholics emphasized that they had existed to establish the truth of Christ's teachings—that is, doctrine. Once doctrine was established, the argument went, miracles could seem superfluous. Post-Tridentine Catholicism included new strictures for testing and evaluating miracle claims, while Protestant orthodoxy emphasized the doctrine of cessation. Thus, if "a doctrine was disputed, a miracle could no longer settle the issue."[77]

Thus, the naturalization of the preternatural banished the modern supernatural in favor of doctrine, which in turn validated the existing authorities in a process Daston dubs "the centralization of divine power." In other words, consolidation via naturalization meant that wonders, portents, and miracles that *did* occur could *not* be brought under the rubric of the Church of England; by definition, such movements would be sectarian at best and heretical at worst. Or to put it another way, if miracles were outside official churches, only those outside the church would see miracles.

Postrevolutionary America offered an ideal environment for such miracle-mongers; the weakness of official churches provided the right kind of environment for sectarian movements to swell like toadstools in the damp dark. By 1789, Virginia's Statute of Religious Freedom—politically backed by a host of dissenting sects—and the First Amendment had opened the floodgates. Even in recalcitrant New England, the anarchic period following the Revolution meant that what establishments existed were not taken very seriously; though Congregationalism was the state church in Vermont until 1807, a Baptist became a lieutenant governor in 1779, and Baptists received a share of the trusteeships at the state university from 1791.[78]

If churches were trapped in ecclesiastical anarchy, they possessed a surprising degree of intellectual commonality. Even Stiles and Paine agreed on miracles, and the debates swirled around the relative worth of witnesses, senses, miracles, and facts. The struggles that emerged cannot, therefore, be interpreted as a struggle of reason against faith or rationality against emotion. Those who argued about the supernatural instead attempted to show the weight of sense evidence and witness testimonies—the probabilities—were on their side, even if they held that new miracles had occurred. The approach was rather close to what Hume suggested in "Of Miracles," but with a very different outcome than Hume endorsed. It was probabilism against itself. New miracles emerged from the center of American religious thought, not its edges.

As often happens when disputants agree on fundamentals, the debate devolved into scorn. Paine, for example, accepted that people would think the story of Jonah and the whale marvelous, but to be truly miraculous, why not have Jonah swallow the whale instead of vice versa? The biblical miracle of creation, Allen wrote, was "better calculated for the servile Israelitish *Brick-makers* than for men of learning and science in these modern times."[79] The debate turned less on fine points of reason than on broad stereotypes of the age; it was a cultural battle more than an intellectual one. When the Temple Patrick Society of Philadelphia hosted a debate on witchcraft in 1788, it was the case *for* witchcraft that cited "the testimony of our own sense and observation" as proof of the evil eye and other magic. The counterargument based its appeal on ad hominem attacks, denouncing the presumed character of those who believed in witches, "the prevalence of ignorance and superstition," enforced by "the fury of barbarous enthusiastic multitudes" as the evidence against it.[80] The debate was no idle fancy for Philadelphians: a year before, outside the Constitutional Convention, a mob lynched a woman for witchcraft, cutting her forehead to break her curses. She died from her injuries.

Intellectual history and the history of science have, for the past two generations, jettisoned the notion that ideas rise and fall on their intrinsic merit, that "good" ideas succeed and "bad" ones fail.[81] Ideas usually made claims to intrinsic merit or "better logic" (whatever that might mean), but their appeal and success, or lack thereof, were often tied to larger cultural shifts and values. The republican case against witchcraft was no different. There were in its tenets and judgments numerous notions that fit well with the broad Atlantic Anglophone culture of the eighteenth century, and especially with the postrevolutionary ethos of the developing American state and a host of its cultural (and political) factors.

Those political factors mattered; the fight over miracles was also a political battle. The state could not interfere to prevent heresy, but it could stop treason or threats to public order. Indeed, John Spencer had figured out the state's vested interest in discouraging supernaturalism back in 1653. His *Discourse on Prodigies* argued that "men may quickly be frighted by such images of straw, as the relations of monsters and strange sights are" turning them into zealots for bad causes. Keeping a lid on prodigies and supernatural reports therefore required political intervention, so as to preserve "the quiet and tranquility of the State."[82] William Pinchbeck, an ex-flimflam man, wrote 150 years later to explain "how dangerous such a belief [in the supernatural] is to society, how destructive to the improvement of the human capacity, and how totally ruinous to the common interests of mankind."[83] The intellectual debate on miracles had brought the American religious firmament to a place where new miracles could be—and were—justified by the same kind of evidence the biblicists claimed. The republican position on miracles and the supernatural, however, took a very different tack and offered a far more probing response to new supernatural events. The battle over miracles was not going to be just a struggle over souls but a struggle over the nature of the state.

TWO

The Practice of the Supernatural

Around 1814, Barbara Powers of Chesterfield, South Carolina, turned a young girl into a horse. Powers rode the ersatz steed through the town of Lancaster; once there, she entered several shops "through the keyhole," stole their goods, rode home, and turned the horse back into a girl again. As a consequence of this witchcraft, the girl's "health and strength greatly declined." Concerned citizens formed a mob, rounded up Powers, forced her "to touch the abused girl, and say over her 'God bless you!'" whereupon "the girl instantly recovered." Powers sued for assault. The judge listened to the testimony and threw the case out of court. Powers would have no legal recourse. The witch hunt was successful.[1]

The witch mob of 1814 exemplifies the complexities of the Jeffersonian supernatural. Some aspects of witchcraft were old (animal transformation by witches, countermagic in the name of God). Some were new: this witch made use of her rights as a citizen of the republic and took her assailants to court. The decision to throw the case out might be interpreted as a validation of the rights of the mob over the rights of Powers, a perverse kind of majority rule.

Alternately, Jeffersonian witch-hunters arranged their own courts. In 1792, the Carolinas faced a witch outbreak reported as far away as New England. It is not clear what precipitated the accusation of witchcraft, but "many a poor girl was thought to be sadly afflicted," and "to relieve the sufferers, it was deemed necessary to give the witches a trial." A mob of perhaps fifty convened "a court comprised of witch-doctors" at Winnsboro. Three or four witches were whipped, then tortured by applying their feet to a fire "so that the soles came off." When taken to court themselves, witch-hunters of 1792 used their numbers as a defense and paid only nominal damages to their victims.[2]

The Carolinas were not finished with witches. A Charleston newspaper reported in November 1793 that "a negro man, the property of Mr. Green," had been tried "for *witch-craft*, before two magistrates and several freeholders, who condemned him to be hanged, and he was accordingly executed."[3] A South Carolina lawyer suggested that England's 1604 laws against witchcraft remained valid in the state.[4] In North Carolina, Duncan McFarland commanded a mob assault on a suspected witch, cutting her across the forehead to end her curses. McFarland had business and political contacts in both Carolinas, and the timing of this attack (between 1787 and 1800) suggests links to the other outbreaks (if not directly in the chain of accusations, then indirectly in the spread of witch fears). Like the Winnsboro witch-hunters, McFarland was also countersued; he was exonerated and was later elected to Congress.[5]

The question of the supernatural was no mere academic problem in the early republic; these cases reveal active witch beliefs that often took violent turns. The Carolina outbreaks brought together ideas about witchcraft, republicanism, and law: believers determined to protect themselves from perceived crimes and dangers acted in the name of the people. Their assaults on witches then had to be tried in courts that acted as the legal embodiment of the same people. In a disestablished state, who could act for the citizenry when supernatural crises loomed? Perhaps sensing the tenuous nature of their authority in such overlapping claims, courts rarely pursued the purveyors of violence against witches with great vigor. Indeed, early U.S. courts sometimes stood with the supernaturalists—accepting ghostly testimony in 1807 in Maryland, or letting two witch executions stand in Pueblo territory in 1854.[6] Ministers and jurists moralized against witch hunts, but as with so much else in the early United States, the people would have the final say. Magic and the supernatural were republican activities, often construed as an exercise in freedom and a defense of the populace. Indeed, constitutional protection of the press and a diversifying market gave Americans greater access to magic and esoterica. Johann George Hohman relished the freedom that, he believed, made his book of magic more trustworthy and verifiable: "I sell my books publicly, and not secretly as other mystical books are sold."[7]

Rather like magic itself, the republican encounters with the supernatural could be fickle; patchy evidence inveighs against chronological or systematic analysis, but the depth and extent of these episodes—and their presence among Americans of all sorts—suggests a dynamic and fruitful supernaturalism in the early republic. Beliefs might overlap or contradict one another;

belief in ghosts did not equate to belief in witches, which did not require belief in angels. Nevertheless, these inchoate ideas shaped private behavior and intruded into the public sphere. Alongside the strident religious conflicts of the early republic were similarly vibrant debates over the nature and presence of magic, witchcraft, ghosts, divination, and angels. If these beliefs were not universally practiced, they were at least *openly* considered and frequently encountered, and they represented an alteration and adaptation of previous beliefs rather than a wholesale renewal.

This low-level supernatural mattered because discussions about miracles in the early republic did not take place in a disenchanted universe. Enlightenment narratives and the politics of superstition emerged in a world where witch beliefs persisted and where fortune-telling and treasure digging almost certainly *increased*. Fewer people believed in witchcraft as a demonic conspiracy in 1825 than in 1625—but that does not mean that people did not believe in witchcraft or in the supernatural.[8]

An overview of American approaches to magic and witchcraft places the miraculous in the broader context of popular cultures of belief. Magic and witchcraft are here selected to stand in for a host of supernatural beliefs; early Americans also experimented with alchemy, investigated the fascinating power of rattlesnakes, and unearthed vampires.[9] The ways in which supernatural beliefs percolated and functioned in the early republic in turn formed the context from which both the American critique of miracles and the new miraculous sects emerged.

Historians should resist the effort to classify magical practice or other supernatural beliefs as discrete systems. Richard Weisman identified magic and Christianity as "two belief systems" with "fundamental disagreements";[10] Jon Butler similarly treated magic as a learned, self-contained tradition that must be taught and that "challenged Christianity." For Butler, magic exists apart from and in distinction to Christianity rather than as a disparate collection of beliefs and practices.[11] John Brooke has maintained that the "occult tradition" in colonial and early republican America represented the sustained presence of the Radical Reformation in the New World. Later, the descendants of these Radicals flocked to Mormonism for its purported combination of hermeticism and Christianity. This formulation equates Christianity with orthodoxy (particularly Calvinist orthodoxy), but Christians had been practicing all kinds of magic for centuries without abandoning their faith. Indeed, faith in Christ was essential for many kinds of magic.[12]

Early republican magic instead represented a collection of religious and supernatural assertions picked up piecemeal and frequently combined in new and unusual ways; bricolage is much more common to magical practice than historians have thought. The republic's magic was handmade rather than organized into the systematic tiers described in printed occult works of the nineteenth century.[13] Theologians might preach against it, but the Christian character of Western magic went back centuries before the Reformation.[14] Most American practitioners of magic saw no contradiction between their faith and their use of spells; Christian faith actually gave efficacy to magical incantations, which were supernaturally powered by the holy letters of sacred names and Scripture. Nor did the practice of divinatory magic strike many in the early republic as heretical. In 1804, the Cane Ridge revivalist Robert McAfee sought out a "water witch" to stop a drought, then headed back to the revivals.[15]

Furthermore, observers of magic in the Age of Jefferson found middle-class and wealthy Americans in the chambers of the fortune-teller and the circles of the treasure diggers. Quitman despaired that "respectable people resort to the closet of a fortune-teller to have a secret discovered."[16] Q. K. Philander Doesticks (pseudonym of the humorist Mortimer Thompson) discovered "men engaged in respectable and influential professions, and many merchants of good credit and repute" meeting with diviners, and noted that they "are actually governed by their advice in business affairs of great moment."[17] The Complete Fortune Teller (1799) went through five printings in the early republic, but William Frederick Pinchbeck's exposé Witchcraft, or the Art of Fortune-Telling Unveiled only one.[18] Magic was a going concern, and its critics had good reason to worry.

Among the most obvious forms of magic in the early republic was the trade in grimoires—books of charms, spells, conjurations, and/or instructions for the creation of magical devices such as amulets. Freedom of the press and freedom of religion provided the opportunity for both publishers and curious inquirers to satisfy their cravings for these strangest of volumes.[19] The authors of the Complete Fortune Teller relished the chance to publish for the masses; the erudite style of previous fortune-tellers ("so embarrassed with scientific words, that the greater part of readers cannot understand them") would not taint the American grimoire.[20] Chloe Russel boasted that her book of dream divination was "plain, clear, and full."[21] Hohman claimed his magic was built "upon the broad platform of the liberty of the press and of conscience."[22] By 1835, the Library Company of Philadelphia listed more than seventy titles under "Occult Philosophy, Alchemy, Astrology, Demonology, &c."

Admittedly, some of the works were volumes skeptical of the supernatural. But interested readers could also find Sibly's *New Illustration of the Celestial Science of Astrology* (1784), Heydon's *New Astrology* (1786), Barrett's *Magus* (1801), and Kirchendoffer's *The Book of Fate, Formerly in the Possession of Napoleon* (1823). Patrons could also find more traditional grimoire fare: Heinrich Agrippa's works on occult philosophy, Raphael's *Sanctuary of the Astral Art,* and Reginald Scot's *Discoverie of Witchcraft.* (Scot's work, though purportedly skeptical, contained numerous details on how to perform magical acts and create magical items; it was used by cunning folk in England and was possibly employed by treasure diggers in the United States.)[23] Most of these magical texts were new arrivals; the 1807 *Catalogue* listed only Agrippa and Scot. The rest were acquired in the thirty intervening years. American appetite for magic was on the rise.

American grimoires focused on astrology and fortune-telling. Texts purported to possess infallible ciphers for the interpretation of dreams, though they also taught readers how to read fates from cards, palms, and moles. Few American texts had a clear author; *The Complete Fortune Teller and Dream Book* of 1824 identified Chloe Russel, "A Woman of Colour, in the State of Massachusetts," as the author. It included a brief biography of Russel—purportedly born in Africa, enslaved, and freed through her fortune-telling. Eric Gardner has determined that a free African American woman named Chloe Russel did live in Boston in 1824, where she was one of only six black women to own property. That in turn seems to support the *Dream Book*'s claim that Russel made enough money reading fortunes to buy her own home. (As Gardner notes, the *Dream Book* also claims that Russel encountered tigers in her African childhood, which seems less likely, since tigers are native to Asia.)[24] Other authors, such as Ibrahim ali Mahomed Hafez, were certainly apocryphal. Hafez, the purported author of 1797's *Oneirocritic,* was supposedly a seventeenth-century Persian, writing in Arabic, whose works found their way into Isaac Newton's library.[25] Erra Pater—whose *Book of Knowledge* went through eighteen editions under various titles from 1767 to 1809—claimed to be "A Jew Doctor" born "near Mount Olive, in Judea."[26]

Dream books borrowed heavily from one another. Hafez and Russel included almost the same introductory comments. Lists of dream subjects and their interpretation were repeated volume to volume; the publishers of the *Oneirocritic* complained that "many will go so far as even to copy it as closely as the law will permit." Counterintuitive diagnoses of certain dream images also suggest shared understanding. To dream of death indicated an approaching wedding; to dream of treasure deep in the earth meant trouble ahead. Dreams of riding horses indicated great fortune. Sometimes there were cautions: to dream of slipping on ice meant bad luck, for example. Yet most dream interpretations connoted success. In the 1816 *New Dream Book*, readers learned that "to dream of the neck signifies power, honour, riches, and inheritance," "to dream one sees a stately oak signifies to the dreamer riches, profit, and long life," and "to dream of peas well-boiled; denotes good success"—and that in only three pages. Few authors had the courage of Hafez, who admitted that "to dream you have an ague, denotes nothing very particular."[27]

Dream books and astrological works might also contain practical spells, magical lore, or other esoteric content. An 1815 dream book concluded with a spell to compel lucid dreaming; practitioners should write the subject they wished to dream of on a piece of paper, "fold it in the form of a heart, get a gill of red wine and dip it in it, then drink the wine in three draughts, just before you go to bed, and put the paper under your pillow." Russel's *Complete Fortune Teller* included rituals to compel love and to learn the fate of absent friends. The 1815 *New Dream Book* vouched for the reality of angels who placed the images in dreams with the purpose of "either forewarn[ing] you of some approaching evil" or "giv[ing] you a foreknowledge of some good that is shortly to happen." To dream of an angel was not merely a subject for interpretation; it was a directed message from above.[28]

Ebenezer Sibly's *New Illustration of the Celestial Science of Astrology*—an English volume for sale in the United States—went further. The enormous *New Illustration* functioned like an encyclopedia; everything a seeker might need was in there. Sibly's volume is most famous for its astrological birth chart for the United States. Taking July 4, 1776, as the date of birth, Sibly found that due to the relative positions of Jupiter, Venus, and Saturn, everything "effected under this [American] revolution . . . shall be supported by those three grand pillars of state, wisdom, strength, and unanimity." Furthermore, "America shall in time have a flourishing and extensive commerce . . . great fecundity and prosperity amongst the people." Sibly's happy predictions have remained popular to the present.[29]

Americans who read further in the *New Illustration* would discover Sibly's darker chapters on witchcraft, exorcism, and demonology. After a warmed-over Swedenborgian summary of angels and the afterlife, Sibly's book enumerated types of demons and angels, and methods for obtaining the favor of each. Sibly insisted that "it is neither safe nor prudent, nor consistent

An astrological birth chart for the United States—carried by an angel—in Ebenezer Sibly's 1795 *New Illustration of the Celestial Science of Astrology*. (L. Tom Perry Special Collections, Harold B. Lee Library, Brigham Young University)

with the well being of society in general, that I should dwell so extensively" on the "particular forms, manner, method, rites . . . requisite to call up and enter into compact or familiarity with spirits." Doing so would "put a weapon into the hands of the blood-thirsty or revengeful" and was "forbidden by the word of God."[30]

Such protestations were pro forma, for Sibly immediately launched into extended discussions of the forms and means necessary to compact with

The protective ward of the angel Jubanladace, from Sibly's *A New and Complete Illustration of the Occult Sciences*. (L. Tom Perry Special Collections, Harold B. Lee Library, Brigham Young University)

the devil or familiar spirits. Despite promises to the contrary, Sibly included details down to the level of the dimensions of the circles and shapes of sigils necessary to capture and compel the spirits. In case a reader should be confused, Sibly added illustrations. Sibly provided directions for the creation of a *"magical candle,* which being lighted, foretels the death of the party of whose blood it was prepared."[31]

Sibly condemned such demonological work as "repugnant to common sense, and incompatible with religion and morality"; it was the opposite of astrology and natural magic, which was "the workmanship of nature, made manifest by art." Though he marketed his work as natural magic, it was not secular in any sense, for Sibly also instructed readers on the various names of angels watching over humanity, and how their power could be harnessed for countermagical protection. Sibly explained, for example, that the angel Nal-gah was "devoted to the protection of those who are assaulted by evil spirits or witches." Anyone who wore Nal-gah's magical symbol around the neck would be safe from witchcraft and suicide. If readers needed a charm of a different sort, Sibly had six other angelic symbols that could be worn as wards.[32]

Angelic sigils were not the only countermagical offerings available. The first true American grimoires—collections of spells rather than astrological and dream books with spells—came from the German American powwow tradition, which produced *Der Freund in der Noth* in 1793. Written by Tobias Hirte, *Der Freund* collected magical charms to dissuade thieves and improve firearms, and claimed to contain knowledge from the Old Country, "from an old Spanish manuscript, which was found at an old hermit's." Hohman's *Long-Lost Friend* proved the most enduring entry in the American grimoire tradition, with eleven distinct editions (in German and English) between 1820 and 1860. Hohman lived a peripatetic and threadbare life, but his *Friend* was a contribution of lasting significance. Incorporated into both powwow and conjure traditions, the magic in the *Friend* continues to be performed in the twenty-first century.[33]

A major source for Hohman was the *Romanusbüchlein,* a purported collection of Romany magic that appeared in Europe in the 1780s. Hohman repeated some of the charms verbatim and in the same order as the *Romanusbüchlein.* He also borrowed some paragraphs from *The Book of Aggregations,* a series of eighteenth-century works attributed to the thirteenth-century author Albertus Magnus. It was certainly not a collection of Native American magic; the name "powwow" derived more from presumed associations of magical power with Native Americans than with the content of the magic, which came almost exclusively from European sources. Even the herbs recommended in the *Friend* were Old World imports. As with many collections of magic, Hohman included magical phrases to be recited during the casting of the spell or charm. These phrases were sometimes orthodox prayers, nonsense words, onomatopoeia, or *nomina barbara,* words recopied from an original so long lost that they have become corrupted.[34]

Most of the spells in the *Friend* mixed religious, herbal, and magical elements to varying degrees. For victory in court, petitioners ought to take "the largest kind of sage and write the names of the 12 apostles on the leaves, and put them in his shoes before entering the courthouse." Protection against fires could be obtained by placing a chicken's stomach in a pot with a shirt from a virgin and an egg laid on Maundy Thursday. If these were buried in wax at the threshold of a house, then if the house caught fire, the conflagration would "do no injury to you, nor to your children. This is done by the power of God."[35]

Some items were simply botanical. Hohman recommended fern juice to heal burns and advised readers to graft cherry twigs to mulberry trees to prevent the fruit from ripening before Martinmas. Other "charms" were purely religious; a ward "Against Danger and Death" was a quotation from Job written on parchment and "carried about the person." A more complex protection involved keeping the "right eye of a wolf fastened inside of his right sleeve" to avoid injuries. To remove warts, Hohman suggested, "Roast chicken-feet and rub the warts with them, then bury them under the eaves."[36]

Several of the charms and spells offered countermagical protection from witches. One charm was to be placed in stables, "to prevent Witches from bewitching Cattle." The same charm placed above a bedstead would protect people. "A Charm for Bad People"—a German euphemism for witches—involved sticking a shoemaker's wax-end on the underside of a chair in which the witch sat: "He will immediately make water, and in a short time die." Hohman made use of the ancient SATOR square—a first-century charm—in yet another spell "To Be Given to Cattle, Against Witchcraft." Farmers were to inscribe the following on paper:

S A T O R

A R E P O

T E N E T

O P E R A

R O T A S

The paper was fed to the cattle, and all would be well. SATOR squares could be found over stable windows into the twentieth century.[37]

There were also handwritten grimoires. Silas Hamilton recorded the money dreams of his neighbors and the arcane instructions for obtaining such buried treasures as they dreamed of: "Tak[e] Nine Steel Rods about ten or twelve Inches in Length Sharp or Piked to Perce in to the Earth, and let them Besmeared with fresh blood from a hen mixed with hogdung." Placed in two concentric circles, the rods would cause the treasure to move closer to the treasure seekers. Hamilton led regular meetings of like-minded treasure hunters—unsurprising, since he was a leading citizen of Whitingham, Vermont, and "held the highest offices the town could bestow," according to his 1890s biographer.[38]

In the 1780s, Joshua Gordon of South Carolina wrote a slim volume of spells now known as the "Witchcraft Book." His spells had a clear didactic function, written (like Hohman's) in the second person. Gordon's work resembled Hohman's in the combination of medical, religious, and magical remedies for common complaints. Victims of rheumatism could apply a mixture of rum, bacon, and salt to the aggrieved location for "one hour every night before you go to bed and with the blessing of god you will git easd." A cure for the "riptur in children" involved killing a buck deer "in the old of the moon," removing its penis, and boiling it "in half a pint of new milk until it begins to crud." The afflicted child should drink this unusual mixture for three mornings "between cock crow and day."[39]

The "Witchcraft Book" is misnamed, since what Gordon wrote was largely countermagic: his guide unhexed spells and reversed witchcraft. In other

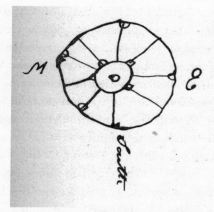

Silas Hamilton's diagram of the necessary arrangement of rods smeared with hen's blood required to recover buried treasure. (American Antiquarian Society)

words, Joshua Gordon's book assumed that *other witches* were already present in the early republic and that readers would require defensive magic against them. For example, "for a gun that is Spel'd," Gordon instructed practitioners to recite the name of the Holy Trinity while loading the weapon. Several spells dealt with the protection of livestock. "If you have Cow or Hors or any other Creatur[e] die through witchcraft," the book advised cutting out the dead animal's bladder and locking it away; "you will thearby Shut up the blather of the Person that hurt your Beast and justly turn thir Mischief upon their own head." Elsewhere, Gordon described means to fool witches into exposing their identities to their victims, presumably as a way to catch them and break their power.[40]

Christianity pervaded countermagic. Gordon placed handwritten appeals to Christ across the front and back of the book, in addition to its internal references to God and the Trinity. Hohman's work, too, relied on the premise that the divine name and sacred prayers were a failsafe against malefic witchcraft. Hafez justified dream interpretation by referencing the story of Joseph and Pharaoh. Hohman referred to the Psalms, which encouraged believers to call on God in times of trouble. The frequent references to God, Mary, and Christ, Hohman believed, made his work the same kind of plea—divine and not demonic—and would therefore answer critics who "persist in denouncing them as something wrong."[41] Sibly's angelic wards drew their power from the Christian God, even if they were not strictly biblically based. Many of those who employed magic and fortune-telling saw no contradiction between Christian belief and magical practice. The astrologer Sullivan Sheffield defended his practice by quoting Moses and Job, and noted that his science led to "predestination . . . agreeable to Christianity."[42]

It is unclear how far readers of these texts incorporated or performed the rituals within. Many must have tried Russel's recipe for finding love; few if any would have taken Sibly's instructions to head for the crossroads to summon a demon. Nevertheless, handwritten notes and occasional diary references demonstrate that these volumes were not mere entertainment. A note on a surviving 1856 edition of Hohman's *Long-Lost Friend* has the words "very good" penciled next to the charm to cure scurvy and sore throat.[43] The American Antiquarian Society's copy of William Pinchbeck's *Witchcraft* contains handwritten notes only on the section wherein Pinchbeck explained the art of reading fortunes from playing cards. At least one reader, then, used Pinchbeck's prescriptions against witchcraft as a guide for fortune-telling.[44] Hohman's spells show up in handwritten account books, personal notes, and on flyleaves of other books, sometimes written in cipher. One of the charms in his book—a cure for rabies—was submitted to the Pennsylvania legislature by Valentine Kettring of Dauphin County.[45]

Memoirs and church records provide further anecdotal evidence of magical cures and spells in frequent use. A Revolutionary War veteran, James Potter Collins, attempted a magical cure for his fever in the southern backcountry. He was advised that when he felt "the shakes coming on," he should take a string to a fruit tree and "tie a knot for every shake." Though Collins "had no faith in the project," he also "thought there could be no harm in it; I tried it." The spell worked.[46] North Carolina's Moravians worried that their branch in Bethabara was attended by "a conjurer who cures illnesses" and "the like has been done by communicant members."[47] Sheffield owned an entire library of magical books, obtained with "great trouble and expense," which he used every day and eventually donated to the American Antiquarian Society.[48] Joseph Doddridge found practices in Appalachia that repeated Gordon's magic exactly; those seeking to cure a bewitched child would take "the child's water, which was closely corked up in a vial and hung up in a chimney." This countermagic would afflict the witch with strangury.[49]

Countermagic presupposed witchcraft—a perennial form of American supernaturalism. Combining data from newspapers, folkloric sources, court records, and memoirs produces an early republican archive of witchcraft, according to one scholar, "every bit as rich and important as that of the seventeenth century."[50] Sometimes the fear of witches remained vague or resolved itself peacefully. A man named Wiley Horn was brought before a Kentucky church discipline committee on the charge of witchcraft; his crime involved shooting a deer that would not die: "after taken its intrails out it got up and walked and bleated at him."[51] Horn subsequently stabbed the deer and it died; the committee exonerated him. Other animals were also witchcraft targets; an 1805 outbreak of bovine disease in Maryland was blamed on witchcraft. Fears of witchcraft led to the burning of cattle in Delaware in 1810.[52] In New Jersey in the 1780s, witches afflicted sheep.[53] Yet another of the manifold Carolina witches kept her fellow Methodists in check by threatening their livestock. The worried Methodists explained: "We are afraid of her. . . . She had killed in a moment every fowl in the yard of some woman whom she had a grudge against." Rev. Richard Jenkins confronted the witch, who "shook herself with a strange, wriggling motion, not unlike a turkey in the sand, muttering something like boo, boo, woo, woo, woo." Jenkins thought it was funny; other church members were terrified.[54]

Witchcraft was an obvious evil, yet the early American legal apparatus was ill-equipped to handle it. The Court of Common Pleas in York, Massachusetts (now Maine), heard a witchcraft case in 1789, when Alcut Stover called Eleanor Estes a witch for cursing livestock, and swore, "I'll have her hanged." Estes's husband took Stover to court for slander. The colonial law against witchcraft never having been formally repealed, however, Estes soon found herself tried for witchcraft. The judge in the case instructed the jury that "witchcraft had never existed since the time of the Saviour's advent" and that moreover, it was a crime impossible to prove in law. The jury followed these instructions and determined "that the declaration was bad and insufficient," and Estes "recovered a large bill of costs."[55]

Unlike Stover, most witch-hunters lacked legal recourse to pursue their ends. Great Britain had jettisoned its witchcraft laws in 1736, radically altering the relationship between witchcraft and the state. When witchcraft was criminal, Owen Davies writes, "elite authority and popular justice maintained a symbiotic relationship with regard to the threat of witchcraft"; popular fears could obtain hearings from clerical and judicial powers, which in turn benefited from their ability to remove witchcraft from the body politic. Such action need not involve a mass trial and panic; regular trials, sentencing, and occasional execution also rid the countryside of witches and thereby signaled divine approbation of the magistracy.[56]

By the end of the eighteenth century, that was no longer possible, though American jurisprudence was not always clear on the matter. George Webb's eighteenth-century Virginia lawbook *The Office and Authority of a Justice of the Peace* was still in use in the early republic and maintained that witchcraft was a capital offense, though "plain and direct Evidence is not to be expected in these Works of Darkness."[57] Some of this confusion continued into the republican era. An 1831 Tennessee court tried Stout, a suspected conjurer, for witchcraft. Stout's accusers argued that Tennessee had never specifically repealed the 1604 English statute against witchcraft, and therefore Stout could be punished. (The case was dismissed.)[58]

More typically, courts ran into witchcraft as part of slander and fraud cases, as when a New Hampshire man sued his local conjurer in 1824. The cunning-man had ended the client's bewitchment but had then altered the bill from nine dollars to ninety dollars.[59] In 1787, a Revolutionary War veteran, Samuel Smith, begged the Maryland State Council for mercy, for "through ignorance he was induced to believe in Witchcraft, which belief drew him into a Riot, for which he was charged." The council agreed to reduce the fine.[60] More ominously, courts might deal with witchcraft in the form of poisoning, as, for example, in the Illinois Country in 1779, where two men, Manuel and Moreau ("negroes belonging to MM. LeComte and Beaulieu") were accused of administering poison to several people. Magical arts were readily apparent in the case. Manuel and Moreau apparently buried their poison "under the threshold of the door." An enslaved woman named Janette was reported as owning "a horn in which there was some boiling blood," which she had apparently procured from Manuel "to put her master and mistress to death." The men were hanged for murder.[61] Whether or not the courts believed the witchcraft, Manuel and Moreau certainly did.

The deaths of Manuel and Moreau presaged the retaliation against the most notorious necromancer of the early republic—Gullah Jack Pritchard, executed by South Carolina in the 1822 Vesey conspiracy. Pritchard arrived in the United States as a slave from Angola in 1805. His first owner, the Floridian radical Zephaniah Kingsley, understood that "Gualla Jack or Jack the Conjurer was a priest in his own country" who managed to bring "conjuring implements" with him across the Middle Passage. He was purchased by Paul Pritchard of Charleston in 1806; he earned his master's goodwill and the respect of both the Angola-born slaves and members of Charleston's AME church. Though the members recognized Jack as a "conjurer by profession and by lineal heritage," they did not seem to mind. Jack Pritchard's supernatural leadership appeared to be an open secret in Charleston between 1806 and 1822. His participation in the Denmark Vesey conspiracy was less public.[62]

Pritchard's contributions to the rebellion included the creation of magical charms. According to one testimony, he ordered conspirators to eat a special diet on the day of the planned revolt, and "when you join us, as we pass, put into your mouth this crab claw and then you can't be wounded." Pritchard also commanded the rebellion of the Angola-born slaves working on the outskirts of Charleston. He seemed fully aware of his authority—a witness claimed that "all his country born promised to join because he was a doctor (that is a conjurer)"—but also of its potential limitations: Pritchard also apparently claimed that "his charms would not protect him from the treachery of his own color." That is precisely what happened; the conspirators were betrayed to the white authorities by an African American slave.[63]

Pritchard's magic made his trial different. A witness for the prosecution feared Pritchard's supernatural powers; court records indicated that "it was not without considerable difficulty that the Court satisfied him that he need no longer fear Jacks *conjurations*."[64] A letter in a contemporary newspaper explained and possibly exaggerated the demonological case against Gullah Jack: "Gullah Jack was considered invincible; he could not be hurt or killed, but a blow from him would do instant execution. At one of these meetings they had a fowl dressed and put on a table. Gullah Jack performed some ceremony of witchcraft over it; when he was done an instant scrabble was made for the fowl."[65] Court records noted only that Jack "positively denied that he ever pretended to be a Doctor or Conjurer"; he and his colleagues otherwise left no writings by which to clear their name.[66]

The court singled Jack out for special opprobrium in sentencing: "You were not satisfied with resorting to natural and ordinary means, but endeavored to enlist on your behalf, all the powers of darkness, and employed for that purpose, the most disgusting mummery and superstition." Such efforts had been intended to sway "the ignorant and credulous." Enlightenment, the judge explained, would prevail with Pritchard's death: "Your Altars and your Gods have sunk together in the dust. The airy spectres conjured by you have been chased away by the superior light of Truth, and you stand exposed, the miserable and deluded victim of offended Justice." Other conspirators received lectures on their ingratitude and specific biblical verses they were meant to live up to. Jack received no such warning. Instead, the judge proclaimed, "You will shortly be consigned to the cold and silent grave; and all the Powers of Darkness cannot rescue you from your approaching Fate!" The state had defeated a dangerous demonologist and his plot against ordered liberty. Pritchard was offered the counsel of any minister of the gospel he might choose; there is no record that he chose any.[67]

Pritchard's sentence was treason, but the context was witchcraft: the end of legal witch trials did not mean the end of witch fears. In most cases, however, the state refused to perform witch executions—and so republicans took the defense of the people into their own hands. Vigilante violence against witches continued throughout the early republic—even during the Constitutional Convention itself. A mob lynched an elderly woman known only as "Korbmacher" in Philadelphia in 1787, just blocks away from the Founders debating at Independence Hall. "Upon the supposition she was a *witch*, she was cut in the forehead," following a common countermagical act of violence designed to break charms. Following the attack, Korbmacher appealed to the authorities. It did little good, for she was attacked again the next week, carried through the streets, and "hooted and pelted as she went along." This time, the injuries proved fatal.[68]

In 1795, Polly Willey of Thornton, New Hampshire, began to exhibit "things . . . to us unaccountable by any natural or ordinary causes"; she received wounds from unseen hands, and perceived invisible creatures, some of whom she named as witches. Fifteen men signed an affidavit acknowledging that "there is reason to suspect the agency of evil spirits in the affair." Yet they counseled "great caution," not because witchcraft was impossible—"it is not beyond the power of Satan to effect such wounds and scratches"—but because "if her case is real possession of the Devil he may present to her imagination innocent persons for the purpose of destroying peace in Society."[69]

Witchcraft fears were rife in New England that year; Paul Coffin heard that a New Hampshire boy "was tormented in the air by a number of witches and then left him in the crotch of a tree."[70] In October 1796, Elizabeth Smith's Maine neighbors came for her.[71] John Hilton encountered Smith on the road, whereupon his ox goad slithered out of his hand of its own accord. Hilton suspected "the power of witchcraft." He "attempted to strike" Smith, but "instead of doing any injury to the Complainant, he himself received a violent blow on the lower part of the back." Another man believed Smith had bewitched him into madness, for his condition subsided when Smith appeared: whenever "she was in the house he appeared to be much better, and talked very rationally." Hilton and others first attempted the countermagical charm of boiling Hilton's urine. When that failed, they sought "to obtain *some of her blood* as an antidote." Hilton and the conspirators beat Smith and forcibly scratched her forehead—just as happened to Korbmacher. Smith sued her attackers, but she received nothing substantial in her attempt to redress her grievances.[72]

Witches also found their way to court as plaintiffs. Elizabeth Smith's own efforts were one of several "reverse witch trials," where suspected witches sued for slander or assault, making the witch accuser and not the witch suspect the focus of legal redress. A witch assault went to court in Maryland in 1832; the supposed witch was accused of causing crockery to break and (with an accomplice) of hexing her victims and fetching "rats alive out of cellar at night by tails, and let[ting] them loose." The judge dismissed the case as "nonsense."[73] An unnamed woman in New England received a more favorable judgment; when her Irish neighbor attacked her for bewitching his goat in 1830, a Portland, Maine, court fined him for the assault.[74]

More egregious violence also got courts' attention. In 1822, Joseph Lewis of Deep Creek, Virginia, murdered Jack Bass, a suspected witch. Lewis believed Bass had bewitched him. Lewis consulted with a fortune-teller to confirm that Bass, a free African American, was indeed the supernatural culprit. Lewis shot Bass dead with a shotgun and received an eighteen-year prison sentence.[75] After much practice, a man named Marsh attempted a witch murder in far southwest Virginia in 1838. The witch in question was a man named Yates, whom Marsh blamed for his scrofula and for cursing other people and animals. Marsh admitted to drawing "the likeness of Yates with chickens blood." He then prepared bullets "into which a small quantity of silver was put" and shot the bullets at the bloody effigy "under the impression that if he could strike it with a silver bullet, he should forthwith knock all of Y.'s 'conjuring' powers into atoms." When countermagic failed to break the spell, Marsh shot Yates instead. According to newspaper reports, one of the bullets employed in the murder "bore upon its surface certain cross marks" intended "to make them take effect and break that power of enchantment with which he [Yates] was supposed to be invested."[76]

The power of silver was part of a body of countermagical protective charms in oral tradition. Doddridge noted the belief that shooting "a bullet containing a little bit of silver" at a picture of a witch "transferred a painful and sometimes a mortal spell on that part of the witch corresponding with the part of the portrait struck by the bullet." Silver bullets shot into trees bearing crude chalk drawings in 1828 testify to the ubiquity of this belief—as does

Marsh's murder. Other forms of countermagic involved food. Jacob Stroyer, writing about slave life in South Carolina, noted that witches who changed their shape could be stopped by repeating the holy Trinity or by a concoction of red pepper and salt spread across a room.[77]

The practice of magic among slaves has received more attention than magical practice among free whites. Several well-known cases of magical activity are found in antebellum slave narratives. In Maryland, Frederick Douglass learned about "a certain *root*" that, when carried in a ritual manner, would protect him from the violence of his overseer.[78] Henry Bibb, who escaped from Kentucky slavery, wrote that numerous slaves in his experience "believe in what they call 'conjuration,' tricking, and witchcraft," which "can prevent their masters from exercising their will over their slaves." Bibb himself purchased a powdery composite intended to prevent his master from harming him.[79] (Bibb and Douglass subsequently abandoned their magical experiments.) Belief in the power of conjure transcended the boundaries of race and enslavement, as in the remarkable case of Dinkie, an African-born slave well versed in conjure. Dinkie's supernatural powers gave him vast autonomy on the Gaines plantation. "No one interfered with him. . . . The whites, throughout the neighborhood, tipped their hats to the old one-eyed negro, while the policemen, or patrollers, permitted him to pass without a challenge," as William Wells Brown recalled.[80] A new overseer, who like many of his ilk made it "a point always to whip a nigger, the first day that I take charge of a farm," took Dinkie out to the barn to flog him. Dinkie had other ideas. He informed his fellow slaves, "Ef he lays the weight ob his finger on me, you'll see de top of dat barn come off." Both men went into the barn as the entire plantation gathered to watch. After a while, both men came out. Dinkie had not been touched. "Dinkie's got de power," one of the slaves remarked. "He knows things seen and unseen, an' dat's what makes him his own massa."[81]

The procurement of magical goods and services via conjure also crossed racial and legal lines. William Wells Brown paid twenty-five cents to consult "Uncle Frank," a slave fortune-teller consulted "not only among the slave population, but also the whites."[82] An African American named Fenda told fortunes in the neighborhood that later burned in the War of 1812—and became Thoreau's Walden. George Izard recorded the 1816 case of Lucy Terry Perkins, who, upon marrying her husband, discovered that one of her rivals "by the ministry of a female Slave . . . cast a spell on him, since which Time he languishes a miserable Being." When doctors did no good, "a Conjurer has undertaken his Case." Izard could not hide his disgust that "otherwise sensible People" would give "serious account of the Wizzard's Prescription and Proceeding," but they did.[83]

These exchanges demonstrate that magic was a tradable commodity in the new republic. The most visible magical merchants were the fortune-tellers. Under the pseudonym Q. K. Philander Doesticks, the humorist Mortimer Thompson wrote an exposé of the practice in *The Witches of New York* (1858). The book was not, he explained, "merely a funny book" but was, rather, a serious attempt to convince his countrymen that fortune-tellers should "be no longer classed with harmless mountebanks, but with dangerous criminals." Doesticks went undercover to numerous establishments in New York, providing the address and price list for each of these "two and sixpenny witches." That number included witches of Brazilian, French, African, English, and Dutch ancestry.[84]

Doesticks inadvertently recorded a panoply of divination practices of mid-nineteenth-century America. According to Doesticks, the witches took precautions to protect their investments. "Madame Prewster" had a shop on the Bowery and was "professionally known to the police," who turned a blind eye while she "engaged in the swindling trade of Fortune Telling" and "has borne a principal part in other illicit transactions of a much more criminal nature." Some diviners, he alleged, also engaged in other forms of questionable economic activity: abortion, prostitution, counterfeiting. Those were bad enough, but fortune-telling was inherently immoral, Doesticks wrote, as it preyed on "ignorant servants, unfortunate girls of the town." Doesticks estimated the fortune-tellers of New York City were "visited every week by an average of *sixteen hundred people*," of all classes and backgrounds.[85]

Commentators confirmed this brisk trade in divination. Americans might have *feared* witchcraft, but they *went* to fortune-tellers. An English visitor complained that "a conjuror or fortune teller has more influence over the people given to vice in America, than either courts of justice, or places of worship."[86] Henry Tufts admitted to feigning fortune-telling skills across the Northeast and found he "gained much celebrity, as a conjuror; sometimes my fees amounted to eight shillings in an evening."[87] Another resident Englishman expressed astonishment that "captains of vessels make it a practice to go to one of these oracles before embarking, to know their success." The visitor was amazed to find the fortune-teller was "a respectable-looking woman, with a family, in a well-furnished house."[88]

The most "celebrated New England witch" was Moll Pitcher of Massachusetts, a legendary figure who made her living as a fortune-teller on the Massachusetts coast until her death in 1813.[89] Even her first biographer— Alonzo Lewis, in his 1829 *History of Lynn*—had difficulty separating the fact from fiction regarding her trade and reputation. Lewis noted that her visitors came with the usual problems people brought to fortune-tellers: "affairs of love or loss of property." She apparently possessed "an unusual degree of discernment"; research by Lewis (and Whittier) confirmed that her only magic was tasseomancy—divination by tea. Lewis described Pitcher's arts as merely "uncommon": educated guesses unrelated to a discourse with evil spirits.[90] Others were less sure. William Bentley wrote that Pitcher "has been commonly resorted to by this neighborhood as a fortune teller," but he also noted local worries that she might be something more: "Some dared to insinuate she was a Witch, but there was no fire or halter in the Law for her."[91]

Whatever fears the public may have had, there was no doubting her influence. Her predictions—told from a house with a gate made out of "two bones of the great whale"—had profound effects on local commerce.[92] Lewis wrote that Pitcher "was connected with some of the best families in Essex county" and "to her came the rich and the poor." "Respectable merchants" could avoiding admitting they wanted to consult Pitcher "by asking in what part of town he could find the bones of the great whale."[93] Samuel Knapp's biography of Timothy Dexter ascribed some of Dexter's unwitting financial acumen to predictions from Pitcher.[94] Amasa Delano recalled a sea journey in which most of the hands "left the ship in consequence of a prediction by . . . Moll Pitcher of Lynn, that the *Massachusetts* would be lost. . . . The majority of them believed the prophecy, and were actuated by it in their conduct."[95]

Pitcher left little by her own hand to defend herself, although a "Moll Pitcher" of Lynn wrote in 1803 to the *Boston Weekly Magazine* to vindicate her profession. A flippant remark by a correspondent (asking "Mrs. Pitcher, to conjure up her infernal agents" to discover the secrets of a wig) brought down the ire of the fortune-teller. Pitcher's letter proclaimed she had "often been the victim [of] that vulgar prejudice" and derided her accusers' poor manners and lack of Christian charity. She admonished them to follow the golden rule, act like the Good Samaritan, and otherwise live by biblical precepts. Pitcher—if it was indeed Pitcher and not an impostor—never mentioned her own purported powers in the letter, but she defended herself by writing that although she had "but few helps towards improving my mind or manners," still she was familiar with "serious and solid authors." Pitcher herself, therefore, defended her work as respectable and saw no contradiction between Christianity and her divinatory profession.[96]

Fortune-tellers were particularly called upon to find lost property; if the property in question was *very* lost—as in left behind by fleeing Tories, legendary pirates, or mythical pre-Columbian empires—the early republic supplied a different species of magical expert. The treasure digger was a legendary figure in the early republic, providing supernatural expertise for Americans who were sure buried riches lay just beneath their feet. The historian Alan Taylor has identified dozens of such episodes in the early republic, stretching from Maine to Ohio.[97]

Unlike other elements of early republican supernaturalism, treasure hunting has no modern analogue. People have not stopped looking for treasure—in 2009, amateurs with metal detectors unearthed the largest Viking hoard ever discovered—but most modern treasure hunts have no supernatural or spiritual component. In the early republic, however, the search for lost treasure involved the mysteries of hidden knowledge and life beyond the grave. Part venture capitalism, part Christian ritual, the treasure hunt was another supernatural bricolage, an occupation that bound together ghosts, demons, divination, magic circles, and (occasionally) animal sacrifice.

The supernatural laws governing treasure hunts often required a nominal secrecy among a brotherhood of seekers; such precepts discouraged written records of the quest for gold. If not widespread, however, treasure seeking was a perennial supernatural activity, often bringing a wide swath of people into its orbit. Silas Hamilton—one of the few treasure seekers to keep careful notes—recorded more than forty dreams or visions of buried treasure from among his fellow Vermonters. What evidence remains of early republican treasure hunting may represent a fraction of the total quests undertaken in the period.[98]

At least four treasure seekers left deep ruts in the historical record—"The Commodore," Ransford Rogers, Joseph Smith Jr., and Daniel Lambert. Commodore led several treasure hunts in New England and Ohio in the early republic; Smith did the same in Pennsylvania and New York in the 1820s. Rogers and Lambert were con men. Lambert's stratagem involved wearing expensive clothes and wantonly spending money, thereby convincing his neighbors he had dug up Captain Kidd's gold. Using his presumed wealth as collateral, Lambert took out massive loans from other settlers, then absconded with the cash.[99] Rogers convinced Americans that he could communicate

The deceased crew of a whaling ship, guarding a magical treasure, from *The Old American Comic and the People's Almanac*, 1841. (American Antiquarian Society)

with spirits who guarded treasure and so demonstrated by bringing forth confederates disguised as ghosts. Once established as mighty to find treasure, he had no trouble procuring smaller amounts of cash from believers, which he then kept for himself. He pulled the ruse in New Jersey in 1788, in Pennsylvania in 1797, and in New Hampshire soon thereafter. He repeated his trick in Montreal in 1801, where his nighttime excursions looked more like American espionage than spiritual activity.[100]

Most treasure seekers claimed supernatural abilities. Smith divined treasure with a peep-stone; Commodore used a magical rod. A "clairvoyant girl from Albany" led a treasure hunt in Oswego, New York, in 1851; an African American known as "Mike" saw treasure through a magical stone in Maine around 1812.[101] American treasure seekers also fought supernatural guardians—hobgoblins, apparitions, ghosts, an "evil spirit" who "would rise up and blast them with his vaporous breath," and in one case, an entire deceased crew, "rowing the spirit of their mouldered boat."[102]

Supernatural powers were necessary because treasure was magical. Treasure "was not some inanimate object," as Johannes Dillinger writes; it had "a life of its own."[103] It seemed to decide whether it *wanted* to be found. When unworthy or unrighteous seekers came close, the treasure could move. Alternatively, as the 1850 account of Commodore put it, "the human voice irritates the evil spirit who has charge of hidden treasures, and they vanish away." Thus, "searches must always be conducted in silence."[104] An 1815 treasure hunt ended when, after hours of silent digging, one man struck the hoard and cried, "Damn me, I've found it!"—whereupon the treasure vanished.[105] William Stafford went on a treasure hunt with the Smith family in the 1820s; the elder Joseph Smith made several concentric circles, but the treasure failed to materialize. Smith Jr. explained the circumstance by informing Stafford that a spirit "caused the money to sink."[106]

These ideas had deep roots in European supernatural beliefs, where treasure could transform itself into rocks, dirt, or glowing embers, and where some experts learned to lure the treasure like game, by placing a few coins on the ground and waiting for the treasure to surface. That belief formed the core of Rogers's ruse; he convinced the money diggers of Morristown, New Jersey, that "they must deliver to the spirits, every man, twelve pounds, for the money could not be given up by the spirits until the sum was given to them." A little money would allow the spirits to relinquish their larger hoard, and be set to rest.[107]

European treasure beliefs posited the presence of spiritual forces surrounding the treasure—ghosts and demons in particular. Treasure hunts in Worcester, England, can be traced at least to 1288, where a wizard conjured up a devil who then showed a young boy the location of a treasure. In 1465, two English monks faced charges of summoning demons to reveal treasure. Authorities allowed a treasure hunt at Trifels Castle in 1723, in part because the castle, being haunted, seemed a likely spot for treasure hunting. In *Hamlet*, Horatio asks the ghost "if thou hast uphoarded in thy life / Extorted treasure in the womb of earth / (For which, they say, you spirits oft walk in death)." In early modern and medieval Europe, demons and buried treasure were natural allies; the subterranean world was the abode of demons, while money had ambiguous moral associations and thus inherently attracted demonic interest.[108]

Treasure hunting was not a praiseworthy activity, but it was not *maleficium*. European practitioners could (and did) make a case for the Christian benefits of treasure seeking. A ghost condemned to guard a treasure had likely escaped from purgatory; finding treasure released the spirit and thereby set a Christian soul to rest. Treasure seeking was therefore both a morally ambiguous search for treasure and a Christian duty—even though treasure hunters openly cast spells, practiced countermagic, and used rods, mirrors, and crystals to keep demons and ghosts at bay.[109]

American treasure hunts drew from these antecedents. Commodore sought treasure on Jewel's Island, off the coast of Portland, Maine, but confronted "the malevolence of the devil, or evil spirit, who was put in charge of the money." The pirates who buried the treasure had killed a person or animal and poured the blood into the pit, Commodore believed, to keep the treasure secret.[110] Commodore studied under a German expert, performing rituals such as drawing circles, dropping new nails into a hole, and reading from "the Apocrypha, where the angel Raphael exorcises the devil"—a reference to the Book of Tobit, wherein Raphael provides a charm to banish the demon Asmodeus. Sometimes blood was needed to counteract the blood left by pirates, opening the question of sacrifice. Silas Hamilton used chicken blood. In 1833, Stafford suggested that the Smiths proposed cutting a sheep's throat "where the treasures were concealed."[111] (Stafford gave them the sheep but suspected the animal was merely eaten for supper.) By contrast, Thurlow Weed saw an all-too-real sacrifice when he accompanied a search for Kidd's gold: "The throat of a black cat was cut, and the precise spot was indicated by the direction the blood spurted."[112]

Whispers of witchcraft occasionally followed treasure digging; one man, observing the Commodore at his work, asked, "Is your old friend a witch or a wizard?" The reply was, "He comes very nigh to one."[113] Rogers's scheme in 1788 nearly came apart when the wife of a treasure seeker feared witchcraft in the harmless powder Rogers shared.[114] Yet the treasure seekers rarely came under formal accusations of witchcraft, because treasure seeking had always been something different from witchcraft.[115] The masculine nature of the activity also protected the treasure diggers. Money was also associated with men, and virtually all early modern European treasure hunts were performed by men. Early republican treasure diggers were also mostly men. The treasure seeker might "come nigh" to witchcraft, but he was not a witch: he was part exorcist, part cunning-man, and part Christian servant, laying souls to rest.

Dowsing rods, seer stones, and other esoteric practices joined in the macadamized magic that was the American treasure hunt. Fundamentally, however, it was a religious effort, though not tied to any particular confession. Rogers put especial care into stressing the religious benefits of the search; his ghosts (really associates in disguise) repeatedly informed the diggers: "I am the spirit of a just man, sent from Heaven. . . . I can have no rest until I have delivered great possessions into your hands." A constant refrain from the apparitions was, "Look to God!"[116] Mormonism's rise is not attributable to Smith's treasure digging (though critics made it regular grist for their mill). Rather, both Mormonism and treasure digging were Christian concerns, though American historians have insisted on seeing treasure digging as "occult" and therefore antithetical to Christian activity.

Treasure hunts seemed to swirl around churches and churchmen. Bentley—the embodiment of upright Yankee churchmanship—provided a Bible and psalm book to the treasure-hunting efforts of a conjurer in 1808.[117] The Universalist preacher Miles Wooley "formed a company, and engaged the services of one of those impostors who, by looking into a mysterious . . . stone, pretended to be able to discover hidden treasures." The conjurer led the company "to dig for subterraneous wealth, which he could plainly see by looking into his dark hat, having this stone in the crown." The Universalists first warned Wooley, then expelled him.[118] In 1789, Vermont Congregationalists did the same to Nathaniel Wood. He set up his own church of New Israelites, who later contracted with a conjurer to find treasure and learned divine truths through their divining rods.[119]

Despite all the esoterica, a democratic simplicity lurked at the heart of American treasure digging. Commodore compared his divining rod to "the priests of the Oracle at Delphos," but with an important difference: "His talismanic oracle, however, was never ambiguous like theirs, but always gave a plain answer."[120] Anyone could be a treasure digger; an entire company of African American men once sought for gold on the Boston Common—an egalitarian assault on the bluest of blue-blood locales.[121] When John Harriott bought his farm on Long Island, the former owner described how he and his sons "worked hard for hours and hours" in those "particular suspected parts, that seemed to answer the description where it was reported so much money was buried during the war!"[122] Treasure digging offered an egalitarian ethos among men, where skill and perseverance could result in riches. "The Money Digging fraternity may be considered, at present, as a democratic body," declared the *Herald of Freedom* in 1788.[123] Idealistic treasure seekers committed to share their knowledge of ghosts, witches, and other forms of magic, so that all would gain as they pressed forward to the treasure.

Treasure digging was also one of the forms of magic most susceptible of proofs. Although most treasure hunts ended in failure, treasure was unearthed at various times in the early republic, or at least it was so reported. Stephen Grindle stumbled across "some four or five hundred pieces of the currency of France, Spain, Spanish America, Portugal, Holland, England, and Massachusetts" on his farm in coastal Maine in the winter of 1840–41.[124] Caleb Atwater reported Roman coins found in Tennessee before 1820. Chloe

Russel maintained that her dreams had led to the discovery of a vast hoard in 1824.[125] Numerous books described ancient American burial sites, where presumed lost civilizations (that is, not the Native Americans) had filled mounds with "quantities of human bones . . . also instruments of warfare, broken earthen vessels, and trinkets."[126] Newspapers reported other tales of secret hoards. In 1810, the *Massachusetts Spy* reported from its foreign correspondent that the governor of Konigsberg had unearthed "an immense treasure of gold, silver and diamonds" by following the legend told him by an old man.[127] The *Haverhill (MA) Gazette* informed its readers that just south of Albany, New York, Kidd had buried "50 boxes of gold, and laid upon them 13 human bodies."[128] Great family names were connected with treasures, too; in 1856, George Brent and Amory Edwards discussed plans to recover the lost treasures of the daughter of Aaron Burr, who had been lost at sea in 1813. Edwards had it on good authority that Theodosia Burr's treasure had been reburied by pirates in a "vault of stone & mortar, each end. North and South will explode if digging there," so Edwards advised approaching through the east wall.[129]

The fungibility of magical ideas in the eighteenth and nineteenth centuries possessed a certain sympathy with the democratic tinkering under way in the Age of Jefferson. As ideas of liberty and freedom reworked government and society to reflect the needs of "the common man," so, too, did magic begin to express itself as a popular tool. American magic was do-it-yourself—or if you could not, in good capitalist fashion, some other expert could be paid to do it for you. If American Christianity "democratized" in the Age of Jefferson, as Nathan Hatch put it, then it should not be surprising that magic and counterwitchcraft democratized as well.

W. J. Rorabaugh once described alcohol in antebellum America as an expression of individual liberty: "To be drunk was to be free." Drinking, especially to excess, implied self-mastery. No king, father, or minister could tell a true yeoman what to consume or how much. A similar logic may have guided early republican use of magical charms and other low-grade supernaturalisms. No judge or minister could tell a citizen what manner of supernatural rites to follow; if magic could be proven to someone's satisfaction, no social concerns or Puritanical qualms about diabolism made a whit of difference. Indeed, magic could wield its own moral force for liberty. Chloe Russel's autobiography claimed she received her freedom from slavery when she dreamed of buried treasure and told the rightful owner where to dig for it. The beneficiary was so glad when he found the specie that he bought her and freed her—thus through magic "I was fairly rid of one of the most tyrannical masters on earth!"[130] Hohman specifically invoked First Amendment freedoms to defend his *Long-Lost Friend:* "The publication of books (provided they are useful and morally right) is not prohibited in the United States, as is the case in other countries where kings and despots hold tyrannical sway over the people."[131] To be magical was to be free.

The early republican sympathy between magic and liberty meant that people from almost all backgrounds became involved in supernatural activities. Nineteenth-century magical practice did not become "confined to the poorer, more marginal segments of society." The early republic had no court necromancers, yet people of wealth and education frequently attempted to "make a gain of soothsaying," as Whittier put it. McAfee—later the historian of the War of 1812—could engage in water witching while reading Locke, Stackhouse, and Edwards. The astrologer Sheffield was an Andover graduate. Whittier reported that a woman in Poplin, New Hampshire, dreamed of gold, and "twenty or more grown men, graduates of our 'common schools,' and liable, every mother's son of them, to be made deacons, squires, and General Court members" were busily digging for the treasure.[132]

It was not that the poor and vulgar became heirs to magic in the early republic but rather that that magic as an *idea* became pejoratively associated with such groups through the republican campaign against magic, the process of setting standards, differentiating peoples, and setting boundaries.[133] It is perhaps because of this process that a democratized supernatural existed uneasily within the emerging republican state, and why the response to supernaturalism seemed well out of proportion to the actual threat faced. Why should anyone care if free white citizens got drunk and spent a midnight ramble digging for buried treasure—which, by the way, they routinely failed to find?

The answer had to do both with the kind of state and the kind of citizen demanded by a republican ideology. Republicanism meant more magic, but republicanism also feared magic; it was both an anxiety and embrace of a world of crumbling hierarchies. The "Old Whig," writing in the wake of the 1787 witch lynching in Philadelphia, made the connection explicit. The death of a witch "repeatedly wounded with knives—mangled and at last killed in our streets" provided "an example to warn us how little we ought to trust the unrestrained discretion of human nature." The Old Whig took Korbmacher's death as an opportunity to call for a Bill of Rights.[134] The belief in witchcraft and magic led to unrestrained passions and violent consequences. Popular belief in witchcraft could kill, and the Old Whig worried that the government was being handed over to popular believers. Witchcraft as an idea threatened the republic as surely as it threatened the life of Korbmacher. The republic needed to control supernaturalism, lest supernaturalism corrupt the republic. It is to this formulation that we now turn.

The Politics of the Supernatural

Andrew Oehler had been a carpenter in Switzerland, a vagabond in New Orleans, a soldier in Napoleonic France, and a balloonist in Havana, but he outdid himself one night in Mexico City. Invited by the governor to present an evening's entertainment, he dressed a suite of rooms in black, drew down lightning, and "converse[d] with a departed spirit"—all via sleight-of-hand techniques, as he explained in his mawkish autobiography, *The Life and Unparalleled Sufferings of Andrew Oehler*. For his trouble, the authorities threw him into prison for witchcraft and trafficking with demons. His hosts, Oehler wrote, "could not but believe I must be assisted by supernatural agency," given that Mexicans were "ignorant of philosophy and the powers of nature" and believed "these appearances to be real and substantial facts," which they looked upon "with a mixture of jealousy and admiration, as though it had been something supernatural." A chance visit from an enlightened Spanish marquis secured Oehler's release. In remorse, the governor offered Oehler Mexican citizenship and a monetary reward, but Oehler hesitated to "take the oath of allegiance to the superstitious laws, and I suppose religion too, of the country." He returned to the United States, where he was promptly robbed and forced to flee naked across an open swamp.[1]

Oehler's book makes for quite a read. It not only has him imprisoned in Mexico but also wrongfully accused of murder in Frankfurt, shipwrecked off the coast of China, battling lions on a tropical island, and commanding a legion of rebellious slaves alongside Toussaint Louverture in Haiti. Sadly, Oehler's description of his stage magic repeats almost verbatim the description of a much more successful and well-known magician, the phantasmagorist Robertson (Étienne Gaspard-Robert)—who *did* perform in Mexico City, in 1798, and was *not* thrown in prison. Oehler's unparalleled sufferings were fictional.[2]

The woebegone odyssey of Oehler sounded familiar themes in Jeffersonian America; the author went through some trouble to mention the exciting events and faddisms of a world at war: Bonaparte, Egypt, ballooning. The absence of referents for Oehler's wild itinerary is secondary; whether readers read the *Sufferings* as true or false, they would have understood it as an admonition about the political consequences of superstition. Belief in the supernatural, Oehler assured readers, was the lynchpin of tyranny. Only free men understood that miracles, wonders, and magic were so much sleight-of-hand or mythology. By the same token, belief in magic or the supernatural would poison free men, reversing their climb to civilization and liberty.

Oehler was not alone in issuing such warnings. In 1812, a year after the *Sufferings* was published, a congressional debate on war preparation veered into a discussion of the supernatural sources of the recent New Madrid earthquakes. The venerable John Randolph of Virginia informed the House of Representatives that the quakes proved "we are on the brink of some dreadful scourge—some great desolation—some awful visitation from that Power whom, I am afraid, we have as yet, in our national capacity, taken no means to conciliate."[3] John C. Calhoun issued a swift and bitter response: "I did hope that the age of superstition was past, and that no attempt would be made to influence the measures of Government, which ought to be founded in wisdom and policy, by the vague, I may say superstitious, feelings of any man, whatever may be the physical appearances which give rise to them. . . . It would mark a fearful retrograde in civilization; it would prove a dreadful declension toward barbarism."[4]

Taken together, Calhoun and Oehler outlined the republican thesis of the politics of the supernatural. This coherent, well-articulated body of thought gilded the new republic, running through sermons, tracts, lectures, plays, novels, speeches, and manuals for stage magic. This interpretation rarely came in the form of a fully articulated theory; it was perhaps less an ideology or a system of thought than a *way of thinking* about certain things—nature, senses, liberty, the nation, God. This theory of magic touched on most of the great subjects of republican discourse and addressed the popular and intellectual anxieties of the revolutionary shift to qualified popular rule and the more terrifying implications of the farther shift to democratization. It was the republican language of the supernatural.

Neither Calhoun nor Oehler fully explained this language, but then, they did not need to: one does not explain what one expects an audience to understand. The tenets, however, emerged from the same Baconian assumptions that caused the rise of American miracles in the republic: a trust in sense evidence to report accurately on the natural world, the assumption of a clockwork universe, the fetishization of "fact." Both Oehler and Calhoun assumed the supernatural was entirely false; indeed, *magic* (not faith) was the antithesis of reason. And since reason was the basis of free government, magic or the supernatural could have no place in the decisions of the republic (thus Calhoun's complaint and Oehler's refusal to remain in Mexico). Oehler and Calhoun further adduced a theory of stadial development; all nations existed on a spectrum from civilization to barbarism and might progress toward the former or slide to the latter. Needless to say, white Americans had civilization (and therefore liberty), but if they embraced supernatural belief, they would tilt toward barbarism (and therefore tyranny). Finally and perhaps most importantly, both Oehler and Calhoun employed their arguments about witchcraft as part of a larger attempt at invective and ridicule. As the Unitarian minister Bernard Whitman wrote, citizens who encountered believers "in fortune-telling and witchcraft, in apparitions and ghosts" must convince them of their error: "And if we cannot produce conviction by sober sense and sound argument, I think we shall be justified in this particular case, in resorting to ridicule."[5] Whittier similarly acknowledged "the slightly disguised sarcasm and ridicule" of his own invective against superstition.[6] The charge of supernaturalism was not simply a mild corrective; it was an assault on the moral and intellectual fiber of one's opponent. Calhoun and Oehler did not believe, and they did not expect any reasonable republican to believe, in magic, divination, or the supernatural activities of higher beings in the earthly realms. Superstition and witchcraft came from foreigners and slaves, Catholics and tyrants, and to believe in such things would tear the nation from the sacred place of liberty down through the stages of civilized development to a state of monarchy or theocracy.[7]

The case against miracles had international analogues. The French state worried about *séducteurs* who promised magical abilities and the *crédules* who believed them in the wake of the Affair of the Poisons.[8] In the Hapsburg Empire, the Enlightenment mavens of the court of Maria Theresa urged the abolition of witch- and vampire hunts in the 1750s, in an effort to chase "barbarous superstitious ignorance from the brains of the people."[9] A burst of Polish trials in the eighteenth century prompted Enlightenment elites to urge decriminalization, which passed in 1776.[10] This "imposture thesis," as outlined by the historian Frank Manuel, laid out the basic lines of the antiwitchcraft thinking of the American nineteenth century: priests and politicians utilized the magical panache of oracles to keep their charges in thrall.[11] The problem of designing impostors out to steal the will of the people assumed added weight in the American context of republican revolution and disestablishment.

"Superstition" in early modern Europe did not refer to ephemera like throwing rice at weddings or knocking on wood; superstition possessed pernicious, even lethal, connotations. Superstition implied false belief—traditions of heretics, use of fraudulent relics, or rites "beyond what was customary and official." It was a common charge of Protestants against Catholics (and vice versa). Given the need to police confessional boundaries, a wide array of practices and popular traditions became classed as superstitious. Local healers, magic charms, and even counterwitchcraft became "superstition."[12] The very concept of "superstition," therefore, had its roots in problems of belief and the process of "cultural disapproval and exclusion," as Clark writes. These associations and patterns remained in the United States as the case against superstition adapted—like the supernatural itself—to a republican society.

"Superstition" lost its association with hellfire, but it still implied false belief, and so it was still dangerous. "When ignorance and bigotry cooperate," wrote the revolutionary veteran James Thacher in his *Essay on Demonology*, "the pure fountain of truth is polluted, and the most preposterous tales of antiquity are held in veneration by every fiery zealot. From this cause, millions of innocent lives have been sacrificed."[13] Indeed, Whitman wrote in 1829, if people believe "the devil works miracles, that witches exist," or that "religious excitements and commotions of the present day are occasioned by the miraculous effusions of the holy spirit," then "trials for heresy, blasphemy, and witchcraft would once more disgrace the annals of our nation."[14]

Whittier called it "supernaturalism"—"matters beyond and above the conception of his sharpened five senses." For Whittier, the term was linked to superstition, derived from "Puritan ancestors," whom he accused of "agitating their entire community with signs, and wonders, and dark marvels—poisoning the fountains of education, and constituting part of their religion." Worse, he found "scarcely a superstition of the past three centuries which has not at this very time more or less hold upon individual minds among us."[15] Whittier's 1847 *Supernaturalism of New England*—along with his 1831 *Legends of New England*—joined works by Thacher, Whitman, and a handful of others on the supernatural and its dangers as the "demonologies" of the early republic.

Though American demonologies lost their association with witch trials, they continued to prescribe certain forms of *communitas* and political action. They ascribed the problems of the supernatural world to particular groups within the republic and advocated particular public measures for the eradication of the supernatural threat. David Reese dedicated his *Humbugs of New York* (1838) to "the constituted guardians of the public health, public morals, and public peace," and explained the "reign of humbug" as a political crisis, the "serious and important bearing on the public weal which certain impostures in our city are likely to exhibit." Reese also noted that it was "the more enlightened portion of our population" who needed to watch out for impostures such as phrenology, mesmerism, and Mormonism, or else "the prevalence and success of these impostures in the lower walks of life, will neutralize civilization itself."[16]

Whitman classified as superstitions all things that "cannot be proved realities by rational and scriptural evidence."[17] In some ways, scriptural evidence *was* sense evidence, for as Thacher pointed out, demons *did* exist in apostolic times, but "holy scriptures tell us of no such tales . . . which confound the laws of nature and absolutely destroy the testimony of our senses."[18] Whitman maintained earlier European theological concerns; superstition was "pernicious, because it turns your attention from God to fate and chance and devils."[19] Yet it also threatened the government, as Thacher wrote, because the "mind that is imbued with a superstitious temperament, is liable to incessant torment, and is prepared to inflict the most atrocious evils on mankind; even murder, suicide, and merciless persecution, have proceeded from, and been sanctioned by a superstitious spirit."[20] Or, as the epic poem *The Village* (1816) eulogized:

> For when in States neglected virtues faint,
> And catch from vice its all corrupting taint;
> In freemen's hearts when love of country fails,
> And careless negligence of right prevails . . .
> Superstition, with its thousand creeds,
> Frowning on Reason as for Truth she pleads,
> Spreads wide confusion and to rage excites,
> In discord triumphs and in strife delights.[21]

Superstition was the opposite of patriotism.

The case against supernaturalism denied the power of magical or divine forces in the human world, attributing reports of such powers to deliberate falsehoods or to epistemological error. A professional set of impostors emerged, according to the new demonologists and other writers, who manufactured wonders to mislead others and thereby obtain monetary and political power. As the printer David Young wrote about Ransford Rogers's hoax, "The more ignorant and superstitious part of mankind, have been, and still are . . . to a greater or lesser degree, subjected to like impositions." Therefore Rogers, with "an intention to extract money from their pockets, endeavored to secure the veil of ignorance upon their minds," pretended to see buried treasure, and arranged the exhibition of faux ghosts, until at last his victims would "revere Rogers, believing him something more than a man: and such was the influence which he possessed over them, with a despotic power." All the miracles since the apostles were fakes; all the witches in history were liars.[22]

That was the trouble: witches had no magical powers, yet people acted as though they did. If there was no longer a "shared assumption at all levels of society that powers existed beyond everyday physical powers," as Diarmiad MacCulloch describes the world of the Reformation, the very fact that this belief was no longer *shared* troubled the minds of some in the early republic. If people still believed in magic and witches, the argument went, then they were mistaken. If they were mistaken, they could be tricked into acting against their own self-interest. If people acted against their own self-interest, the polity was doomed.[23]

The evil of supernaturalists therefore came from the harm they inflicted through belief; the power of delusion was no vanishing nightmare under a republican order. "There is power in a popular delusion and general excitement of the passions of a community to pervert the best of characters," wrote Charles Upham in his history of the Salem witchcraft trials; it would "turn the hearts even of good men to violence."[24] The somewhat reformed charlatan William Pinchbeck wanted "to oppose the idea of supernatural agency in any production of man"—once his own moneymaking hoaxes were finished. He wrote a book explaining "how dangerous such a belief [in the supernatural] is to society, how destructive to the improvement of the human capacity, and how totally ruinous to the common interests of mankind." In Pinchbeck's mind, each of his astute readers, on learning the threat of superstition needed to "reclaim the obstinate believers in ghosts."[25] Whittier insisted that "that stern duty which the true man owes to his generation, to expose error" required constant vigilance against "the evil of impressing the young mind with beliefs, unwarranted by reason or revelation."[26] Upham assumed that a republican would inevitably "do what he may to enlighten, rectify, and control public sentiment . . . to accelerate the decay of superstition."[27]

Thus, inquiry into the nature of the supernatural was not ancillary to the politics of the early republic; such inquiry was essential to the perennial Jeffersonian and Jacksonian dilemmas about the problems of freedom, tyranny, and reason. Witchcraft "belongs to the mind-enslaving and misery-creating family of superstition, and is twin sister to priestcraft," intoned the *Boston Investigator*.[28] Fortune-telling, wrote a critic in 1812, "destroys the tranquility of many . . . fetching the last penny from the purse of indigence." Therefore, "the legislature of New-York has acted wisely in making this a subject of prohibition . . . an example which ought to be imitated by every State in the Union."[29] Some states did: "every juggler and fortune-teller" was classed with prostitutes by Maryland law. Connecticut classed as vagrants "all persons using, or pretending to use any subtle craft, juggling . . . or feigning themselves to have knowledge in physiognomy, palmistry, or pretending they can tell destinies, fortunes, or discover where lost or stolen goods may be found." (The law recommended the workhouse for all of them.)[30]

The historiography of witches and witchcraft provides numerous studies of the ways in which societies perceive "the other" or "otherness." By defining abnormality, witches as others helped establish acceptable behavior. This definitional process is often thought of by historians as operating in a broadly social or psychological plane, crafting personal affectations and taboos, but it could also function in concrete ways—as when early modern states campaigned against witches to prove themselves and their reign to be of God. Dispossession "validated the authority in whose name it was made," as Stuart Clark writes, thereby making the classification and prosecution of certain individuals as witches a political process (among other things).[31] Citizens of the American commonwealth, however, were more likely to hear a warning against the way superstitious fears would alter election outcomes, such as this bit of early-republican doggerel:

How often I have seen fanatic zeal,
Where superstition rules the public weal
Call a town meeting, and request a vote;
To send for a young candidate in haste,
To have him come forthwith and peddle out
Brimstone, and fire, and supernatural war.[32]

If witches were "others" in a nation that had destroyed monarchical rule, it perhaps makes sense that witches ceased to be agents of the devil warring against God and his righteous monarchs and became instead conniving individuals whose actions defrauded the public. The "sacred" power that opposed them, in this formulation, were republicans and enlighteners, bearers of truth who "tried" witches in the court of public opinion and exposed them rather than executed them. In short, as Clark and Bengt Ankarloo have discussed, witchcraft remained an "other," but the "other" of an age of reason, an "other" of "eighteenth-century rationalism, a much-despised example of all that was deemed to be wrong with traditional religion and unenlightened societies."[33] Thomas Jefferson did not believe in miracles; indeed, he spent part of his presidency editing the New Testament by removing all of its references to supernatural powers. Nevertheless, Jefferson called the Federalist ascendancy of 1798 a "reign of witches": "Our present situation is not a natural one," Jefferson explained, because Alexander Hamilton had blinded the people by manipulating "the irresistible influence & popularity of Genl. Washington" to put the government into "antirepublican hands." In the end, though, Jefferson pledged that "we shall see the reign of witches pass over, their spells dissolve, and the people recovering their true sight." Jefferson did not fear magical spells, but he feared those who could manipulate and command factions among the people, and he called that witchcraft.[34]

One such place in which early Americans could have found that lesson was in the incipient American literary establishment. Fiction—especially popular fiction—both creates and reflects the culture in which it is produced; Philip Gould has described how early American novelists used Salem as a metaphor for the political dangers of their own time; Gretchen Adams has shown the ways in which that metaphor shifted and changed through American history.[35] Yet the rhetoric and explanations of magic were not merely metaphor. They did not only explain politics; they explained and defined *magic* to the first generations of U.S. citizens. While these writings did not represent any singular uniform "commonly held" notion of the supernatural in the early republic, they did represent *a* conception of the supernatural. As James Sharpe wrote about Shakespeare and *Macbeth,* "even in plays where witchcraft and magic were not central themes, the language of the occult, of astrology, even of alchemy is frequently to be found. This is not to say that playwrights or their audiences were obsessed with magic" but rather "that their audience would be familiar with such issues and at least some of the discourse surrounding them," particularly when "the playwrights of the period were for the most part professionals, aiming to meet current tastes and reflect rather than lead opinion."[36]

Theater's importance had not diminished in the years between Shakespeare's Globe and Joseph Jefferson's Astor Place. Theater expanded in the early republic; the increased wealth of the colonies made theatrical performances a luxury good that more and more people could afford, and as theater historians have noted, this shift made the stage an important site of American self-definition.[37] The newly independent audiences clamored for American plays, and theater managers and playwrights took up the challenge.

What did the American theater of the early republic assume its audiences would understand about magic? Playwrights portrayed witchcraft as a tyranny encouraged by charlatans and enforced by the mob. *The Tragedy of Superstition* features a Salem-esque Puritan village in thrall to its minister, Ravensworth. When the public clamors for witch trials, Ravensworth obliges, despite the warning that,

> If reason in a mind like yours . . . can bow down
> Before the popular breath, what shall protect
> From the all-with'ring blasts of superstition
> The unthinking crowd, in whom credulity,
> Is ever the first born of ignorance?

Nothing, of course, can save the crowd from itself, since,

>   such folly,
> When it infects the crowd, is dangerous.
> Already we've had proof what dreadful acts
> Their madness may commit, and each new day
> The frenzy spreads.[38]

The public demands witch trials; Ravensworth obliges, and disaster follows.

In 1809, John Howard Payne published the first translated American edition of Voltaire's *Mahomet*, in which the prophet of Islam is portrayed as a religious dictator justifying his claims by false miracles. The American introduction to the text explained that the prophet Muhammad had offered his revelation solely to obtain personal power, and the prophet knew it, too, since he "foresaw that an impostor might be obeyed—adored;—and that no extravagance of mystery or miracle, was too wonderful, or too ridiculous, for a people's belief." In *Mahomet*, Americans saw the prophet portrayed as both heretic and tyrant, with the two crimes clearly related; the play declares its purpose in the prologue as "To point what lengths credulity has run, / What counsels shaken, and what states undone." The prophet is condemned as "Thou poor deserter of thy country's gods / Thou base invader of thy country's rights." If the audience had any further doubts as to the quality of the prophet's character, the play goes so far to have him hold up a copy of "the alcoran" and declare, "Glorious hypocrisy!"[39]

The play takes place inside the still-pagan Mecca of the 620s CE, under siege from the armies of Islam. The Mecca of *Mahomet* bears a marked similarity, in the English translation, to antebellum America. It is ruled by "the senate" and follows "true religion . . . always mild, propitious, and humane." Such "principles like these, which reason dictates" are compared to Christianity, which the pagan Alcanor remarks "may be right." The mob threatens to ruin the peace of this republican-pagan Mecca. The followers of the prophet are "untutor'd reptiles . . . more credulous still / Of what is most incredible." Moreover, popular pressure afflicts the imaginary democracy of this fictional Mecca, as an advisor warns, "say, is the senate sound? / I fear some members of that rev'rend class / Are mark'd with the contagion." Indeed, it is through a vote in the senate that the prophet (meant to be seen as a tyrant) finally gains entrance to Mecca.[40]

Credulity and the supernatural did not always result in tragedy. In 1797, audiences in Philadelphia and Baltimore enjoyed the adventures of Sir Credulous Testy in *The Comet*. The dashing Belmont hoaxes the aptly named Credulous in order to marry the old man's ward, the lovely Emily. Belmont and the Lady Candour team up to use an "electrical jar" to stage a faux Armageddon for Credulous, and "while his senses are bewilder'd . . . he will imagine a thousand horrours, and may perhaps give his consent to your union." The tricksters succeed, and Emily is liberated from her superstitious guardian, "whose preposterous ignorance, joined to his extreme tyranny, render[ed] the pangs of separation from Belmont doubly poignant."[41] A similar ending resolved the 1820 production of *The Magician and the Holy Alliance;* at the play's climax, "A Huge Black Snake supposed to be the grand papa of the '*Sea Serpent*' lately seen in the east" swallows the nefarious magician Katterfelto. The lesson from the author, one "Tobias Alltruth," is that "in the end, we always see . . . TRUTH triumphs over hypocrisy."[42]

Thomas Forrest twice wrote *The Disappointment, or the Force of Credulity* for the American stage, in 1767 and 1796. The play's prologue declares: "Theatric business was, and still should be, / To point out vice in its deformity ... / No matter which, the pulpit or the stage, / Condemn the vice and folly of the age." To do so, Forrest seized on "a knave and a conjurer" who "Quit solid sense for airy golden dreams." The plot revolves around a team of japesters tricking a pack of immigrants into digging for treasure and making fools of themselves. All the usual errata of treasure digging make appearances: hazel rods, iron pieces, the zodiac, magic circles. The marks dream of improving themselves without work; the conspirators laugh about making "proselytes of half the town" as long as "credulity and love of money prevail." After learning of the imposture, the victims forgive the prank and take the moral lesson: "dis is my own fau't for being too credulous," says Raccoon in his Swedish pidgin. "I bill take de resolution to lead a new life and follow my bid'ness wid honesty and industry." The dupe Washball concurs and ends the play with this speech: "Let it be a warning to others not to listen to idle schemes and give way to vain imaginations." Those "weak enough to listen to artful, designing men, stands upon a dangerous precipe. . . . They tread unsure, who 'gainst their senses run." Forrest went on to serve two terms as a Federalist congressman.[43]

The theater featured more than plays. Traveling exhibitions made similar claims. Pinchbeck himself first displayed astounding marvels, then exposed them. He toured the early United States with the famed "Pig of Knowledge," which could respond to certain questions by picking correct answers out of a hat. (There were reports of several learned animals at the time, including at least one "learned goat.")[44] Pinchbeck turned in the 1800s to displaying miraculous contraptions exposed, the most famous of which was the Acoustic Temple shown in Boston in 1804, the point of which, one broadside declared, was to make citizens "Attend, and never after give credit to the improbable tales of Witchcraft and Supernatural Agency!"[45]

Ghost stories in the early republic went to great lengths to assure readers that such things did not exist—and that anyone who thought otherwise was foolish at best and dangerous at worst. A collection of ghost stories appeared with the revealing if lengthy title *Ghost Stories Collected with a Particular View to Counteract the Vulgar Belief in Ghosts and Apparitions and to Promote a Rational Estimate of the Nature or Phenomena Commonly Considered as Supernatural.* The introduction thereof assured readers that in ancient days, "the vulgar were afraid of spirits, and wiser heads left them under the influence of that apprehension, which they sometimes employed for good, at others for sinister purposes."[46] Whittier gave several accounts of ghosts—all of

An illustration of a faux ghost—a turnip in disguise—from the 1810 volume *Tales for Young Children*. (Courtesy, American Antiquarian Society)

them merely a byproduct of imagination or intoxication.[47] Both *Amusement for Good Children* (1808) and *Tales for Young Children* (1810) featured stories entitled "The Ghost"; in each story, the fearsome specter is revealed to be a hollowed-out turnip. Frightened children get a lecture from their mother on the nature of apparitions: "Do not, I beg of you, my dear children, by such weak ideas, tempt my serious displeasure. I have ever endeavoured to impress upon your young minds, the folly of encouraging such idle opinions."[48] Thacher related the story of a young woman whose "disturbed imagination" mistook a white robe for the revenant of a smallpox victim, yet who insisted she had seen the ghost, complete with the telltale scarring.[49]

The Witch of Endor became a symbol for the republican dangers of the supernatural. King Saul, for example, had been misled by the phantasmagoria of the witch. "She was probably possessed of some secret knowledge of natural properties," Upham explained, and "had perhaps the peculiar powers of a ventriloquist, and by successful imposture, had acquired an uncommon degree of notoriety and the entire confidence of the public."[50] Upham, Lathrop, and Quitman all gave exegeses on 1 Samuel 28, and found within the passage the evidence of the witch's theatrical tricks. Quitman found imposition "every where visible . . . she causes a cloud of narcotic vapors to rise from the earth, at the sight of which she cries with a loud voice, to increase the fear of the spectators."[51] The theologians disagreed to details, but they all followed Lathrop's general line regarding the tendency of supernatural claims to "dissolve our mutual confidence and subvert our social security."[52]

Similar pronouncements crossed the Atlantic. Hannah More's *Tawney Rachel* (U.S. editions in 1800 and 1807) recounted the crimes of the titular Rachel, who "was continually practising on the credulity of silly girls" by claims to divinatory powers, and "took advantage of their ignorance to cheat and deceive them." William Godwin found magical imposition across all Western history; the *Lives of the Necromancers* (U.S. editions published in 1835, 1847, and 1865) declared its intention "to observe the actual results of these imaginary phenomena, and the crimes and cruelties they have caused us to commit." Godwin explained the trickery behind more than a hundred historical witches and wizards. Macbeth "addicted himself continually to the consulting of wizards," a practice that destroyed his reign. Merlin "exhibited a very criminal sort of compliance" in helping Uther bed Ygraine. Paracelsus fooled people into believing his magical prowess so that he could engage "in beastly crapulence with the dregs of society." More and Godwin shared few political sentiments, but both writers agreed on the danger and "the power which superstition has over the weak and credulous mind."[53]

Then as now, Salem was the preeminent example of American witchcraft. In the early republic, Salem became a morality tale of credulity run wild. The witchcraft trials had long served as a warning-piece to the colonials; immediately after the proceedings closed, Cotton Mather and John Hale both wrote books declaring that the devil had been in Salem (though the authors disagreed on Satan's tactics). Robert Calef thought the devil had stirred up Puritan imagination to create a delusion, and then "Witchcraft became a Principal Ecclesiastical Engine (as also that of Heresie was) to root up all that stood in their way."[54] Eighteenth-century histories leaned toward Calef but found the fault less in the devil than in the political leadership that succumbed to clerical demands.[55] These works indicted the courts and the laws of the land for their failure to protect the innocent. Thomas Hutchinson's 1767 account blamed the shoddy law of the court of oyer and terminer, the use of decades-old accusations, and the acceptance of spectral evidence.[56]

Beginning with William Bentley's 1799 *History of Salem*, however, the fault no longer lay with the judges who listened to the people but with the people themselves. "Witchcraft," Bentley wrote, "soon proved itself to be an evil to be corrected in the public opinion, and not in a court of justice." The "terror of the imagination was so great" that people confessed, especially under threat to their life, and "confessions blinded the judges." But the blame from Bentley still went to "the public clamours" that urged the judges on, "till nineteen innocent persons were victims of the public credulity."[57] So the story of Salem became the story of a superstitious public overrunning the established law of the community. Hannah Adams's 1806 history of New England lamented the execution of nineteen people, but "even this circumstance was insufficient to open the eyes of the people," who presumably could have stopped the trials had they wanted to. Yet "the prevailing credulity of the age" prevented them.[58]

The Supreme Court justice Joseph Story wrote in 1828 that the executions at Salem derived "partly from blind credulity, and partly from overwhelming fraud. The whole of these proceedings exhibit melancholy proofs of the effect of superstition in darkening the mind." Story described the trials as the reign of "fanaticism, acting under the influence of preternatural terror," which once let loose, led to a general dissolution of social bonds: "We find parents accusing their children, children their parents, and wives their husbands, of a crime, which must bring them to the scaffold."[59] The historian and politician George Barstow, too, found in witch trials a collapse of state and civilization: "Contrary to the laws of nature and the laws of civil society, husbands were permitted to accuse their wives, and wives to bear witness against their husbands. What can be more revolting than a superstition thus deaf to the voice of humanity; arming itself with supernatural terrors." Barstow believed witch judges were "infected by the popular belief"; indeed, "the public excitement rose to such a pitch that all legal principles seem to have been . . . effectually destroyed," and "judges partook of the frenzy which bore the multitude away."[60]

Charles Upham completed the early republic's most extensive scholarly treatment of the trials in his 1831 *Lectures on Witchcraft,* which stitched together the varied elements of the early republican critique of superstition and the supernatural.[61] Upham began with the falseness of witchcraft: "It is, at present, the universal opinion that the whole of this witchcraft transaction was a delusion, having no foundation whatever but in the imaginations and passions." Imagination triumphed over reason, courts credited the accusations, and the result was predictable: "Whenever a community gives way to its passions . . . and casts off the restraints of reason, there is a delusion that can hardly be described in any other phrase."[62]

For Upham, this state of affairs made an opening for an unscrupulous and conniving politician to seize control of the state and capture liberty; Upham cast Cotton Mather in this role. Mather's plan had been to incite a witchcraft panic "in order that he might increase his own influence over an infatuated people, by being regarded by them as mighty to cast out and vanquish evil spirits." Mather himself "combined an almost incredible amount of vanity and credulity, with a high degree of cunning and policy; an inordinate love of temporal power and distinction, with every outward manifestation of piety and Christian humility; and a proneness to fanaticism and superstition with amazing acquisitions of knowledge." The people of Salem, under the influence of imagination, became captives of Mather's controlling interest. Upham clarified the allusion to the developing party system of his own day, writing that Mather, "like other ambitious and grasping politicians . . . was eager to have the support of all parties at the same time." Nor was politics the only danger: "The clergy were also instrumental in promoting the proceedings. Nay, it must be acknowledged that they took the lead in the whole transaction." Where credulity ruled the public, priestcraft and politicians thrived.[63]

A medley of early American novels also took Salem for their subject, and of those, virtually all of them made the conjunction of delusion, superstition, and power their theme. In the 1824 novel *The Witch of New England*, the title character's power comes from the influence she wields over the ignorant: "Over common minds, she invariably obtained an influence and stern mastery that she seldom relinquished, and often used with heartless and unrelenting disdain."[64] *Rachel Dyer*, John Neal's 1828 story of Salem, describes Samuel Parris as "a shrewd, artful, uneducated man" who became "head-ruler in the church" through the influence of those "who believed in witchcraft as a familiar thing."[65] Similarly, Jonathan Scott explained the logic of his 1817 epic poem, *The Sorceress, or Salem Delivered*, as the usual story of priestcraft: "It was the grand object of the clerical body to be able to obtain the assistance of the civil power; on this circumstance much of the following tale depends."[66] Eliza Lee's *Delusion, or the Witch of New England* (1840) informs readers that the demoniac children of Salem deliberately invented their lies: "They had concerted this diabolical plot, and had rehearsed and practiced beforehand their contortions and convulsions." The saintly heroine Edith explains witchcraft this way: "God suffers us to be tempted by our own passions and unrestrained imaginations, but not by invisible or visible spirits. O, listen to me: go no further in this mad, this wicked delusion. . . . Bigotry and power are all around us."[67] In Elam Bliss's comedy about the witch trials, *Parson Handy of Punkapog Pond*, the Mathers become both tyrants and tyrannized, although in this case they are prompted on by their own doltishness rather than cruelty. Bliss makes it clear that cleverer common people have duped the Mathers; Increase and Cotton inadvertently abet a humorous subjugation of justice by playing into the intricate plots of the jilted Beautiful Hobbes (who is ugly) and Remarkable Short (who is six feet tall) to implicate the innocent Patience Peabody as a witch.[68] In William Dunlap's "Tom Bell," an 1836 story set in the eighteenth century, Benjamin Franklin arrives just in time to stop a treasure-digging hoax and rescue the intended victim "from delusion and ruin." Dunlap also joked that George Washington had similar powers of dispossession; New Jersey "in the good old time was famous for witches" (or at least, the "housewives" who believed in them) "until Washington made it his winter headquarters, and put the devil, as well as his agents to flight."[69]

Sometimes it took a magician to catch a magician. Professional stage magicians advertised their shows as educational and improving; in 1808 the amazing Rannie declared that he could show the audience "INGENUITIES . . . so that they will be able to exhibit the same for their own amusement, and what had too long passed in the world for *Magic, Necromancy,* or some other Occult Science, but which is in reality no more than the effect of a certain agility," would be exposed. Rannie thereby warned the public against "the arts of unprincipled men who would apply such means to corrupt their morals, warp the understanding, & in the end lay snares for their property."[70]

Magic manuals were similarly wary about magic.[71] There was a broad stock in trade in books and pamphlets that explained tricks that could be done at home by amateur performers; these instruction manuals came with a heavy dose of warning and opprobrium. *The Art of Conjuring Made Easy* taught its readers how "to make a room seem all on fire" but insisted practitioners "have a care there be no women with child in the room, for *you yourself would be frightened, if you did not know the trick.*"[72] One "Day Francis the Great" wrote a book of magic that explained the secrets of lodestones and then mocked a story he had heard about "the coffin of Mahomet, which is iron" suspended between two lodestones "which the bigotted Musselmen look upon as a miracle."[73] The anonymous author of *Ventriloquism Explained* hoped that "by calling the attention of youth to the subject, to diffuse some information respecting jugglery [that is, sorcery] among those, who, while too much enlightened to practice it, have not been sufficiently enlightened, in many instances, to avoid being deceived."[74] Unlike earlier magic guides— which tended to be a hodgepodge of general household advice—and the later works of performers like Barnum and Blitz (which reveled in the credulity of their audience), early national magic marketed itself as a republican venture. Magic shows, magicians insisted, were the best education about magic.

Antisupernatural writings borrowed the predilections, anxieties, and taboos developing in white society. Rationality (and natural philosophy) of the eighteenth century became associated with gentility, refinement, and masculinity. The case against superstition adopted the same tenor and shifted the blame for superstition to those nonpersons in republican society: women, children, and "savages," that is, those without votes in the American democracy. Alongside, and possibly even stronger than any academic argument, came the denunciation of belief in witchcraft and superstition as vulgar, the province of lower classes, primitive peoples, and women. Bentley knew where to lay the blame when he explained how people of Salem lost their heads; they spent too much time listening to people who were not white men: "Children, below twelve years of age, obtained a hearing before magistrates. Indians came and related their own knowledge of invisible beings. Tender females told of every fright, but not one man of reputation ventured to offer a single report."[75]

Whatever the other nuances of their position, writers who opposed "superstition" all agreed that women were particularly susceptible to superstition, and therefore men ought to guard against its pernicious influences. A 1788 published debate on witchcraft explained that "if the male nature had been as subject to nervous weakness, or spasmodic affectations, as the female," then men, too, would have been seized as witches in earlier times.[76] Rachel of *Tawney Rachel* made sure to visit farmhouses only "when she knew the master of the house was from home," and More concluded the story by reminding readers that "God never reveals to weak and wicked women those secret designs of his providence."[77] William Lloyd Garrison's *Liberator* praised Wendell Phillips's 1838 lecture on witchcraft for the "manly and dignified ridicule" it heaped upon "that silly notion, which credits the existence of ghosts and demons."[78] David Reese particularly bemoaned the influence of humbug upon women, "intoxicating the 'weak sisters and female brethren' whose intellectual imbecility renders them an easy prey to delusion."[79]

In particular, old women were often singled out as troublemakers; the crone figure shifted easily from a confederate of the devil to a teller of pernicious stories that ruined the mind. The *Sorceress* opined that "the deference paid to the opinions of old women, forms a striking feature in the New England character. . . . And there is not one of them but has, at some period of her life, seen the Devil in the shape of a white horse, a green pig, or a red gander."[80] Quitman worried about old women because "their minds are weak and their imagination lively."[81] Edward Bickerstieth's account of African superstitions informed readers that "the power of darkness and ignorance . . . works upon the minds of the old people," instigating superstition that was then passed to the next generation.[82] Pinchbeck, too, feared (literal) old wives' tales; the power of stories of monsters and goblins "has been known to be so deeply implanted, and lasting, that even manhood itself could not erase its power."[83]

Indeed, "manhood" and masculinity were often the victims of superstition. The 1802 popular tract *False Alarms* consisted of a number of "false" ghost stories told by a father and uncles to a group of children, wherein (as in any good Hanna Barbera cartoon) the perpetrator is always unmasked as something harmless or criminal. Credulity is set against masculinity. The servant girl swoons on seeing a white ghost in the basement. Although the apparition is revealed to be only a leg of mutton wrapped in a napkin, she persists in her supernatural belief: "It was several minutes before she could be convinced of her ridiculous mistake. At first, she would insist upon it, that the phantom stared at her in the face with eyes as large as saucers." Another story tells of a brave sister who investigates and finds out the true nature behind a ghost; but the lesson in the story is clearly for little boys, not girls, for the main character of the tale is the brother John, who is humiliated by his sister's bravery: "This had such an effect on little John, that he never more gave way to the idle imagination of ghosts and apparitions."[84] ("When such impressions are made upon the minds of children," Whitman warned, "the effect is most baneful and lasting.")[85] In "The Haunted House," a mother and daughter are terrified by a screaming ghost; the local (male) farmer discovers the sound comes from a tomcat trapped in the house, and "a worthy family [was] delivered from their fears of goblins, spooks, and apparitions."[86]

The campaign against superstition was unequivocally aimed at whites, and the humiliation of other peoples formed part of the effort. Here, a different stage art proved an ally—ventriloquism. The anonymous author of *Ventriloquism Explained* (1834) warned that "colored servants are invariably addicted to telling stories of ghosts and goblins to their master's children. . . . A colored nurse was once detected in his own family, in the very act of personating an evil spirit, to frighten a child."[87] An 1851 prank told the story of Signor Von Blitz disrupting an African American revival and so fooling the "cullered bredderen." A story circulating in the 1840s told of a ventriloquist

John Quidor's *The Money Diggers*, 1832. Quidor's illustration of a story by Washington Irving shows an African American, a Dutchman, and a German frightened out of their wits as they dig for legendary treasure. (Brooklyn Museum)

frightening a caricatured slave (and his credulous master) by pretending to make a horse talk and eggs cluck.[88]

The bearing of these interpretations of race, gender, age, and gentility on the larger republican questions of self-rule and liberty is exemplified in Washington Irving's "The Legend of Sleepy Hollow," a mainstay of American literature that only makes sense as a story when considered in light of the American campaign against the supernatural. The plot of the tale, when seen in relation to the other faux ghost stories of the era, is not particularly original: a superstitious man is tricked into seeing a false ghost and consequently loses both reputation and ingénue. Ichabod Crane, the principal character, has all the qualities of intellectual and martial weakness that endanger republicanism. He is physically weak ("one might have mistaken him for the genius of famine"), gluttonous ("a huge feeder, and though lank, had the dilating powers of an Anaconda"), proud and overcultured ("a kind of idle gentleman like personage, of vastly superior taste and accomplishments to the rough country swains").[89] He is also a gold digger, out to marry Katarina Van Tassel for her father's money and farm. Irving pits Ichabod against Brom Bones, the "burly, roaring, roystering blade" whose strength and "hardihood" are legendary, who wears a fur cap and ruffles the feathers of society with boyish good humor—Jacksonianism personified.[90]

Moreover, Ichabod has the flaw of superstition: "He was, in fact, an odd mixture of small shrewdness and simple credulity. . . . No tale was too gross or monstrous for his capacious swallow." He owns a copy of Cotton Mather and believes every word, spending his time with "the old Dutch wives" by the hearth, drinking in their stories and superstitions that then terrify him on his journey home. Perhaps this gives Ichabod his "soft and foolish heart." Brom Bones, dressed as the notorious Headless Horseman, so terrifies Ichabod one night that the schoolmaster leaves Sleepy Hollow forever, his reputation broken; Bones weds Katarina. When the good citizens of Sleepy Hollow examine the effects Ichabod leaves behind—"Cotton Mather's history of Witchcraft, a New England Almanack, and a book of dreams and fortune telling"—they consign the lot to the flames.[91] The moral, then, of this very American tale, is that credulity, weakness, and femininity are not to be tolerated in American society. Those who believe in goblins get what they deserve, and the yeomen get the girls.

Of course, Ichabod Crane was a fictional character. So were Washball, Remarkable Short, Credulous Testy, and (in all likelihood) the "colored servant" of Ventriloquism Explained. However, what James Sharpe has written about demonological tracts in early modern England might well apply to the early United States: "These pamphlets did not merely describe witch beliefs and witch trials; they also located them in a moral framework."[92] These were warning pieces with a didactic function: everyone in a republic needed to know how supernatural belief bred chaos and disorder.

That connection explains why so many sects and cults were accused of credulity and witchcraft—people had come to expect it. When supernatural claims arose—as they did with Catholics, Mormons, Shakers, and other wonder-working sects—the cultural and political bias was that all supernatural doings were inherently fake, inherently tyrannical, and inherently close to barbarism, femininity, and the members of the human race born with darker skins. It was "witchcraft" not because it dabbled in dark arts but because it threatened republicanism with the supernatural. These are exactly the objections raised against Joseph Smith, Ann Lee, Richard McNemar, Jemima Wilkinson, and others; the objection against new, supernatural sects followed a common theme, though many American historians, examining radical supernatural groups one at a time, have seen these objections as particular only to their own subjects. In fact, the argument against the religious and political dangers of the supernatural occurred in numerous contexts.

The question of interpreting marvels and performing fantastic things was, therefore, intimately connected with the challenges of the republican experiment. The good yeoman who trusted to his reason and from whom power extended in a democracy was beset by a thousand enemies—including "witches." These were general ideas and associations flitting through republican culture and discourse about the supernatural and the threat it posed. When these ideas actually met miracles—as with Shakers, Native American prophets, Mormons, and a host of minor sects—the results could become far more dramatic and violent.

For under the glare of republicanism, a "witch" had become a conniver. The threat to the citizen and the state was not that supernatural powers were real but that they were false: they took advantage of the ignorant, they poisoned morals, and they doused the fires of natural government. So, too, with those who saw signs in nature beyond a mild, natural providence: they filled the public mind with falsehoods and thus set the republican ship adrift. Politics and religion were connected not simply through policy but also through epistemology. The supernatural was a problem because it was *not* true.

PART II

The Sectarian Impulse

FOUR

Shakers

In 1810, James Smith branded the Shakers "a political evil, under the pretext of divine worship." Shaker pacifism was a front; the order secretly planned "to raise and pay an army of Tories." Smith was an ex-frontiersman and legislator with extensive Indian-fighting credentials; he and his confederates whipped up an Ohio mob five hundred strong intent on destroying and exiling the Shakers. The Shakers, Smith explained, "can see angels and spirits which to others are invisible" and used these pretended supernatural powers to keep "many of the lower class . . . infatuated" and fearful of leaving the sect. The Shaker leadership thus turned loyal white Americans into "voluntary slaves . . . seduced, bewildered, and lost, under strong delusion." At the head of Smith's mob was the Presbyterian preacher Matthew Wallace, who (as one Shaker remembered) gave a blistering harangue on how the Shakers poisoned civil society. Wallace "began in the name of the people, to state their grievances, that our [Shaker] principles & our practice had caused great disturbances in the minds of the people, & led to the extinction of civil & religious society which they are determined to uphold. That our system was a pecuniary system, & led mankind into bondage & oppression." A sect "in every respect destructive to mankind, to soul and body, to church and state," Shakers and their miracles meant to demolish America.[1]

The Ohio Shakers survived Smith's 1810 mob, as numerous Shaker communities survived similar vigilantism in the early American republic. Yet the Ohio mob typified the conspiratorial logic of anti-Shakerism, a logic that both developed from and contributed to the larger republican invective against the supernatural. Just as purported magicians and false prophets secured the loyalty of the weak-minded with promises of supernatural warrants, so, too, the Shakers intended to deploy supernatural claims to assume all power in the republic. "According to their scheme civil and ecclesiastical government are blended together," Smith explained; "theirs is a despotic monarchy."[2] Those who believed in miracles were surely out to turn the credulous into an army to drown the republic.

Shakers—officially designated the United Society of Believers in Christ's Second Appearing—denied any designs on state power, but they never backed away from their supernaturalism. Indeed, their foundational miracle was the greatest possible: the claim that Jesus Christ—or at least the Christ Spirit—had returned to earth, revealing the fullness of the gospel in a blacksmith's daughter named Ann Lee. As a Shaker hymn went, "Christ in one part was revealed," but "his last manifestation in female as well as in male." For this belief—and the ecclesiastical and social demands that accompanied it—the Shakers faced repeated harassment, violence, political fracas, and lawsuits.[3]

Critics routinely seized on Shaker miracles, wonders, and healings as evidence against the Believers. Lee was derided as a "deluded fanatic" who "worked miracles of all descriptions," "a false prophet working miracles," and a "fortune-teller."[4] The case against the Shakers was the case against the supernatural: Shaker belief in the supernatural was a front to blind the weak to their tyrannical ends, its "superstition and fanaticism" bred "clerical as well as secular tyranny," according to one critic.[5] The whole Shaker system, Ezra Stiles wrote, was a "cloud of religious Dust while they are acting as Spies among us."[6]

Shakers themselves imbibed the other side of this Enlightenment discourse on the miraculous. Strewing Baconian proofs and appeals to sensory testimony throughout their written and oral testimonies, Shakers repeatedly stressed the value and trustworthiness of sense evidence and witness testimony. The "public testimony of facts," delivered from "eye and ear witnesses," the Shakers said, verified that a new age of miracles had begun, and as was the case with miracles, had brought with it new dispensations and religious instructions for humankind.[7]

Thomas Brown, for example, sought out the Shakers, "a strange people" he had heard performed miracles. Brown interviewed Shakers who held forth about "the miracles wrought on their own bodies." "One man in particular," wrote Brown, "had been a cripple . . . instantly healed by the power of God, through instrumentality of his brethren." A Shaker from England confirmed that Ann Lee spoke "twelve different languages, to the astonishment of many present; particularly some of the learned." Another Shaker recalled an instance when a crowd had gathered to hear the Shaker message, and in imitation of Matthew 14, provisions enough for five had fed fifty. Brown heard of Ebenezer Cooley, a Shaker who found his arm pointing of its own volition, pulled by the power of God. When Cooley walked in the direction his arm had shown him, he found an injured man and healed him. "I should not mention these things," Brown wrote, "if they were only the faith, or the opinions of a few individuals."[8]

Scholars have understandably been drawn to the heteroclite aspects of Shaker life—what made the Shakers stand out, then and now. Shaker theology revised the godhead, reworked marital and sexual ethics, and constructed a new architecture and culture to impart those principles. Such queries have unearthed much about Shakers and the early republic. Lee's spiritual equality of the sexes did not always translate into equality in Shaker ecclesiology— the Hancock Shaker village "laid it by," according to Isaac Youngs—but as Glendyne Wergland writes, Shakerism's very "pursuit of the ideal made a difference in sisters' lives." If Shakerism did not make women full equals to men in ecclesiastical matters, it provided far more authority to women than almost any other Christian group at the time, and their pursuit of consensus gave the majority-female membership great weight in decision making. Looking at miracles and Shakerism does not change these observations about Shaker theology, architecture, or ecclesiology.[9]

But such things were effects, not causes. The Shaker edifice came into existence as a result of a continued series of miracles. Only great revolutions in the supernatural world could justify a faith so radical, and the supernatural in turn troubled the body politic. The Shakers were no quaint stub of Americana; they were a fundamental case study in the American supernatural, the first and—in some ways—the most significant.

The source of Shaker religion was obvious: "Christ was again revealed," declared the *Testimonies of the Ever Blessed Mother Ann Lee,* one of a host of Shaker holy books, "in England, to a gentile nation, and in the person of a female."[10] For Shakers, however, the Second Coming was not the end of history but a transformation, "for by Christ the Shakers understood not a person or a being, but a condition of endowment," according to one scholar. As a Shaker elder explained, "the same spirit and word of power, which created man at the beginning" also "dwelt in the man Jesus" and "was revealed to a woman . . . ANN LEE."[11] The Christ Spirit had returned and could be infused into any true believer; Lee did not claim she was Christ, but rather that it was "Christ who dwells in me."[12] Critics (and potential converts) might be forgiven for missing the subtlety. When the ambassadors of Shakerism gave their first address in Kentucky in 1805, they announced that "Christ hath made his second appearing on earth" and "God had raised up to Himself witnesses and gave unto them the same gifts of the Holy Spirit that were given to the Apostles in the day of Christ's first appearing."[13]

The first Shakers had broken away from the English Quakers; later historians have cited the arrival of the French Prophets in England as an inciting cause for the fracture. Whether Quaker or Camisard in origin, Shakerism emerged in England under the direction of Jane and James Wardley by the 1740s. Shakers disrupted Sabbath services of other Christian groups and proclaimed signs and visions. By 1772, leadership had descended on Lee, then only thirty years old. Arrested at least twice for her proselytizing, Lee moved her religion to the colonies in 1774.[14] Lee and a handful of others kept silent for six years, until May 19, 1780, "the most Remarkable Day Ever known in this Land," when darkness fell across the New England coast. According to the diarist John Gates, "it grew very Dark," so much so that "many people lit up candles. . . . Every appearance seemed like night." One Weston man "spreading Dung in his Field, was obliged to leave his work, not being able to discern the difference between the ground and the Dung."[15] In Providence, the wind stank of sulfur and soot. Ashes fell from the sky. It seemed "a kind of Egyptian darkness . . . almost impervious to the rays."[16]

New Englanders called it the Dark Day; neither eclipse nor thunderstorm, the event remains mysterious.[17] Religious interpretations of the phenomenon abounded. In Worcester, Massachusetts, "people came flocking to the Meeting House," reported the minister David Hall. The president of Brown University told a friend that the darkness was "a prelude to that great and important day when the final consummation of all things is to take place." Issachar Bates remembered that "the people were out wringing their hands, and howling, 'the day of judgment is come!'" One group in particular, Bates recalled, had great discernment concerning the event: "And what next!—Right on the back of this—On came the Shakers!" With "singing, dancing, shouting, shaking, speaking in tongues," the Shakers explained the Dark Day as a supernatural invitation for the world to join them. And Bates did.[18]

The Dark Day was the catalyst for the opening of the Shaker gospel; it was, according to New Hampshire Shakers, Lee's "signal from Heaven to send forth her Elders to preach the everlasting Gospel." Lee and others undertook missionary treks across New England, demonstrating as they did a penchant for the supernatural: healing, exorcizing, and speaking in tongues.[19] Hundreds joined the church as Shaker missions turned the curious into converts.[20]

Within weeks of this supernatural transformation, Shakers found themselves imprisoned for treason. No sooner had a supernaturalist group gone
public than the revolutionary political order clapped some of them in prison
on suspicion of espionage. New York's Commissioners for Detecting and
Defeating Conspiracies rounded up the Shaker David Darrow with other
likely suspects and accused them of "Collecting a Number of Sheep ... to
convey them to the Enemy." Darrow's fellow defendants swore an oath of
loyalty to the Patriot cause, but Darrow declared "that by his religious principles he is restrained from taking up Arms in defence of the Country." The
committee accused him of "pretending" to a religious faith and imprisoned
him. The commissioners later investigated rumors that the pacifist Shakers
had stockpiled weapons for use by the British.[21]

By December 1780, a pamphlet connected the presumed miracles of the
Shakers to an insidious political conspiracy. Shakers, according to the pamphleteer, insisted "that they have all the apostolic gifts that were ever given,"
gifts they demonstrated by praying in tongues, speaking with angels, and
casting "evil spirits out of the house." The author of the pamphlet would
have known; he was the former Shaker Valentine Rathbone. Rathbone also
warned that Shakerism convinced those who had given "vote and money
for the defence of the country" to revoke support for the Revolution, and to
"throw down their arms, and cry out against the means of defence made use
of against the common enemy, and appear most obstinate against all the
proceedings of the country." Rathbone had even "heard some of them say,
that all our authority, civil and military, is from hell."[22] The Shakers were
enemies within, whose "delusive charms" represented a danger to the Patriot
cause. From the very beginning, Shaker politics and Shaker supernaturalism
were bound together in the public sphere.

That supernaturalism took numerous forms. A convert met James Whit-
taker at a prayer meeting, wherein Whittaker claimed to "have Cast out
Thousands of Devils in this meeting. And whenever I touch any one of you
I See the Evil Spirits Come out of you in Swarms."[23] Francois Marquis de
Barbé-Marbois (traveling with Lafayette in 1784) found that the Shakers "cure
wounds and claim to cure even fractures, by mere laying on of hands."[24]
Issachar Bates could not make up his mind about religion until "some invisible being" asked him in the woods "will you be willing, to go and lead
mankind, into the way of righteousness." Bates immediately vowed he would
follow the Lord. Later, a flash of power like lightning confirmed Bates's faith
and cured him of a sore lump.[25] In 1783, Lee imbued John Hocknell with the

power to exorcise a small child. Lee had the ability to read minds, as when she identified the source of a cattle plague as a man who had been "defiling himself with the cattle. He confessed his sin, and the plague ceased."[26] Benjamin Silliman later wrote that Shaker Elders had apparently inherited Lee's "power of inspecting their very thoughts, and their most secret actions."[27]

Other gifts abounded. In Shakerism's early days, Lee herself recollected the "names of some that she had seen rise from the dead." Sarah Kendall saw Ann Lee do "the same work and performed miracles in the same spirit that Christ did." When Elijah Slosson hosted a Shaker gathering, people thronged and "upwards of one hundred horses" grazed his pasture clear; by the next week, the pasture had grown back fuller than before, and "the quantity of butter and cheese made by the family, from four cows" who fed on that new grass "was considered as miraculous." Jemima Blanchard reported that she could fly "over stone walls & swamps without any effort; & that she had been entirely supported & upheld by the power of God, without touching any material substance."[28]

Thomas Brown experienced supernatural episodes himself and found them convincing: "I began to have operations of shaking, trembling, and stamping . . . likewise a gift, as it is called, of speaking languages, or unknown tongues. At one time I had a gift to sing but no one understood what I sung, nor myself neither." Brown eventually left Shakerism and renounced his faith, but not his supernatural experiences: "These things I did not do as a sham. . . . I really and sincerely believed I was under the influence of divine power."[29]

Shakers were understandably distraught in September 1784, when Lee, "having finished the work which was given to her to do, *she was taken out of their sight.*" ("In honest English, she died," sneered Timothy Dwight.)[30] After Lee's death, James Whittaker and then Joseph Meacham led the Society, and under their leadership, Shakers developed the blueprints of what became their classic style of living. Whittaker encouraged the sharing of possessions and the centralization of Shaker converts, insisting that Shakers live together and pool resources on land owned by the church. Lee's successors also exhibited supernatural powers: Whittaker cast out demons, and Meacham, while in a pasture, entered a trance so powerful that even the cows left off feeding to watch with "reverential awe."[31]

Lucy Wright became prelate upon Meacham's death in 1796 and began a phenomenally successful pontificate in the Shaker church. Under Wright, Shaker villages crossed the frontier, appearing in Kentucky, Ohio, and Indiana. Wright also oversaw the publication of three sacred volumes, each one an account of and rumination on the life of Ann Lee and the rise of the Shaker church. The 1808 *Testimony of Christ's Second Appearing,* the revised 1810 *Testimony of Christ's Second Appearing,* and the 1816 *Testimonies of the Ever Blessed Mother Ann Lee* all emerged from a complicated east-west collaboration of the far-flung Believers. The 1808 *Testimony* began with four hundred pages of Christian history, explicating Shaker belief that Christ was not a person but an aspect of God. The final two hundred pages detailed the arrival of the Christ Spirit in Ann Lee. The 1810 revision left most of the material intact. Stories referenced in the 1808/1810 *Testimony* prompted some Shakers to seek the direct word of Lee, spurring the creation of the 1816 *Testimonies,* a less theological volume that provided narrative detail and wisdom stories about Mother Ann and the early Shakers.[32]

All three books are rife with miracle stories, and with good reason: "God has, in every dispensation of his grace, addressed their external sense, with evidences of his divine power," the *Testimony* argued, and the current dispensation "has by no means been lacking in such kind of evidence."[33] The Shaker church possessed the same "extraordinary gifts [as] were in the primitive church, such as gifts of healing; working of miracles;—prophecy—discerning of spirits—divers[e] kinds of tongues." The 1816 volume quoted Lee herself: "The signs which Christ spoke of follow them that believe. They speak with new tongues; the sick are healed, and the wonderful power of God is made known by divers[e] operations." The signs to living witnesses were evidences of the new soteriology; indeed, the 1810 *Testimony* noted: "We are far from expecting, or even wishing any of our writings to supercede the necessity of a living testimony."[34]

Both versions of the *Testimony* devoted an entire section to healing: "There were many instances of miraculous cures of diseases, of almost every kind." The healings listed in the text "are but a few out of many, which were of such a nature as could not be hid." These "outward gifts have been abundantly ministred through our Mother" in "sufficiently . . . close relation to the work that was manifested in the primitive church" to suggest the opening of a new dispensation connected to Lee's person. Indeed, "the same power over diseases, which Jesus and his apostles manifested, was given to Mother, with other apostolic gifts."[35]

Though these texts spoke with biblical idiom, their explanations were thoroughly grounded in early nineteenth-century understandings of miracles. Witnesses and critics could only "judge according to their outward senses" as to whether or not an event was supernatural. The 1810 *Testimony* added a note wherein it accepted proofs as "something like legal attestation" and included its healing stories in the form of affidavits: "We have stated these evidences, after the manner of depositions, signed and witnessed." The *Testimony* even noted that its opponents agreed that "they would believe upon the evidence of such mighty works," except that "hatred of the truth" made them into disbelievers.[36]

The 1816 *Testimonies* replaced the lengthy theological introduction with a biography, following Lee from England to North America, illustrating how her teaching and ministry were punctuated by the supernatural. Imprisoned in England, Lee survived on milk and wine passed "through a pipe-stem, that was put through the key-hole." She survived on this mixture for two weeks "as a favor of God." When her enemies assaulted Lee, a magical balm covered her body to protect her from injury; when released from a long imprisonment, she was as spry as a healthy young girl: "The world were astonished at it, and said it must be a supernatural power that attended her." Daniel Goodrich, according to the *Testimonies,* was despondent because he was "feeling a lack of that visible power and operation of the spirit, which was perceptible among other Believers." Lee healed his daughter to give him a sign.[37]

Then there were the long lists of disasters that befell Lee's opponents. Reuben Rathbone, who had issued one of the more virulent anti-Shaker pamphlets, was crushed to death by a tree; Thomas Law, who led an anti-Shaker mob in Massachusetts, "afterwards lived as a vagabond upon earth . . . despised by all that knew him." Ephraim Bowman "came to nothing. . . . He died in a most deplorable state; not even a friend to close his eyes," whereas Selah Abbot Jr. died "with his eyes wide open, nor was it in the power of his friends to close them." Eleazar Grant, meanwhile, "was taken with a strange disorder: first his fingers, and then his hands and arms began to perish." He "was obliged to leave off the gratification of his lust with his wife. . . . Thus he became a Shaker in judgment." Indeed, the whole town of Harvard, Massachusetts—which had treated the Shakers shabbily—had "a blast and a curse upon the town" with suicides, floods, and fires: "The whole town seemed to be in continual perplexity and vexation; and it has never appeared to be in a flourishing condition since."[38]

The *Testimony* and the *Testimonies* must be used with great care; they are oral histories collected thirty and more years after the events they purport to describe. They are sources for the early days of the church, but they are equally sources for nineteenth-century Shakerism. The decision of that church to collect and teach from its miracle stories—indeed, its compulsion and desire to *have* miracle stories—speaks volumes about the importance of miracles to the Shakers. The tales collected from 1808 to 1816 cannot be taken as the exact words of Lee, any more than gospel accounts written decades after the crucifixion necessarily represent the exact words of Christ, but they can be taken as the words from which Shakers learned and in which they believed. Indeed, the compilation of miracle stories and recollections of Ann Lee undertaken between 1808 and 1816 were themselves miraculous; the 1816 *Testimonies* declared that some of the testimonies—"the most important"—were not in circulation in the 1810s but rather were "brought to remembrance by a special gift of God, after having been, as it were, entirely forgotten, for many years." The Shaker gospel was miraculous in both subject and compilation, for God had arranged for "the act which he intended to bring to pass, was to be *a strange act,* even a *marvelous work and a wonder.*"[39]

These new annals also laid out an argument for miracles as theology. "Divine miracles ... carry to the minds of the lost children of men, the strongest evidence of the sacred messenger's divine authority." Therefore, "many miraculous gifts, of various kinds, attended Mother's ministry." The proof for miracles came in sense evidence, for "the testimony of living witnesses," declared the 1810 *Testimony,* "is considered of the highest authority, and superior to any written record whatever." This position buttressed the traditional Shaker emphasis on oral communication and experience over written creeds, but the emphasis on "eye and ear witnesses" also affirmed the standard American philosophical position on the reliability of the senses.[40]

The assertions of the 1816 *Testimonies* were not outliers; nineteenth-century Shakers repeatedly defended the theological and phenomenological validity of new miracles and pointed to those miracles as justification for their church and its authority. Before he joined the church, Brown interviewed a Shaker and asked why he believed in Mother Ann's gospel. Brown was told: "We have abundant proof, both external and internal," that "all the apostolic gifts are in the church, as the gifts of miracles. . . . The other churches are not the churches of Christ" because "miracles are all ceased among them."[41] In 1827, a correspondent asked the Shaker William Byrd whether "God has given to man any other revelation of himself and the way of salvation besides . . . the bible," and if so, "by what miracles was it authenticated?" Byrd replied that "an infinity of inspirations and miracles have existed not contained in the bible, the bible itself authorizes us to believe. 'Many other Signs truly did Jesus in the presence of his disciples which are not written in this book.'"[42]

In 1826, Abijiah Worster outlined the connection between miracles, faith, and obedience; he "was desirous of some Stronger Confirmation," while investigating Shakerism, and God "Laid his Blessed Power upon me, and dropt me on my knees, where I was Shook like an Earthquake: and under this operation, I was fully confirmed, that it was the way of God." After he became a Shaker, "God in deep condescension Blest me, (the unworthy) with the Gift of Healing." Though his gift was erratic, Worster once healed five Shakers in a week. And Worster had no doubt from whom the power came—and, therefore, where his allegiance lay: "These manifestations of Power were Received, through obedience to, and faith in that Holy Anointing, that dwelt in our Blessed Mothers Soul."[43]

Shakerism grew rapidly in the trans-Appalachian West after 1805, coaxed from the embers of the Cane Ridge revivals. It did so despite terrific opposition. One opponent threatened that "if any Shakers came to his house, to delude & draw away any of his family, he would Shoot them with his Riffle." Those who come to jest often stay to pray: the rifleman and his wife later joined the Shakers, as did hundreds of others. All sorts of revivalists joined the Shakers, from the enslaved Anthony Chosen to some of the revival's leading organizers, including Richard McNemar and Malcolm Worley.[44]

Other revivalists were less than pleased. Barton Warren Stone likened the Shakers to Simon Magus, the seller of magics in the New Testament, for the Shakers "said they could perform miracles, and related many as done among them," but "we never could persuade them to try to work miracles among us." (Stone maintained his caveat that the ecstatic exercises of his own denomination were only "so like miracles.") Stone's venom may have been the bitterness of a former convert; his confederate John Dunlavy wrote that Stone "was at first very much taken with" Shakerism, but "finding the cross against the flesh too great for him . . . fell back" and "denounced their religion as a delusion."[45]

Some frontier converts experienced miracles or preternatural events with the coming of the Shakers. Stone wrote that Shakers claimed conversations with angels "and all the departed saints." A western outbreak of tongues in 1815 made Issachar Bates wonder whether Sinai "manifested more awful signs of the divine majesty than the place in which we were assembled." A fire set by a mob burned a stack of wheat without consuming it.[46] At other times, western Shakers looked east. "I cannot help still wishing that a gift of healing was imparted to some member or members of our Society," Charles

Willing Byrd admitted in 1828, for "at Watervliet in New York those gifts have been received even within the last two years."[47]

Yet most scholars have pointed to a crisis in Shaker fortunes by the end of the 1820s. Shaker growth leveled off, and then began a long decline that has lasted to the present day. In the late 1830s the church embarked on a profound intensification of supernatural activity. Institutional change, novel ceremonies, and a voluminous host of new writing and artwork emerged from this period. During these years, spiritual visitors descended upon Shaker communities—the ghosts of Shaker founders, spirits from Christian history, and shades of American political leaders, including George Washington, Tecumseh, William Penn, and others. Angels joined these spirits, and all of them took possession of certain instruments (Shaker Believers) and communicated advice, instruction, and prophecy, initiating a denominational revival from Kentucky to Maine.[48]

The visitations brought forth "many supernatural gifts, such as shaking, turning, bowing, speaking with tongues &c," according to one Elder. This period was known as Mother Ann's Work. In every Shaker village, sensitives received spirit communications in the form of messages, stories, dances, songs, and drawings. According to Elder Rufus Bishop, "The gift of Visions has had a powerful effect in removing doubts, and establishing the faith of such as were weak and wavering." Orren Haskins similarly testified that manifestations came "to encourage both the weak and the strong. . . . I received much that was given, and believed it was truly from the invisible world." These communications likely constituted the longest sustained supernatural event in antebellum America.[49]

The phenomena began with a series of visions among young Shakers in Watervliet, New York. On October 1, 1837, Ann Mariah Goff "fell into a trance & had to be carried out to the waggon like a lifeless person."[50] Goff became one of the first "instruments." Shaker instruments reported being covered in golden cloaks, meeting angels, and seeing Mother Ann and Joseph Meacham.[51] Sometimes visionaries would see the words of heaven descend on golden sheaves, and they would copy the spiritual words onto earthly paper, "written partially in English and partly in unintelligible jargon, or unknown tongue, having a spiritual meaning . . . understood only by those who possess the spirit," wrote an 1841 correspondent.[52] Ghosts and angels swarmed over the Shaker landscape. Goff, for example, was taken by Mother Ann in a vision to a women's prison, where "evil spirits came out of the women, and they began to grow white. Each one of them had an evil spirit which looked just as they did." On her way home, "I met two or three evil spirits. I stood my ground and made them turn out."[53] Jefferson White, at the village in Enfield, Connecticut, wrote that he "saw 500 spirits assemble over the West families house." They were "as bright as the sun."[54] One Shaker deacon went to his own funeral; after his death, "The Deacon with many good Spirits attended the Funeral, & went to the Grave."[55]

Often those receiving inspiration manifested the gift of tongues: "Several young sisters have been unable to speak a word in their own tongue for several weeks together, except they were in vision," wrote Oliver Spencer.[56] Shakers sometimes recorded the glossolalia verbatim, such as "vi O ville ve ving ving" or "I lo le viteca vum vole os ca nere von." Sometimes spiritual language accompanied English to form a hymn, as with, "O we will praise our maker, yea, we even will, / Ki lo vin sa vo van vos onena vil."[57]

Some scholars have interpreted Mother Ann's Work as a charismatic outgrowth intended to solve purported problems in Shaker society, psychology, or economy.[58] The Work in this formulation was a religious response to nonreligious problems.[59] Such a view repeats the basic fallacy regarding the supernatural in early republican historiography; it also misreads Shaker history. Supernatural events had long played a role in Shaker belief, liturgy, and scripture. Even the notion of returning spirits passing through Shaker worship was not new; early opponents accused the Shakers of "frequent dialogues" with "angels, devils, and departed souls."[60] In 1796, Moses Guest wrote of Shakers seeing "the souls of all those persons who have died . . . daily appearing before them."[61] William Haskett noted that Shakers believed George Washington had "returned in spirit" and joined the Shakers by 1828.[62] Mother Ann's Work may have represented an intensification and generalization of supernatural practice, but it was not a fundamental change.

The career of Rebecca Cox Jackson offers a telling illustration. A free African American, Jackson (1795–1871) wrote an autobiography detailing her religious experiences, first with the African Methodist Episcopal Church and later with the Shakers. Jackson formally joined the Shaker church during the Era of Manifestations. Yet supernaturalism had marked Jackson's entire life. At a New Jersey revival in 1832, a fire broke out in Jackson's tent but was extinguished by "an unseen hand." A pile of ashes—sitting on a pine table in the middle of a cloth tent—provided evidence that the fire had come and gone without igniting a general conflagration. Jackson then received the word of the Lord: "And by this miracle they shall know I am with thee." Jackson also performed healings and at least once controlled the weather through the power of God. She learned to read supernaturally; she was illiterate when she prayed to God while holding the Bible, then opened it and began to read. When she first visited the Shakers in 1836, she felt an overwhelming sense of love and swiftly used her "gift of power" and supernaturally "bound" her companions, preventing them from speaking ill of the sect.[63]

When Jackson joined the Believers, she entered into Mother Ann's Work; in January 1843, she healed the scalded hand of a Shaker sister. Two months later, she healed a sister's eye; a Shaker eldress healed Jackson in turn.[64] Elsewhere among the Shakers, visionaries "bound" other mockers and skeptics. The Shaker schoolteacher Hervey Elkins wrote of a Shaker named Henry who participated "derisively" in the Work. One of the instruments "passed his hands with great rapidity over him, as though binding him with invisible cords." Henry found himself paralyzed, "bound fast by invisible manacles."[65] Meanwhile, a story circulated about a group of non-Shakers who could not *stop* their mockery near Canterbury; when they "sung, danced, turned, &c." in satire of the Shaker worship, they soon discovered they "could not stop when they wished to, but kept on till they became sick, spewed, fell to the floor, and rolled and wiped up their vomit with their broad cloth coats."[66]

The Era of Manifestations therefore represented a continuation and intensification of Shaker supernaturalism. Yet the accounts of healings, exorcisms, and glossolalia were few compared to the wider reports of visions. Healings, exorcisms, and other physical phenomena—what had been known as "miracles"—continued during the manifestations, but visions and subjective phenomena far outpaced them. In that sense, Mother Ann's Work may represent a changed supernaturalism rather than a resurrected supernaturalism, in keeping with a general trend toward internal spiritual life as the American nineteenth century wore on. Internal proofs were replacing external proofs. As Mother Ann's Work declined in the later 1840s and 1850s, Shaker supernaturalism dwindled. As it did, public perceptions of Shakerism lost their political edge, and Shakers began their long drift into nostalgic Americana. The Era of Manifestations was the last and longest chapter of Shaker supernaturalism.

Shakers tested their miracles and wonders, as would be expected of Baconians in the nineteenth century. In 1824, Abigail Crosman experienced tongues and found it "enough to confirm my faith beyond doubt, that mortal and immortal spirits could commune with each other." Nevertheless, when she became an instrument in Mother Ann's Work several years later, she had doubts as to their divine character. She proceeded to test the spirits and asked for "certain signs of my own chusing. . . . These requests were granted." Like other Americans who tested the supernatural, she felt "like Thomas" and "could not believe without evidence palpable to the physical senses."[67] Freegift Wells warned his Ohio Shakers "to be wide awake, so as to detect if possible, every counterfeit message," but "I have no doubt but we have had many genuine Messages from the Heavens."[68] Similarly, Spencer wrote "in this extraordinary time of the outpouring of the spirit of Christ & of Mother it is all important that the Ministry & Elders keep their eyes open . . . to be able to discern clearly the between the genuine spirit of Mother and that which is counterfeit."[69]

In 1818, John Dunlavy's *Manifesto* made similar claims, borrowing directly from the Enlightenment discourse on miracles: "When impostors understand that certain miracles have been wrought by the true ministers of God, they will endeavor to imitate them, as the magicians in Egypt." Dunlavy continued, "The miracles which were wrought . . . by Jesus Christ and his followers, are, in their own nature and place, incontestable proof of their divine original; *but not direct,* especially to those who have not seen them." Nevertheless, Dunlavy insisted that the power of miracles "no doubt belongs to the Church, and we have no idea of any true Church of God without such power."[70] Miracles were a proof, but they had to be assessed carefully: a good Baconian standard. Elkins dismissed some of the supernatural events he experienced during Mother Ann's Work as practical joking. Yet even after leaving the Shakers, Elkins maintained that "one or two instances occurred in which a superhuman agency, was indubitably obvious."[71]

Shakers rarely got credit for this care in approaching the supernatural. Critics preferred to list secret Shaker crimes, for which little evidence was offered, including the charge that this celibate sect secretly engaged in midnight orgies and naked dancing.[72] Accusations that Shakers murdered or imprisoned their members echoed the contemporary anti-Catholic theories of secret monkish tunnels between abbeys and convents. From the opening of the Shaker gospel in 1780 to the close of Mother Ann's Work, commentators repeatedly warned the public that the threat from Ann Lee and the Shakers was more political than theological. The Yale divine Ezra Stiles thought Lee's followers were spies and saboteurs, "sent over into America by Ministerial Connexions, to excite Confusion & religious Disturbance and propogate principles against fighting & resistg G. Britain."[73] Benjamin West found himself trapped by Shakers' "inchanting influence, by which means I soon became . . . subjected to their lead and government." After leaving the Shakers, West cited a host of biblical texts to buttress his theological objections, but he also took time to attack the politics of Shakerism as "papist" and "vending itself with the attempts of tyranny."[74] The anonymous author of the extended tract *Bath-Kol* (1783) referred to the Shakers as "locusts vomited out of the pit" but blamed their appearance on "the civil and religious troubles that have come upon us after the revolution."[75] Valentine Rathbun wrote a play wherein George III and his advisors export Shakerism to America as a war effort, hoping Shaker pacifism would "cut the sinews of the rebellion."[76]

Early criticism explicitly connected Shakerism to witchcraft, and though some critics meant the demonic variety thereof, intimations of witchcraft as delusion and political gambit filtered through as well. *Bath-Kol* vaguely suggested Shakerism was "the issue of some diabolical influence," while Valentine Rathbun thought it imbued with "the spirit of infatuation and witch-craft" and "the most powerful of any delusion I ever heard."[77] The *Theological Magazine* of 1795 derided the reports of Shaker tongues-speaking, describing them as "betwitching charms" that "deluded people" and "wholly swallowed up all their attention," rather than as a demonic wonder.[78] Similarly, when the visitor St. John Honeywood saw the Shakers dancing in white clothing, like "a throng of discontented ghosts hovering round the gloomy shores of the *Stygian* lake" and compared them to "*Lapland* hags performing their nocturnal orgies," his primary concern was not demons but rather "the iron hand of Superstition" marked on their faces. (Honeywood was also linking Shakers to the presumed primitivism of Lapland.)[79] Citing Nahum 3:4, Benjamin West indicted Lee by saying she "selleth families through her witchcrafts." The citation is telling, for Nahum's prophecy also denounced witches as those who "selleth nations through her whoredoms."[80] Witches destroyed nations as well as souls; the indictment suggested imposture and black magic si-multaneously. Amos Taylor's 1782 tract barely mentioned witchcraft—only insofar as to explain that he, as yet, had no reliable information on that topic. Instead, Taylor's central concern was the "deep design at the bottom" that kept "a few Europeans" in control of an American religion.[81] The fear of Shaker witchcraft was as concerned with national power and delusions as much as with *maleficium*.

Later critiques connected Shaker tyranny to Shaker miracles. "Its miracles, visions, revelations, superstitions," wrote David Lamson, were the means "by which the elders obtain unlimited sway over the minds of their subjects."[82] Timothy Dwight similarly assessed Shaker leadership, beginning with Lee's

"pretension to miraculous powers," which preyed on "ignorant persons, especially those, who have warm feelings and lively imaginations." The "love
of domination," Dwight wrote, "appears to have taken a final possession of
the elderhood; and absolute submission, of the brethren."[83] Isaac Backus
enumerated Shaker "abominations," including the notions that Shakers "must
believe as the church believes, and do as they say" and that Shakers "propagate
their scheme with a strange *power, signs, and lying wonders.*"[84] Other printed
discussions of Shakerism regularly referred to the Believers as "deluded,"
"madcap," and "fanatical . . . governed by the whims of the imagination."[85]
William Haskett's treatise charged Shakers with anti-intellectualism, the
source of its "superstition and fanaticism" that bred "clerical as well as secular tyranny."[86] Only those who were drunk, "too young to have any rational
choice of their own," or "children *in the science of social life,*" said the *Western
Star* in 1796, would accept "their pretended theocracy."[87]

The great attack on Shaker theocracy came with the long campaign of Mary
Marshall Dyer. Dyer joined the New Hampshire Shakers in 1813 but found
she did not care for the institution. The feeling was mutual. On leaving the
Shakers, however, Dyer discovered that her husband, Joseph (who remained
a Shaker), by law owned the children. A fierce legal and pamphlet battle
ensued. Mary Dyer wrote several books attacking the supposed horrors of
Shaker life; Eunice Chapman made a similar claim against the Shakers of
New York, and the two women collaborated on further works. Dyer reprinted
the inflammatory works of Smith in her publications, to show how Shaker
"principles and conduct are in several respects, not only subversive of christian morality" but also "detrimental to the well-being of society."[88]

The Dyer campaign culminated with a petition drive on New Hampshire's
legislature, which resulted in a series of hearings on whether the Shakers
committed "gross and inconsistent practices, subversive of the public good,
which require the interference of the Legislature to suppress." The depositions
accused the Shakers of violence, arrogance, tyranny, and even murder—but
they also made it a point to show how Shaker supernaturalism permitted
such evil deeds to occur. Theresa Willard testified that she "was *always* taught
to obey my Elders, in every particular," and that "Shakers pretend, and are
understood, to have the power of healing diseases." The ex-Shaker James
Partridge described one man gagged by an angry Elder, and another Believer
compelled to crawl on all fours by the Elders, because "he did not believe
in inspiration, and would not speak in unknown tongues." James M. Otis,
another apostate, described beatings of Shakers and gave a lengthy description

of tongues-speaking.[89] In their defense, the Shakers employed the counsel of the future U.S. president Franklin Pierce (who did a better job as solicitor than as president), and the Shakers escaped unharmed. Shakers also gave as good as they got; they printed numerous public responses, including one by Dyer's husband, Joseph, that lambasted Dyer as a bad mother and a religious zealot.[90]

Other accusations were harder to dismiss. Chapman and Smith both accused the Shakers of providing material support to the Shawnee Prophet and his followers along the Wabash River in Indiana. The western Shakers had instituted economic and religious contacts with the Prophet, exchanges which Smith called "artful measures to excite the Indians to fall upon the defenceless frontiers, belonging to the United States." Chapman warned the readers that "half of the Shakers in the state of OHIO are *Indians.*"[91] John C. Irvin charged the Shakers with colluding with the Indians and firmly declared that Shakers "are equally bent on the DOWNFALL OF CIVIL GOVERNMENT, and the DESTRUCTION OF THE INNOCENT."[92]

It was the *imperium in imperio,* the usual hobgoblin of early republican politics. As Lamson wrote, "Their government is a perfect despotism . . . in the midst of a republic." He feared for the sanctity of individual conscience, since the Shakers, he wrote, believed that "the seat of government is at New Lebanon" and "all other laws and government are regarded as growing out of the depravity of man."[93] Another ex-Shaker, Benjamin Green, asked how the republic could permit within its borders an institution "fond of exercising despotic power, and striving to bring others into subjection to their wills."[94] Some anti-Shakers openly advocated mob justice, should the state not act to protect itself. After all, "Shakerism is a DESPOTIC GOVERNMENT *already* erected within our state."[95]

Anti-Shaker mobs arose to mete out justice in defense of their republic. These violent confrontations were not as dramatic as the Mormon standoff with the militia at Far West in 1838 or the militarized antisupernaturalism that fed the Battle of Tippecanoe in 1811, but in the aggregate, these acts of political invective and violence amounted to a campaign of coercion. As Matthew Wallace explained in 1810, Shakerism "led to the extinction of civil & religious society," which the mobs "are determined to uphold."[96] Violence shaped the Shaker experience from 1780 through the 1820s, as critics versed in antisupernaturalism mounted sustained campaigns to destroy the religion.

Massachusetts mobs made several attempts to oust Shakers from their state. In December 1781, the Shakers attempted to preach in Petersham;

"delusion was the general cry," according to the *Testimonies*. A group dubbed "the Blackguard Committee" attacked Lee at a church meeting, then returned that night, beat several Shakers, and seized Lee, dragging her across the countryside and whipping the Shakers who followed. A Harvard militia in 1782 demanded the Shakers leave town; those who remained were placed, one by one, atop an empty barrel and interrogated. Lee by that time had gone to Enfield, where another militia accosted her. She again left, and the departing Shakers "saw and felt themselves surrounded by hosts of angels."[97]

Following a Harvard meeting where "the power of God manifested" in the bodies of the Shakers, a mob decided to rid the town of them permanently. They burst in upon Shaker lodgings in the early morning; "the brethren and sisters were seized indiscriminately . . . and dragged out." The Shakers were given an hour to pack their belongings and then marched out of Harvard. Once they had cleared the town, the mob formed a circle around them and took turns beating the Believers.[98]

Western Shakers fared little better. Turtle Creek fought off mobs in 1805, 1810, 1813, 1817, 1819, and 1824. Indeed, when Shakers first organized their Turtle Creek settlement, anti-Shakers roamed the territory, "breaking glass windows—cutting down orchards—throwing down fences—burning buildings &c." McNemar wondered how "in any part of a free and friendly republic" citizens could be allowed "to beset the houses of the *Shakers* in the night, assault their persons with clubs and stones," not to mention "destroy their grain . . . disfigure their horses, beat and abuse their bodies." McNemar was probably referring to a series of attacks in October 1805, where anti-Shakers burned down a preaching stand, smashed windows, and mutilated several Shaker horses. McNemar himself was surprised by a gang of opponents and beaten. The Shakers let the burned stand remain as a "monument to remind these ungodly persecutors of there dark & wicked works."[99]

A mob attacked the Pleasant Hill community in June 1825, "the most imbitred persecution that we ever experienced," according to one sister. At the close of a Sabbath meeting, "a mob, from 40 to 50 men all around with Clubs, dirks or pistols" broke open the door and proceeded to bludgeon every Shaker they could lay their hands on, with "a number of Brethren and Sisters . . . inhumanly beaten," some to unconsciousness. The mob sought to release Lucy Bryant, a teenager whose brother Gray had left the Shakers and wanted her to do the same. Lucy spoke with the leaders of the mob and refused to leave. The mob dispersed, but all the next week, the Shakers "were Continewally held under the most Sevearest threats of destruction." That

Sunday the mob regrouped. This time some of them tied the dirks to the ends of their clubs, seized Bryant, and "dragged the girl off without mercy." A year later, Bryant was still trying to return to the Society.[100]

There were also smaller, disorganized attacks. Blanchard remembered a meeting where "pistols were shot into the windows."[101] A Pittsfield mob seized James Whittaker, but "there was a division among them," and cooler heads prevailed.[102] A company of men accosted Benjamin Youngs along the road, informing him that "no Quaker [Shaker] has a right to travel through this country" because they were "leading people into delusion" and "pretended to the spirit of prophecy." The men considered castrating Youngs but in the end merely took his hat.[103] In 1830, a mob fortified with "a keg of cherry bounce" stormed the Harvard Shakers, trying to seize a Believer named Babbitt; when Babbitt struck the mob leaders, the Shakers were put on trial for assault.[104] A Pleasant Hill church record book grimly referred to a child named John Cooney, "Deceased in Fall of 1810, occasioned by the barbarous treatment of a wicked persecutor."[105]

Shakers faced a host of legal battles as well. In 1800, citizens near the New York families sued the Shakers for keeping their young people in "the Condition of Common Slaves" and subject to "influence of their superiors."[106] The Ohio legislature passed a law declaring that "agents, trustees, and elders" of any "associated society whose property is all vested in common stock" were subject to fines for any member of that society who refused to serve in the militia. (In other words, if any Shaker refused to serve, the entire village had to pay the fine.)[107] That law came on top of the 1811 Ohio law that set a five-hundred-dollar fine for efforts to persuade men to join any sect professing celibacy. In 1784, the town of Henniker, New Hampshire, "Voted to Due something relative To those People Called Shakering Quakers." They banned any new Shakers from settling in an incipient Shaker village in the town and established a committee to which the Shakers would have to report if they chose to "strool about the Town." Unsurprisingly, the Shakers left, and the Henniker village vanished before it could begin.[108]

In the long prelude to the War of 1812, Shakers fought laws that insisted on their military service or required onerous financial recompense for avoiding it. Massachusetts officials tried to fine Shakers six dollars for every member who refused to serve. Indiana officials drafted Samuel Swan McClelland for the march on Tippecanoe, notwithstanding his Shaker faith and the fact that he had ripped his fingers down to the bone in a timbering accident. The state charged him regardless, and McClelland had to sell his tools to pay the fine. The militia stayed at the Shaker village of Busro in the wake of Tippecanoe and the broader War of 1812, "without regard to even common good behaviour." They ate the Shakers out of house and home, "cattle and hogs . . . butchered and destroyed in a most savage wasteful manner." Shaker houses were commandeered as barracks, "our nurcerys into horse lots, and our fields into race grounds." The Shakers were forced from Busro, and the "whole place looked as tho a host of Pharos plages had passed over it." The Shakers would return after the war, but the damage was done. Busro closed again in 1827, this time for good.[109]

It is difficult to assess the long-term effects of anti-Shaker mobs and laws. Certainly Busro and Henniker failed because of armed and legal opposition. Yet multiple mobs did little to stem the growth of Turtle Creek or Harvard. Threats of violence may have kept potential converts away, but by the 1820s, Shaker numbers were already declining. Perhaps the dynamic Shaker village seemed less threatening when it was shrinking. Still, for those needing a symbol of the dangers of supernaturalism in a republic, the Shakers remained an easy target. Indeed, the Shakers appeared in some of the leading literary works of the age in just that capacity. Nathaniel Hawthorne's "Shaker Bridal" praised the industry of the Shakers but only because the sect had raised itself from the "wild fanaticism" of its early days, when Mother Ann had (according to Hawthorne) used a hot cattle-iron to discipline her followers. The Shakers play a minor role in Catherine Maria Sedgwick's *Redwood*, where believers fall "under the dominion of Anne Lee."

Shaker miracles even found their way into *Moby-Dick*. When the *Pequod* encounters the *Jeroboam*, Ahab's sailors discover the other ship has fallen under the control of a religious fanatic. The man called Gabriel "had been originally nurtured among the crazy society of Neskeyuna Shakers," and once at sea, followed the culturally prescribed behavior of a miracle-monger: "He set himself forth as the deliverer of the sea and vicar-general of all Oceanica. The unflinching earnestness with which he declared these things . . . united to invest in Gabriel in the minds of the majority of the ignorant crew, with an atmosphere of sacredness." Melville intimates that even at Niskeyuna, Gabriel performed false miracles; at sea, Gabriel soon has the run of the *Jeroboam* and orders "the incredulous captain" to jump overboard. Gabriel declares the white whale to be "the Shaker god incarnate," and the "sailors . . . fawned before him, in obedience to his instructions, sometimes rendering him personal homage, as to a god." It is a telling aside: in a novel suffused with religious themes, when Melville needed a religious tyrant, he turned to the Shakers.[110]

But like the *Jeroboam,* Shakerism was adrift by 1851. Its supernatural experiences, in the form of Mother Ann's Work, tilted toward the interior; a long period of decline had already set in. Of course, Americans had been predicting the death of the Shakers almost since the moment of their founding—a perennial deathbed attitude that must be in part responsible for that heavy mist of nostalgia that still suffuses the sect. Yet the early Shakers themselves saw only promise and holiness in their midst, and they saw and celebrated it because of miracles and supernatural events that filled their lives and the stories they passed on to new converts. Bearing records of healings, exorcisms, mind-readings, and other marvels, Shakers insisted that they had proofs—witness testimony and sense evidence—that Christ had returned, because *miracles* had returned.

Those miracles also shaped the response to the church. The close connection in the revolutionary mind between supernatural claims and incipient tyranny formed the backdrop and language of the case against the Shakers— which explains why a relatively small pacifist sect caused so much trouble. Attacks on the Shakers were forerunners of greater violence against Native American prophets, Mormons, and perhaps even Catholics. The raids by James Smith in 1810 and Gray Bryant in 1825 were in some measure the seedbed for Haun's Mill in 1838 or the Charlestown convent in 1834. Shakers and anti-Shakers set the pattern for wonder-working in the new republic. The Shaker experience suggests that violence against religious groups deemed unacceptable (because supernatural) emerged with the Revolution itself. Proving miracles and punishing miracles were to be part of the republican experiment.

FIVE

Native American Prophets

In the summer of 1806, Tenskwatawa put out the sun. As miracles go, it was impressive stuff. Tenskwatawa (the Shawnee Prophet) had received a taciturn message from William Henry Harrison, territorial governor of Indiana. Harrison demanded an end to witchcraft trials among the Delaware Indians of Indiana. Seeking to discredit Tenskwatawa's witch hunts, Harrison immediately went to the argument from miracles: "If God has really employed him," wrote the governor, "he has doubtless authorized him to perform some miracles, that he may be known and received as a prophet." Miracles, Harrison was certain, served as *the* divine warrant for true religion and a surefire test to discredit "wretched delusion" and "the arts of an imposter." Harrison even suggested a few potential miracles: "Ask of him to cause the sun to stand still—the moon to alter its course—the rivers to cease to flow—or the dead to rise from their graves. If he does these things, you may then believe that he has been sent from God." Harrison's meaning was clear: Tenskwatawa could not, and was not from God. And if Tenskwatawa was not from God, then he had no authority and must cease his confrontation with the duly constituted power in Indiana—Harrison and the United States he represented.[1]

But Tenskwatawa *did* work a miracle that June and thereby improved his standing and his authority, both civil and religious, among the manifold tribes of the Old Northwest. He issued a warning that disbelievers "would see darkness come over the sun."[2] On June 16, it happened. The eclipse was "a matter of great surprise to the Indians," wrote one white observer. Some ran in fear, some fell to their knees in prayer, and some wrapped themselves in blankets and waited to die.[3] From that day forward, recalled one witness, Tenskwatawa's followers "submitted to his dictation, with a confidence that was never shaken."⁴ "We all believe," explained the Shawnee diplomat and convert George Bluejacket. The Prophet "can dream to God."⁵

Other supernatural powers surrounded the Prophet. Followers claimed he could "uncover even the thoughts of people," could "cure all diseases," and knew how to identify witches and other sources of evil magic. Animals gathered about him to facilitate hunting for the faithful. Soon after the 1811 New Madrid earthquakes, stories circulated that "the *Shawanese Prophet* has caused the earthquake to destroy the whites." It was even said of him, according to one report, that "he can fly."⁶

Between 1760 and 1820, a variety of devotees, known to whites as "prophets," preached a novel religious system known in the twenty-first century as nativism. Many particulars set the prophets apart from other "new religions" of the early republic. Most obviously, nativists worshipped a figure called the Master of Life, not Jesus Christ. Nativists preached exclusively to Indian nations; Shakers, Mormons, and Wilkinsonians were predominantly white. Nevertheless, nativism shared in the wonder-working revolution of the early republic. Like other new sects, nativism claimed miracles and wonders as evidence of a new dispensation. When a Catholic missionary lectured Kenekuk, the Kickapoo Prophet, on the validity of the Bible being "proved by miracles," Kenekuk immediately responded by listing the healings and resurrections he had performed. "This is the way," Kenekuk explained, "I got to be believed."⁷

The importance of these wonder-working prophets should not be underestimated: the U.S. government went to war with two of them. With the rise of the prophets in the United States, ideas about Indians, witchcraft, and evidence—always an undercurrent of political discourse—entered directly into the political, legal, and military crisis regarding Indian land claims and white settlement plans. In the midst of deep tensions between British and American forces, the presence of Indians who could talk to God, perform miracles, and (in the case of Tenskwatawa and the Red Sticks) command military forces embodied the worst nightmares of antisupernatural republicans. When Harrison's braggadocio about miracles failed so spectacularly, the governor turned to warfare as an alternative. Harrison launched a preemptive strike against Tenskwatawa at the Battle of Tippecanoe in 1811; this struggle was absorbed into the subsequent War of 1812. False religion would be met with force; Tenskwatawa was undone by the Battle of the Thames, not by religious debate. Red Stick prophets of the Old Southwest suffered a similar fate at the Battle of Horseshoe Bend. Andrew Jackson suggested a forced atonement for the superstitious Indians: "They must be made to

114 THE SECTARIAN IMPULSE

know that their prophets are impostors, & that our strength is mighty & will prevail."[8] Accusing Indians of superstitious practices and its concomitant antirepublicanism—the same critique foisted upon Shakers, Mormons, Cochranites, and others in the early republic—provided an ideal pretext for early republican Indian wars.

The case against the prophets was the broader case against miracles and the supernatural in the early republic; it was the language of credulity and superstition applied to whole populations at once. A belief in stadial development marked the antebellum period, and the perceived primitivism of Native Americans in the white imagination provided a kind of tautological proof of the power of superstition. If Indians were childlike, they would revere wonder-workers, and because wonder-workers were found among them, Indians must be childlike. Benjamin Drake assured readers in 1841 that Tenskwatawa's eclipse "enabled him to carry conviction to the minds of many of his ignorant followers, that he was really the earthly agent of the Great Spirit."[9] The effort to prove that prophets had merely cribbed Christian practices for their own use became a cottage industry in the early republic. The artist George Catlin, among Kenekuk's faithful, wrote that the Kickapoo Prophet must have learned the art of preaching from Methodists, and "commenced preaching . . . pretending to have had an interview with some superhuman mission, or inspired personage," with the intent to accrue "any honor or emolument, or influence to be gained by the promulgation."[10] Prophets like Handsome Lake, Lewis H. Morgan concluded in 1851, simply "adopted the idea of a revelation from Heaven" from the Christians, "to give authority and sanction to his projected reformation."[11]

A related claim about Indian borrowing formed a plank of twentieth-century scholarship on prophets. Anthony F.C. Wallace's theory of revitalization used Handsome Lake as its template, claiming that cultures under duress produced new religious leaders who combined old cultural elements with novel innovations via charismatic revival. In this case, the synthesis occurred between European Christianities and Iroquois traditions. These "hallucinatory" leaders needed the cover of religion to justify changes in the society's way of life even as they claimed to restore traditional practices.[12] This formulation cloaks realist concerns; it is an effort to explain a category mistake—why *did* Indians believe?—rather than an analysis of the components of belief and their change over time. Moreover, it places the generative power entirely within Christendom; nativism becomes a "basically European innovation expressed in native idiom."[13]

A more recent generation of scholarship has argued that "preoccupation with their indebtedness to Christian teachings can too easily divert us from the important task of placing their prophetic messages within their proper contexts."[14] Native American religions often borrowed and adapted ideas from multiple belief systems; any sharing that occurred should therefore be seen as a Native American development rather than a warmed-over Christianity served up by cloying masterminds. Moreover, the nations of the Eastern Woodlands possessed flexible religious systems that shared numerous basic assumptions, a process exacerbated through frequent mourning wars in the long eighteenth century.[15] The accretion of ideas and concepts of divine power was no novelty in Indian religious history; rather it was part of the syncretic tendencies of Eastern Woodlands religions. The prophets did not copy a foreign religious tradition and superimpose it on their own; their own religious system supported the incorporation of many different elements. In this sense, the nativist revival was not (as an older historiography had it) "self-contradictory" by incorporating polyglot Christian ideas about spiritual power into a movement that ultimately opposed Christian settlement and conversion.[16] The religion of the nativists should instead be considered an indigenous tradition, born from Native American experience and religious thought rather than merely borrowed and refurbished from white neighbors.

Moreover, if Native American religions actively incorporated ideas and spiritual power from other cosmologies, then it cannot be maintained that they accepted credulity when they accepted nativism. Native Americans understood notions concerning supernatural proofs, validation, and skepticism. Thus, while it is possible to understand the rise of nativism as part of the long struggle for the Ohio Country between 1754 and 1815—situating the rise of Neolin, Tenskwatawa, and others within the context of scurrilous land sales, invasive white settlement, and military upheavals—the religion can also be understood in the context of Enlightenment-era religious change in North America. Overlooking supernaturalism among the Indians—or isolating it as particular to the Indians—has prevented historians from seeing the supernatural as a driving idea in American religion and politics that crossed communities.

Nativism spread most quickly and significantly among the nations now designated as the Eastern Woodlands cultures, where at least four major prophets emerged between 1750 and 1820: Neolin (also known as the Delaware Prophet, active 1752–1754), Handsome Lake (the Seneca Prophet, 1799–1815), Tenskwatawa (1804/5–1836), and Kenekuk (the Kickapoo

Handsome Lake preaching, as recreated by Jesse Cornplanter, 1905. (New York State Museum)

Prophet, 1819–1836). Farther south, the Red Stick movement among the Creeks was popularly linked to Tenskwatawa and his brother Tecumseh. Such a connection existed more in the white imagination than reality—Red Sticks adhered to a more traditional interpretation of existing religious beliefs and were "best understood as traditional Muskogee sorcerer-shamans"—but they shared in the nativist penchant for miraculous proofs and the rejection of white culture and practices.[17]

The prophets altered Native American religion, but it is not entirely clear how much or how far. There was no single faith system called "Native American religion" (though whites insisted on thinking there was); beliefs and practices changed from nation to nation, clan to clan, village to village, and even person to person. In 1804, Constantin Volney remarked that among Indians, "every individual . . . makes himself a creed after his own manner."[18] Popular culture of the twenty-first century, moreover, has tended to conflate historical Native American religion with modern New Age practices; these reinterpretations have not always pleased Native American groups, nor do they correspond with realities of worship in centuries past.[19] Most data about Indian religious practice in the eighteenth century, of course, comes from white sources, and though some white observers might have accurately reported what they saw and heard of Indian worship, their comprehension often lagged behind their observation.

European misunderstanding of Native American religion was nothing new. As Anthony Pagden has explained, the first generations of Europeans who encountered the Americas "had to classify before they could properly see, and in order to do that they had no alternative but to appeal to a system which was already in use."[20] As reports (and resources) flooded back into the Old World from the New, the image of Indian society as an inversion of Christian society took shape and developed over the sixteenth and seventeenth centuries, complete with strained analogies and outright fictions.[21] The practices of the Aztecs and Incas, wrote the Franciscan Jose de Acosta, were deliberate Satanic inventions designed to mock Christianity, with real cannibalism substituted for eucharistic transubstantiation, and blood-drenched priests replacing the purity of the church.[22] In pursuit of such theories, Diego de Landa investigated Yucatán natives for the practice of human sacrifice; he tortured 4,500 Indians himself, killing more than 150.[23] In Mexico City, Indians and mestizos were grouped with Jews and Moors under Inquisitorial classification. For fifty years after Cortes, mestizos could not receive clerical ordination.[24] Moreover, this association of Indian religions with Judaism contributed to the resuscitation of the myth of the blood libel, the notion that Jews used the blood of Christian children in their ceremonies. The rise of the early modern Christian conceptions of Judaism as an inversion of Christianity paralleled and likely perpetuated the myth of Indian worship as a bloody, anti-Christian affair.[25]

Seventeenth-century English colonies did little better. Cotton Mather worked himself into a lather over Satan's alliance with Native American shamans, believing that "Indians employed their *sorcerers,* whom they call *powaws*" to enact "diabolical *conjurations,* to obtain the assistance of the devils against the settlement of these our English." The Indians' "whole religion was the most explicit sort of *devil-worship,*" and indeed, "The Indian *Powawes,* used all their Sorceries to molest the first Planters" of New England. Such ideas were not limited to the New England colonies; Alexander Whittaker of Virginia remarked of the local Indians, "Their priests . . . are no other but such as our witches are."[26]

The notion of a single Native American religion was an illusion, but the tribes now designated as Eastern Woodlands cultures shared a core of beliefs and practices in much the same way that Judaism, Christianity, and Islam shared beliefs as Abrahamic faiths. The cultural groups that stretched (at the time of the British invasion) from the southern Appalachians to the Great Lakes and into what is now maritime Canada lived in a universe populated by a hierarchy of spiritual beings. Most Eastern Woodland religions featured a high god, but often one who was either distant or easily duped. The power worth seeking in the Native American cosmos usually came from lesser supernatural creatures. The spirits of animate and inanimate objects were closer to the human world and more likely to understand and care about human affairs, and so were usually the ones who received succor. An Oneida Indian described the concept to Jeremy Belknap, explaining that wind, clouds, thunder, and mountains "have an invisible, as well as visible existence, and an agency over human actions."[27]

These beings went by many names but were often referred to in the eighteenth and nineteenth centuries as "manitou." Morgan described the notion among the Iroquois: "Most of the objects in nature were thus placed under the watchful care of some protecting Spirit." Great powers like the thunder had spirits, but so did small things, down to "the Spirit of the Strawberry."[28] Volney's investigation of Indian religion revealed a "great *manitou,* residing on high" who "concerns himself . . . little about the affairs of men." More important were the "subordinate *manitous* or genii innumerable, who people Earth and air, preside over every thing that happens. . . . It is to the latter chiefly, and almost exclusively, that the savages address their prayers."[29]

The nativist revival altered this supernatural balance of power and placed the Master of Life, rather than the manitou, at the center of the spiritual world. "The Great Spirit spoken of by the prophets," writes Alfred A. Cave, "was born in the eighteenth century."[30] Nativists argued that the Master of Life had returned and was preparing to make his favored people, the Native Americans, lords of North America once again. For that to happen, Indians needed to reform their lives. Neolin and Tenskwatawa additionally taught that this renewed religious age sanctioned an end to tribal designations. Henceforth, there would be no separate tribes like the Ojibwe, Miami, or Ottawa; there would be only Native Americans.[31]

Particular religious mandates varied depending on the prophet, but all prophets insisted that the return of the Master of Life foretold a new era in existence. "I am He who made heaven and earth, the trees, lakes, rivers, all men, and all thou seest, and all that thou hast seen on earth," the Master of Life informed Neolin, and further instructed him, "Because I love you, you must do my will."[32] Tenskwatawa learned that the Master of Life had created the world and the Indians, but "the *Americans* I did not make—They are not my *Children.* But the *Children* of the *Evil Spirit—They grew from the Scum of the great water, when it was troubled by the Evil Spirit.*"[33] Similarly, Neolin let his followers know that whites were no longer welcome on the continent: "Send them back to the country which I made for them."[34]

None of the prophets had much experience as ecclesiarchs or leaders prior to their first visions; indeed, Handsome Lake was "considered . . . from his youth as below mediocrity, and indeed as quite deficient in intellect," according to the Presbyterian missionary Samuel Kirkland.[35] That very mediocrity, however, "occasioned a degree of surprize, and gave some efficacy to his first visions." Tenskwatawa, prior to his visions, was "a perfect vagabond" and "a great drunkard."[36] While no clear story of Kenekuk's early years exist, an 1831 reference refers to him as "at one time given to intemperance."[37]

The foundation of each prophet's movement began with a supernatural journey across the cosmos (possibly literal and possibly only spiritual); this journey took them on a long road to the afterlife, where guides and messengers explained the cosmos before leading the prophet to the Master of Life himself. Though uniformly referred to as "visions" by white observers, the journeys as recounted by nativists do not suggest a wholly mental state. Handsome Lake and Tenskwatawa had to die to take their journey, and their returns were therefore more like resurrections than dreams.[38] Neolin's call to prophecy was profoundly prosaic; he first perceived the mystic paths "while cooking."[39] Neolin was not dreaming; he appears to have climbed a mountain physically and met the Master of Life in person. In 1766, Neolin gave a much briefer account of his vision, where he claimed he was simply instructed on true religion by "the appearance of a man who came to him by night while he sat by the fire alone." Even in this dressed-down version, however, Neolin insisted he was "perfectly awake."[40]

The road formed a central image in nativist teachings. Kenekuk described "the straight way" as contrasted to "the crooked path of the bad."[41] Handsome Lake crossed a road descending from the heavens on a great sky journey. That journey was recorded in the Code of Handsome Lake (*Ganiodiio*), read then and now at regular intervals during the ritual year.[42] Tenskwatawa, too, discovered a forked road on his journey; one branch led to paradise, a rich, fertile country where farming and hunting were easy. But he also "saw vast crowds going swiftly along the left hand road," which was lined with houses of punishment.[43]

In the houses of punishment along the evil road, prophets saw hellfire and damnation as vivid as anything from the mind of Dante: drunkards forced to swallow molten lead, gamblers handling heated playing cards that seared their fingers off, a fiddler forced to play his own tendons, an "immoral woman" raped with red-hot implement until "steam [was] issuing from her body."[44] Kenekuk preached about "the broad road that leads to misery," with pits "filled with fire for the punishment of all wicked and ill men; all professed drunkards, tattlers, liars, and meddling bodies."[45] Handsome Lake saw a woman who had used magic cursed with snakes for hair, and quarrelsome spouses whose tongues and mouths had turned to fire.[46] Tenskwatawa heard the wicked "roar like the falls of a river."[47]

The nativist paradise, on the other hand, was comprised of strata based on ethnicity and justice. The Assisink Prophet Wangomend had been permitted to tour the afterlife, where he found three heavens—"one for the Indians, one for the negroes, and another for the white people." The Indian afterlife was the happiest "and that of the whites the unhappiest; for they were under chastisement for their ill treatment of the Indians" and for enslaving Africans.[48] The missionary John Brainerd heard the same story from an unnamed prophetess in 1751.[49] One of Kenekuk's disciples visited heaven and found "four stories," the fourth occupied by "the palace of the Great Spirit."[50]

Getting to heaven required adherence to the new code of nativist ethics. All prophets insisted that followers abandon alcohol. They opposed the use of white customs, trade goods, and animals. Tenskwatawa's followers ought not to sell hides or other goods to whites nor even eat food cooked by a white person. The Seneca Prophet similarly taught that "our Creator, when he made us, designed us that we should live by hunting." A later exception was made for the raising of cattle and Western-style houses, but those were "all that you can adopt."[51] Dogs and cats also represented the intrusion of white culture, and "many killed their dogs," reported the adopted Shawnee John Tanner.[52] Reports of the slaughter of domesticated animals paralleled the rise of the Red Sticks from 1811 to 1814.[53] Magic and sorcery were forbidden; Tenskwatawa taught that traditional medicine bags were demonic, and Handsome Lake condemned compelling charms and personal magic: "A great pile of human bodies lies dead because of this."[54]

A final injunction accompanied all the prophetic teachings: land was inviolable, indivisible, and Indian. The Master of Life told Neolin that "the land on which you are, I have made for you, not for others."[55] Handsome Lake similarly taught that the Master of Life who "made the earth, never intended that it should be made merchandise."[56] In Handsome Lake's visit to the afterlife, he saw some of the dead moving a heap of sand, one grain at a time. This punishment was dealt out to land sellers.[57] The Master of Life had made the lands of North America for Native Americans; its sale to whites was forbidden, or at the very least, required the consent of all the tribes. As Kenekuk explained in 1827, "The Great Spirit told me that no people owned the land—that it was all his, and not to forget to tell the white people that when we went in to council."[58]

All the prophets justified their new teachings by reference to miracles and supernatural events. Kenekuk claimed: "I raised the dead to life. There was a woman . . . who, so every one thought, could not possibly recover her health. I breathed on her and from that moment she began to recover." He also healed an infant "just about to die." A Christian missionary wrote in despair from Kenekuk's country, "the Indians were not to be converted except by men who could work miracles."[59] When Handsome Lake met Thomas Jefferson, the prophet justified his authority through supernatural powers: "Angels empowered me to relieve any man of any sickness whatever it may be, if he be a good man, who looks up to the Great Spirit above."[60] The Red Sticks drew circles around themselves, which maintained their spiritual power; when an outsider entered one, he apparently went mad and died. The Creek prophet Captain Isaacs "continually related the wonderful things he could do and the miraculous things he had done," which included spending several days at the bottom of a river and the ability to "petrify" those who opposed him.[61] Even Andrew Jackson blamed desertion in the Creek War on "The Phisic of the indians prophets" that turned "men, once so brave" into cowards. Jackson might have been joking—but even the joke points to the otherworldly, unnerving powers of the prophets.[62]

Supernatural proofs were not exclusive to the prophets. Believers in the manitou defended their faith in the same way in the nineteenth century. The Sauk leader Black Hawk recalled that in his childhood, "A good spirit . . . with large wings like a *swan's,* but ten times larger" had care of a local island in the Mississippi, and in return for respect and quiet, the spirit allowed the Sauk to forage, feast, and play. Black Hawk knew the spirit was real, because it "has often been seen by our people."[63] Morgan's Iroquois informants similarly noted that some manitou "were made tangible to the senses."[64] The missionary John Heckewelder challenged the Delaware holy man Chenos to produce a miracle in 1799. Chenos promised to make it rain. Several hours later, the ground was soaked with rain, and "the credulous multitude did not fail to ascribe it to his supernatural power." Heckewelder was beaten by his own strategy: he sought a supernatural proof, and Chenos provided one.[65]

Nativist proofs, however, were *expected* as legitimating evidence. Tenskwatawa's validation by eclipse is the prime example. Vacillating Creek leaders "sent a runner" to the Red Sticks asking to "see and hear what you say you have seen and heard. Let us have the same proof you have had." The prophets did not oblige—perhaps because the runner turned out to be complicit in the murder of Red Stick allies and was put to death.[66] According to John Keating's 1823 account, Tenskwatawa met a group of Sauk Indians who demanded he perform a resurrection to prove his power. He refused. (His principled stand managed to impress listeners: "Many were satisfied and did as he bid them.")[67]

The problem of proof and powers was most apparent in the long struggle against witchcraft that formed a central plank in the nativist program. The Delaware Prophet learned in his vision that prayers intended for the Master of Life had instead reached "a wicked spirit, who induces you to do evil." Traditional prayers and chants did the Indians harm rather than good; only the Master of Life was to be propitiated. All other worship was a kind of sorcery.[68] Handsome Lake and Tenskwatawa taught that witches, worshipping an evil god, had infiltrated Indian societies and were purposefully causing harm and the erosion of territory to white governments. Soon after receiving his prophetic office, Handsome Lake declared that witches had sickened his niece, daughter of Cornplanter. When Cornplanter's daughter recovered, Handsome Lake's stand against witchcraft was vindicated and he gained wide-ranging authority over the Seneca, albeit briefly.[69] Shortly thereafter, and farther west, Tenskwatawa oversaw witch trials among the Delaware and Wyandot nations of Indiana. In 1806, with the assistance of the warrior classes of those nations, the Prophet sought "to know & point out those who practise [witchcraft]."[70]

Scholars have attempted to explain Handsome Lake's or Tenskwatawa's trials as the rise of misogyny in Eastern Woodlands cultures, an attempt at cultural reintegration, or a battle between Native Americans who suffered from land sales against those who benefitted.[71] As Robin Briggs has written about the great witch trials of early modern Europe, the more historians learn about individual trials or outbreaks, the less likely broad interpretations become, so a theory of multiple causations becomes the most likely. Certainly ideas about gender, land, and community all combined in the witch trials of Handsome Lake and Tenskwatawa, but none of these explanations alone suffices.[72]

As brutal and terrifying as the executions were, there was a theory and a theology to them. Just as miracles and supernatural powers justified new religious devotions and faiths among whites, so, too, did the supernatural removal of witches justify a faith in the return of the Master of Life and his designated prophets. Clark's observation that "in describing witchcraft as a social evil authors necessarily invoked a conception of the social order, an idea of *communitas* . . . they committed themselves to views about authority and about the general desirability of certain forms of rulership" speaks to the Indian as well as the European context.[73] Witch trials were not merely hunts for outsiders or high political power struggles garbed in religion; they were the working out of old and new conceptions of power and authority. They functioned, in other words, like the supernatural regularly did in the early republic: reestablishing and reorienting legitimacy and power. In this case, the witchcraft trials provided validation for a new political system based on prophetic (rather than tribal) authority.[74]

Neolin's emergence coincided with a witchcraft panic among the Delawares. In the wake of the Seven Years' War, part of the Nanticoke nation had been expelled from Maryland. The fate of the Nanticokes was typical of Indian tribes along the coastal regions of British North America. Despite promises of protection and autonomy from the government of Maryland, Nanticokes faced hordes of white squatters who occupied their land. Colonial governments ultimately backed the whites; the Nanticokes became refugees. Delaware land had been similarly seized by whites through the 1737 Walking Purchase and the 1754 Albany Purchase.[75] By 1763, both nations found themselves in central Pennsylvania. Rumors circulated among the Delaware about Nanticoke sorcery. The substance in question was "called *Mattapassigan,* meaning poison," according to the missionary David Zeisberger. This poison, however, was inert in its natural state. It would only "receive its power for working injury through witchcraft," Zeisberger wrote, and then it might infect "whole townships and tribes with disorders as pernicious as the plague." This poisonous witchcraft had arrived almost at the same time as Neolin's vision, and for two years, the "Delawares have endeavored to extirpate the shocking evil."[76] The trader James Kenny noted in 1761 that a Nanticoke woman had apparently "kept and fed" an "infernal spirit" that grew large enough to kill children, whereupon the spirit seized control of the tribe and the Nanticokes pledged to "obey & serve it."[77]

It is not clear whether Neolin initiated this witch hunt against the Nanticokes (Zeisberger called the effort "in vain"), but he clearly supported a move against Nanticoke sorcery as part of his platform. The struggle against sorcery was almost immediately followed by Neolin's greatest success. Correlation

does not imply causality, but the campaign against Nanticoke sorcery occurred almost simultaneously with a massive pan-Indian uprising across the
Ohio Country in 1763 and 1764. The leader of the revolt was Pontiac—an
Ottawa follower of Neolin's teachings who sought to create a Native American political order that would obscure existing tribal divisions. The Indian
revolutionaries secured sufficient victories to force Britain to announce the
famed Proclamation Line of 1763, legally establishing the Appalachian range
as the limit of white settlement in the West. Though this arrangement lasted
less than a decade, Neolin's upstart religion—and its witch-hunting spiritual
substratum—secured the Ohio Country for the Indians.[78]

Neolin vanished from the historical record in the wake of Pontiac's Rebellion, but once he did, Wangomend, the Assisink Prophet, came into
clearer prominence. A Munsee Indian, Wangomend may have had visions
as early as the 1750s, though Heckewelder dated his emergence to 1766.
Wangomend also forbid witchcraft. He received "general approbation," according to Heckewelder, "when he declared . . . that the wizards were getting
the upper hand, and would destroy the nation." At least one trial occurred, in
1773; the accused woman was exonerated. In 1775, Wangomend approached
the Delawares on the Muskingum with his fear about witchcraft; the Delaware
leadership apparently agreed. It wanted "every conjurer and witch in the
nation brought to an account and punished with death" and appointed Wangomend to uncover the guilty. The witch hunt failed, however, when Wangomend himself fell under suspicion of witchcraft, and, in Heckewelder's
words, "his zeal, in consequence, became considerably cooled." The Delaware
chiefs "were no longer disposed to meddle with this dangerous subject,
justly fearing that it could not but terminate in the ruin of their nation."[79]

Handsome Lake's movement also began in the midst of a witchcraft crisis. Shortly before the first vision, Handsome Lake's niece sickened and
died; suspicions of witchcraft fell upon "a certain woman . . . whom they
suspected to have a familiar Spirit." Cornplanter—a Seneca chief and the
prophet's brother—ordered her execution; his sons carried out the sentence
by tomahawk. A few days later, Handsome Lake fell into his trance, where
he learned that though one witch had died, "yet there remained one like her
who was a man."[80]

The "devil made the witches," Handsome Lake explained, and when the
Master of Life tried to kill them, they fled underground and would return
at the end of the world.[81] Just as Neolin had attacked traditional Indian religious ceremonies as sources of secret magic and illness, so, too, Handsome

Lake decried the venerable secret societies of the Iroquois—including the renowned False Faces. Their ceremonies could accidentally transfer power to some evil being; Handsome Lake wanted all such societies disbanded.[82]

In August 1799, the messengers repeated their insistence that a second witch continued to practice secret sorceries.[83] A year later, Cornplanter's other daughter, Jiiwi, took ill. Cornplanter entreated Handsome Lake to prophesy; eventually, the messengers agreed to give Handsome Lake the ability to find the witches causing the illness. He found them. "Some of the Delaware Indians who lived at Cattaraugus possessed the power of witchcraft," he declared, "and were the cause of their illness." Indeed, "the principle Muncy chief" was one of the witches (and possibly the father of Jiiwi's child). The Munsee Delaware lived on Iroquois land, and the accusation did not sit well with them.[84] They provided their own healer to visit Jiiwi and prescribe a remedy, but the Allegheny Seneca decided instead to hold him hostage. The Senecas stuck by the predictions of Handsome Lake, as they explained to the settler David Mead, because "the man we depend on to discover these things is fully capable of explaining how they are contrived and executed." Mead informed New York's governor. Meanwhile, Delaware military units gathered near Seneca territory. The issue was referred to a council at Buffalo Creek in June 1801.[85]

Witchcraft was not the only item on the agenda. The council—with delegates from all Seneca villages—met to settle the question of the Black Rock corridor, a mile-long stretch of land along the Niagara River. The Seneca owned it; New York State wanted to buy it. Red Jacket, the famed orator of the Buffalo Creek Seneca, wanted to sell the land while reserving to Native Americans the rights to fish and gather in the territory and to travel across it without restriction. Handsome Lake opposed any sale; the messengers had told him so, and he passed their advice to the council. Witchcraft and land became part of the same diplomatic agenda in an internal Iroquois struggle.[86]

Handsome Lake took the lead at the council, accusing "sundry old women & men of the Delaware Nation, and some few among their own tribe" as witches, according to the surveyor Joseph Ellicott. It is possible Handsome Lake accused Red Jacket of witchcraft, although as Christopher Densmore has noted, the only evidence for this claim is DeWitt Clinton's report from 1811, and Clinton's sources are unclear.[87] Handsome Lake did manage to get the council to agree that "those persons accused of Witchcraft should be threatened with Death" if they persisted "bewitching the people." The council adjourned, however, without carrying out any executions.[88]

Nevertheless, the council was decisive. Though Handsome Lake failed to stop the land sales and the road, Jiiwi recovered. The survival of the victim suggested that Handsome Lake's attacks had either frightened the witches off or stymied their supernatural powers. The Delaware and Munsee nations soon retreated from Seneca territory. If some of the Delawares were witches, and the Delawares left, that, too, had solved the witchcraft problem. If so, then Handsome Lake had defeated the witches without further bloodshed.

The Allegheny Seneca soon gave Handsome Lake political leadership to match the new *communitas*. A November 12, 1801, council declared him "High Priest, and principal Sachem in all things Civil and Religious." His supernatural success transformed the political community of the Allegheny Seneca, allowing a heretofore minor political figure to assume religious and political control. As the Quaker missionary Jacob Taylor wrote in 1803, a "principal part of the Sineca Nation have agreed to be under his Government—and nothing in the future of any Consequences is to be transacted without the Knowledge and approbation" of Handsome Lake. The Quakers noted that "his influence is great over most of the Indians of the Seneca nation and even to others of the six nations."[89] Kirkland believed Handsome Lake had more followers (per capita) among the Onondagas than among the Senecas.[90]

Though Anthony F. C. Wallace described Handsome Lake's reign as "that of a dictator," the actual rule of Handsome Lake appears remarkably moderate. He continued to rail against land sales, but once in power, he compromised on accommodation to white culture. He encouraged cattle raising among the Alleghenies, and permitted Senecas who converted to Christianity to remain in the community. He encouraged Quaker missionaries to open an English-language school in his territory.[91]

Handsome Lake's later campaigns against witches are murkier, though clearly finding and destroying witches remained a priority. The Code of Handsome Lake relates the story of two women who used "witch powder" to drive a man mad; they were whipped and then died. It is not clear whether their deaths were intentional; according to the Code, Handsome Lake believed "they would surely live."[92] The Code also stipulated that witches ought to repent rather than die; it commanded witches to confess, either to the public, to the Seneca Prophet, or secretly to the Master of Life, and if done truly, "the prayer will be sufficient."[93]

Despite this teaching, oral tradition connected Handsome Lake to a witch killing in 1807; this event may have been elided with the killing of an Onondaga witch in 1809.[94] Several other witchcraft suspicions cropped up among the Six Nations during Handsome Lake's pontificate. The Tuscaroras apparently suspected a witch in 1805 or 1806, and Mary Jemison reported several witch fears within her own family culminating in the fratricide of her son in 1811.[95] Throughout this time, Handsome Lake continued to preach his religion and lead the Allegheny Senecas; in 1803 he established a new town at Cold Spring, though he had to abandon it in 1809.[96]

That was the same year Tenskwatawa left his ministry in the shadows of the American fort at Greenville to build a new nativist town in northwest Indiana. The Shawnee Prophet—like Neolin and Handsome Lake—had long taught that traditional spiritual and magical techniques were actually diabolical. Tenskwatawa believed medicine bags in particular brought sickness and ruin upon the community. Medicine bags were ubiquitous items among several tribes of the Old Northwest, including the Shawnee, Sauk, Fox, and Kickapoo nations; medicine bundles functioned as repositories of supernatural aid. The medicine bag was "a mystery bag," wrote Catlin; "Every male in the tribe carries this, his supernatural charm or guardian."[97] The bags could be used to heal, and were "indispensable to obtain success against our enemies," as one faithful user put it in 1825.[98] Tenskwatawa insisted, however, that "all medicine bags were to be destroyed in the *presens* of the whole of the people." The bags did not contain spiritual power derived from manitou; they instead contained the essence of the king of serpents, a primeval entity dissected by the world's first witches. The witches combined these parts with offal from other evil beasts and placed them into the medicine bundles. Tenskwatawa insisted the faithful burn their bags and make open confession.[99] Kenekuk later made the same demand of his followers.[100]

These theological pronouncements probably encouraged the participation of Tenskwatawa in the Indiana witchcraft crisis—the same crisis that prompted Harrison's call for a genuine miracle, and Tenskwatawa's subsequent validation by eclipse. The prophetess Beata had brought the teachings of Tenskwatawa to the Delaware community at Woapikamunk, near the Moravian mission to the Delaware Indians. Beata had also encountered spiritual messengers—her vision came when she "swallowed three times a light that appeared to her"—but her monotheism, ban on alcohol, and affiliation with Tenskwatawa suggest that she acted as one of the Shawnee Prophet's itinerants.[101] Beata's preaching proved more effective than the Moravians'. From 1805, when Beata arrived in Woapikamunk, the missionary Abraham Luckenbach recorded a steady decline in the fortunes of his ministry. The "old baptized souls have become heathen again," Luckenbach wrote.[102]

In 1806, Beata informed the Delawares that they had a witchcraft problem. The Delaware chiefs invited Tenskwatawa to their town; given that he had preached against witchcraft, he could presumably detect "who among the people had poison or possessed the unhallowed gift of sorcery to bring about the death of Indians."[103] The results were grim. All Indians in the region were ordered to gather for "the examination." Messengers with black-painted faces forced recalcitrant converts at the Moravian mission to attend on pain of violence.[104] Tenskwatawa discovered ten witches. The witches were a diverse lot—from the high-ranking Ann Charity (a "chief among the women" and likely a member of the women's council among the Delawares), to Teta-patchsit, a former leader of the Ohio Confederacy, to a Mohican Christian named Joshua who lived at the mission.[105] Several of these witches were tortured, "brought to confess through fire," and then executed. Executioners immolated Tetapatchsit in full view of the Moravians. As he struggled, the flames leapt to the nearby prairie, and the whole encampment filled with smoke and fumes. The executioners then demanded food and tobacco from the horrified Moravian witnesses. At least four other witches were killed in the hunt. Not long after this event, the Moravians abandoned their missions and left Indiana.[106]

Tenskwatawa's trials strengthened his support in Indiana. As Cave has noted, "after the witch-hunters were ousted from power at Woapikamunk the tribal leaders did not reaffirm their previous friendly relations with the Moravian missionaries and instead embraced a nativist program."[107] Beata instituted new festivals; the Delawares demanded compensation from the Moravians. The trials had shown Tenskwatawa's supernatural ability to defy the enemies of pan-Indianism: witches, accommodationists, and missionaries. That defiance had measurable results: the removal of the missionaries and the humiliation of Harrison. Within two years, Tenskwatawa would parlay that support into the new Prophetstown settlement in northern Indiana.[108] A similar process occurred with Handsome Lake's campaign; the presumed end of witchcraft when Jiiwi recovered—and the Munsee decampment—justified the efforts taken to remove the supernatural threat. The result was a novel political reign by prophet who, in turn, established a new polity at Cold Spring.

In this sense nativism was political as well as religious—moral behavior and religious truth demanded a particular political program, and miracles and wonders provided proofs needed to justify such radical changes. By dispossessing the country of witches—which transformed the fortunes of the Seneca and Delaware nations, at least temporarily—the prophets demonstrated that they, and not the accommodationist allies of the Americans, knew what really caused the problem. They explained a political crisis and provided the means to solve it. Witch-hunting was not a cover for politics; it was politics, reifying the supernatural and natural realm as only the legitimate authority could.

Prophetic politics were short-lived but profound. Neolin's teachings formed the basis of Pontiac's rebellion across the Ohio Country in 1763 and 1764. No other prophet had such success, but Handsome Lake, Tenskwatawa, and Kenekuk all established towns under their direct rule, and each of them held off white appropriation of their land, at least for a time. Tenskwatawa and the Red Sticks participated in the War of 1812 and its related conflicts, championing political and military leadership that stymied the Americans, at least for a time. Handsome Lake even brought his prophetic authority to Washington—and had it approved by the president. His journey to Washington in 1802 was in part to demonstrate his claim to leadership of all the Six Nations—and therefore, to overrule the sales made by Red Jacket and his allies.

Jefferson and his diplomats were not expecting a visit from Handsome Lake. At the 1802 negotiations, Jefferson and Secretary of War Henry Dearborn expected to see Cornplanter as the principal chief but instead found that role taken by the Seneca Prophet. At the meeting, Jefferson received another lesson on how supernatural agents could direct politics; Handsome Lake repeatedly cited the angelic proofs of his mission as the justification for his presence and authority. Indeed, he referred to himself as one of the messengers: "The Great Spirit has appointed four angels and has appointed me the fifth, to direct our people on earth." Blue Eyes, Handsome Lake's lieutenant at the council, further elaborated: "Your red children have perfect confidence in Handsome Lake, are willing to bend an ear to his instructions, and yield obedience to his precepts. To him they have entrusted all their concerns, to be governed by his direction, wisdom, and integrity." Such a decision had been "deputed by the four Angels."[109]

The angels made specific political requests at that council: "The four Angels have directed that all the lands which have been reserved for the use of your red children, should be secured to them for their comfort . . . and this they desire may be done, by giving them separate deeds for each tract."[110] The angels got what they wanted; Dearborn assured the delegation that deeds would be provided. His letter praising Handsome Lake's reformation was placed in the longhouse as evidence of American sanction of the new faith.

Tenskwatawa's career followed a similar arc, though the Shawnee Prophet spent less time cultivating American contacts and had no interest in tribal authority. Tenskwatawa instead sought to create a pan-Indian movement, centered at an Indian city of his own choosing. He insisted that tribal designations had vanished; the new spiritual order required a single ethnic and political unit: "The Indians were once different people," Tenskwatawa explained; "they are now but one: They are all determined to practice what I have communicated to them, that has come immediately from the Great Spirit through me."[111] The Trout, Tenskwatawa's itinerant, explained that the Master of Life insisted that Indians *never to go to War against each other,* but to cultivate peace between your different Tribes that they may become one great people."[112] From his headquarters at Greenville and later at Prophetstown, Tenskwatawa received visitors and made converts from across the Old Northwest. When white officials questioned his right to establish his own towns, he replied that "it was revealed to him that the place was a proper one to establish his doctrines . . . by the supreme ruler of the universe."[113] Visitors translated into converts; converts made Tenskwatawa a political force on the frontier. William Wells—an adopted Miami on the American payroll—wrote in 1807 that "The Indians are religiously *mad* and beleaves all the Shawnese says to them."[114] His followers certainly numbered in the thousands.

Kenekuk's political career was smaller but more successful. He was already prominent among the Vermillion Kickapoo by 1816; he probably fought on Tenskwatawa's side in 1812. He signed a peace treaty in 1816 but not the scurrilous 1819 treaty by which the Kickapoo "sold" their lands in Indiana and Illinois. (The "chiefs" selected were hand-picked by white authorities to be amenable.)[115] When officials insisted that Kenekuk get his people to remove to Missouri, Kenekuk replied that "God would talk to him again and he would let me know what he said."[116] Though his land had been sold, Kenekuk's calm demeanor delayed the implementation of removal; the Vermillion remained in Illinois and Indiana far longer than other tribes. Kenekuk deftly promised to consult with the Great Spirit, placated white officials, and held open-air preaching to Indians and whites to demonstrate his goodwill, sobriety, and "civilization," building a détente surrounding Kickapoo Removal.[117]

Kenekuk could not stop the Black Hawk War, however, and the 1832 violence sundered his plans. White officials forced Kenekuk and the Vermillion onto new lands in Kansas. Soon whites were after that land, too. Numerous other tribes of the Old Northwest were again torn from their lands in Kansas and thrown into the Indian Territory, yet the Vermillion (and adopted Potawatomi) retained their Kansas cession. There is little doubt the credit goes to the political savvy and religious teachings of Kenekuk—inspired, shaped, and defended by a long pedigree of prophetic Indians and their supernatural experiences.

Prophetic political success lasted only for a season; by 1816, Tenskwatawa had lost most of his authority, and his political movement lay dead with Tecumseh, victim of the Battle of the Thames. Handsome Lake died in 1815, but not before seeing most of his authority whittled away. Cornplanter assumed much of the authority once held by Handsome Lake, whose decision to support a moderate form of accommodation (keeping land communally but learning English and raising cattle) may not have sat well with younger members of the Iroquois. Handsome Lake also continued to pursue witches, and Cornplanter eventually set himself up in opposition.[118]

Still, the decline of nativism was not entirely due to the actions of nativists; consistent political action by whites, and particularly by frontier officials, stymied their efforts. This political opposition was drenched in the language and presuppositions of antisupernaturalism, backed by military force. Military intervention broke the prophetic political stalemate on the frontier.

The road to Tippecanoe, for example, was lined with the apologetics of antisupernaturalism. Harrison's vigorous pursuit of land purchases from Indians—often made under dubious legal circumstances—heightened political tensions with Tenskwatawa, who insisted that any land treaty had to be approved by all tribes (land being a sacred trust held by all Indians). In 1809, Harrison bought a huge tract of land in the Treaty of Fort Wayne; Tenskwatawa and Tecumseh forbid surveyors to enter the lands sold. As political tensions increased, Harrison made sure to emphasize the superstitious and credulous character of the Indians and their prophet. In 1809, he informed the legislature that the Indians must choose between "a scene of savage fury, of misery and superstition, or the delightful spectacle of man in a state of progressive improvement . . . worshipping his Creator in the manner in which he has himself prescribed."[119] In 1810, he warned that Indiana was "threatened with hostilities by a . . . bold adventurer who pretends to act under the immediate inspiration of the Deity." Could Indiana remain "the haunt of a few wretched savages" when it was meant "to be the seat of civilization, of science, and of true religion"?[120] Civilization and true religion went together; threats to one were a threat to another. Harrison appealed for military authorization against the Prophet for years; the Madison administration grudgingly approved it in 1811.[121]

When the Battle of Tippecanoe went wrong—for despite later laurels for

Harrison, the 1811 fight at Prophetstown resulted in significant casualties and calls for a court-martial—Harrison defended the strike on Tippecanoe through the politics of superstition. One of Harrison's first reports following the conflict boldly announced: "The Veil under which he [Tenskwatawa] has practiced his imposture has been completely rent," and even "the most ignorant of the Indians" would realize that nativism was a mere lie.[122] Writing to the governor of Kentucky, Harrison called Prophetstown "this scene of those mysterious rites" where "the Prophet had taught his followers to believe that both his person and his town were equally inviolable."[123]

After Harrison emerged a hero from the War of 1812—and parlayed the stalemate at Tippecanoe into "Tippecanoe and Tyler Too!"—this antisupernaturalism assumed a leading role in the stories whites told themselves about war on the Indiana frontier. Accounts, tracts, biographies, and dramas consistently stressed the idea that because the Prophet's miraculous power had failed in the battle, his political base was therefore also destroyed. In other words, the defense of the nation involved the exposure of false miracles as well as military prowess; indeed, the two went hand in hand.

The political campaign materials of 1836 and 1840—when Harrison sought the White House—made use of Tenskwatawa as a superstitious tyrant, "a shrewd imposter; cunning, artful, and treacherous." Benjamin Drake wrote that Tenskwatawa pursued "that career of cunning and pretended sorcery, which enabled him to sway the Indian mind in a wonderful degree."[124] Biographies claimed that the Shawnee brothers deliberately invented their religion, so that "the savages fought with all the fury of religious fanaticism" until the "moral influence of Harrison's positions subdued this son of the woods." This portrayal, from an 1836 campaign sketch, concluded its discussion of Tippecanoe with the veiled threats of the descent into medieval violence bred by superstition: "Far different would have been the scene had the Prophet triumphed—towns would have been sacked, hamlets burned, and to the peaceful tenement of the settler offered up as a sacrifice to savage fury."[125] The defensive nature of Tenskwatawa's war—Harrison brought the army to the town—went unmentioned.

Antisupernaturalism also shaped the American war against the Red Sticks, 1813–14. George Stiggins, a settler of Natchez and European descent who sided with the Americans in the Creek War, wrote a history of the Creeks in the 1830s which credited the Shawnee Prophet with inspiring the Red Sticks to war: "The Shawanose prophet had convinced them of the overbearing wrongs they had suffered and of the successful revenge the Indians would have. . . .

The Creator would assist the Indians in the recovery of their lands."[126] Stiggins probably overstated the case, as did most of the antiprophet forces in the South. Tecumseh made a diplomatic journey south in 1811. Popular legends and oral histories have described this journey as a thoroughgoing success; it was considerably less. Tecumseh found relatively little support among the Native Americans of the Deep South. He went home with few new followers and with no promises of alliance.[127]

The Red Stick movement was born amid internecine conflicts that prompted the Creek Civil War, which in turn joined the broader War of 1812. The campaign to defeat their internal enemies and the Americans did not go well for the Red Sticks. Despite a rout of the Americans at Fort Mims in August 1813, the U.S. counterattack at Holy Ground that December and Horseshoe Bend the following March scuttled the resistance, though inspired prophets continued to animate resistance movements in subsequent Indian wars in the Deep South.[128]

The white soldiers and politicians who fought the Red Sticks paid little heed to fine distinctions between the Red Sticks and Tenskwatawa. To them, it was all the product of Indian superstition and credulity. The rebellious Creeks were "crazed by the prophecies of your wicked prophets," wrote Andrew Jackson, "tools of great Britain and Spain."[129] Alexander Cornells (an accommodationist Creek) reported that "the plan, whatever it is, must have come from the [Great] Lake Indians," even though "we have not yet been able to find the talks brought from the Prophet of the lakes."[130] The war's first historian (and a veteran of the Battle of Tippecanoe), Robert McAfee, directly connected the two conflicts: "Having witnessed the powerful effects of fanaticism on the northwestern frontier under the management of that miserable vagabond, the Wabash [Shawnee] Prophet, the British agents from Canada had already been careful to inspire some of the Creek worthies with prophetic and miraculous powers."[131] And of course, there was the developing insistence that Tecumseh had caused all the trouble down south, "played upon all their feelings, but principally upon their superstition."[132]

With military victories over nativism in both the North and South, U.S. policies of land appropriation went ahead; post hoc justification for the wars became tinged with the fight against superstition. Whites did not have a choice, the historians and poets wrote; the War of 1812 was fought to defeat superstitious factions of Indians whose credulity posed a threat to democracy. Harrison's actions at Tippecanoe were "measures for the defense of the citizens," wrote McAfee in 1816, whereas the Indians accepted "the most absurd stories" of Tenskwatawa's "power to perform miracles, and no fatigue or suffering was thought too great to be endured to get a sight of him."[133] Red Stick forces were "deluded people, the unfortunate dupes of British intrigue and of their own superstition" who made "easy prey to our [U.S.] united forces."[134] The "age of prophecy in the Creek nation displaced the light of reason," Stiggins argued, led by men who "intended to domineer by prophet craft."[135]

Similar stories emerged about other nativists in the wake of 1812. When Schoolcraft presented the visionary journey of Neolin in 1835, he criticized the way Pontiac had manipulated it "to turn the mythological and superstitious belief of his auditors to political account."[136] Morgan, who recorded extensive observations on the Iroquois, nevertheless dismissed the career of Handsome Lake by writing, "It is singular that the credulity, not only of the people, but of their most intelligent chiefs should have been sufficiently great to give credence to these supernatural pretensions." Handsome Lake himself, Morgan explained, knew his own religion was a sham and merely "professed to repeat the messages that were given to him from time to time by his celestial visitants, with whom he pretended to be in frequent communication . . . thus enforcing his precepts as the direct commands of the Great Spirit."[137] John Berryman dismissed Kenekuk's religion as a political manipulation: "The pretension of these savage politicians are supported in the main by appeals to the credulity of the ignorant masses." The French Catholic reports on the Kickapoo mission were uniformly negative; the Kickapoo Prophet "continues to seduce his people. He is a tyrant who holds an unlimited power over all his people."[138] In 1821, the *National Intelligencer* referred to Seneca efforts to control witches as the "*Imperium in Imperio*"—the same republican bugbear deployed against Mormons, Shakers, and other wonder-workers in the new republic.[139] Any political authority outside the state would unmake the Revolution. The politics of Indian wars were also the politics of the supernatural.

Yet the accusations of superstition overlooked the myriad ways in which nativism used proofs as evidence to defend their claims, adapting threads of legal skepticism as white Christians did in the early republic. Some Indian voices had concerns as profound as any Enlightenment witch court. Cornplanter in 1809 expressed regret for the witch panics since it would be wrong to execute anyone "without being sure that they are guilty," given that witchcraft was "very difficult to prove." Henry O'Bail, Handsome Lake's nephew, held that he "believes, with respect to witchcraft, that it does not

exist," and would voice "his opinion among them, but has to do it with care."[140]
Cornplanter and O'Bail ultimately usurped Handsome Lake's authority. The
Senecas, when faced with a potential witch execution, asked exactly the same
question of a local official that European witch hunters had grappled with
for centuries: "We earnestly request your judgment . . . whether you think it
would be right and consistent with the will of the Great Spirit and the laws
of humanity to take life through or by the medium of such a proof."[141] Such
concerns belie the notion, sometimes still found in the historiography, that
"witchcraft was frightening and uncontroversial" among Native Americans.[142]
Each of the nativist witch hunts provoked an internal debate; witch-hunting
divided Native American nations rather than unifying them and in this way
became further caught up in political considerations over leadership and land.

The notion that Indian prophetic movements created political change is
not new. What has gone unnoticed is the extent to which these movements—
and their religious and political effects—were based on supernatural ideas,
presented as miraculous proofs. Nativism drew on many of the same ideas
about the supernatural that animated new religions among the white population—and the criticism and political riposte they received in turn matched
those faced by Shakers, Mormons, Cochranites, and others in the early
republic. Overlooking supernaturalism among the Indians—or isolating
it as particular to the Indians—has prevented historians from seeing the
supernatural as a driving idea in American religion and politics that crossed
communities.

The response to the Indian prophets was the response to sectarians. In
every case, white observers assumed that the presence of the supernatural
indicated a deliberate effort to mislead and accumulate political power. The
attack on "superstition" formed part of the political response to the prophets
as well, and it is no surprise that violence against wonder-workers came as
part of the answer. Understanding this precedent of armed U.S. response to
wonder-workers (who were also armed) therefore helps explain the broader
history of violence against sects—the mobs who disrupted the Shakers, and
military response to the Latter-day Saints. Nativists were part of the wonder-
working world of the early republic not only in their miracles but in their
fate at the hands of republican authority.

The Age of the Prophets has not ended. After several decades of declining
membership, the Longhouse religion of Handsome Lake began to expand
in the 1960s; indeed, it became a source of activism and leadership for the

emerging American Indian Movement, and today its adherents in the United States and Canada number in the thousands. There are fewer members in Kenekuk's church, but it, too, remains in Kansas. They represent an enduring testimony not only to the power of American supernatural religion but to the religious significance of the wonder-workers and the spiritual meaning their religions continue to impart into the twenty-first century.[143]

SIX

Latter-day Saints

A great steamboat rolled across the sky above Kirtland, Ohio. According to John Pulsipher, "it was a large fine & beautiful boat, painted in the finest style." Its 1838 passenger manifest was a roll of the departed, including "Old Elder Beamon, who had died a few months before . . . standing in the bow of the Boat Swinging his hat & Singing a well known hymn." Field hands quit work to watch the celestial craft, and as it rattled with the "puffing of a Steamboat, intermingled with the sound of many waggons," it "passed right over the Temple & went out of sight to the west," but not without incident: "As it arrived over the Temple, a part of it broke off & turned *black* & went north & was soon out of sight. While the boat, all in perfect shape went to the W[est] more beautiful & pure than before."[1]

The Temple in question was the Kirtland Temple, built by the followers of Joseph Smith Jr. according to God's command. Pulsipher and Beamon were among those followers, who had by then taken to calling themselves Latter-day Saints. Others had more colorful names for them: "ignorant fanatics," "engines of death and hell," and "an impoverished population, alienated in feeling from other portions of the community." Critics complained that Mormons were "a gang of impostors" who "know they utter false predictions. They know they cannot work miracles." Pulsipher, however, believed in the flying steamboat and understood its significance as one of the "Signs & wonders [that] were seen & heard which caused the Saints to rejoice."[2]

The celestial steamboat exemplifies both the centrality of the supernatural to Mormon religious experience and the nature of American miracles. Though Pulsipher only wrote about the event years later, he insisted that the "people of Kirtland" saw the flying ship; like many other Mormon miracles, it cited its public character as part of its defense. The critical historical question, however, is not whether the ghostly ship really did appear in the sky (a theological query), but rather what the appearance meant for the Mormons who saw it, or at least for Pulsipher. Fortunately, Pulsipher recorded that very information: arriving in a season of deep institutional and political turmoil for the Saints, the steamship was a "wonderful Sight" that "encouraged the Saints because they knew the lord had not forgotten them."[3]

Miracles and wonders were rife in early Mormonism, from the founding of the Church of Jesus Christ of Latter-day Saints in April 1830 until the expulsion of that church from Missouri in 1838. Like the Shakers, Cane Ridge enthusiasts, Cochranites, residents of Prophetstown, and a host of others, early Mormons set store by the supernatural, taking the miraculous events that followed them as proof of authority and divine approbation. While some Mormons disdained the gifts of the spirit or claimed they were unimportant in conversion, early Mormon missionary journals and narratives affirm the centrality of Mormon miracles: healings, tongues-speaking, visions, and exorcisms as guides along a sacred mission. And when "miracles were wrought, such as healing the sick, casting out devils," wrote John Whitmer, "the church grew and multiplied in grace, numbers, and knowledge."[4] The Saints collected sense evidence and reliable testimonies and deployed them in a Baconian style that they saw as appealing to both intellect and rationalism.[5] "Intelligence is religion," proclaimed the apostle Sidney Rigdon, "and religion is intelligence."[6]

From the standpoint of the nineteenth-century world of miracles, the Latter-day Saints were hardly unique. Others in the antebellum spiritual marketplace claimed revelations and saw angels; even the Mormon claim to new scripture had precedents in the *Testimonies of the Ever Blessed Mother Ann Lee* and the Code of Handsome Lake. Scholars of American religion and Mormon history have largely overlooked Mormonism's commonality with other religious movements of the day, mistakenly assuming that LDS supernaturalism was unique in the American firmament. One scholar suggests that "conditions" in western New York "made it likely that novel religious ideas—that would have been dismissed out of hand in more settled situations—would here receive serious consideration."[7] Terryl Givens argues that the tactile reality of the Book of Mormon had a factual quality missing from other Christian interpretations of the early U.S. republic, but other sects had their facts and evidences ready, too. In its first decade as an organized church, Mormonism's commitment to miracles made it distinctive—but not alone—in the early United States.

Opponents understood this similarity. From the very beginning, anti-Mormon rhetoric linked the efforts of Smith and his followers to the panoply of wonder-working sects in the early republic. The *Rochester (NY) Gem* opened its vitriolic 1830 assault by saying that the Book of Mormon "partakes largely of Salem Witchcraft-ism, and Jemima Wilkinson-ism, and is in point of blasphemy and imposition, the very summit."[8] The *Rochester (NY) Daily Advertiser* called it "hocus pocus," the *Palmyra (NY) Freeman,* "superstition," and James McChesney, a prolific anti-Mormon writer, described Mormonism as "like Mahometanism, and every other delusion" because "its foundation is hatred to virtue."[9] Mormons themselves made comparisons between the LDS and contemporary sects. "If you start a church with a prophet in it," sighed the Mormon polemicist W. W. Phelps, "every body will be against you, as they were against Ann Lee, Joanna Southcoate, and old Jemima Wilkinson."[10]

Everybody *did* seem to be against the Mormons, or at least, Phelps could be forgiven for feeling that way. Only nativism provoked as violent a response, and like Tenskwatawa's followers, the Mormons were eventually expelled from the United States. Smith was tarred and feathered; Mormon missionaries were beaten and murdered. Mobs and militias forced the Saints from cities in Missouri in 1833 and 1838, and from Illinois in 1845. Later reports and animadversions against the sect attacked its polygamous practices, but in the early years, the repeated refrain was that Mormonism practiced imposture. Isaac Hale declared in 1833 that "the whole 'Book of Mormon' (so called) is a silly fabrication of falsehood and wickedness, got up for speculation, and with a design to dupe the credulous and unwary."[11] On this basis, the Latter-day Saints were effectively expelled from the American republic; their exodus in 1845 took them to the loosely regulated north of Mexico. Only an accident of history—James K. Polk's land grab for California—put the Saints back in the Union.

Early Mormonism therefore needs to be interpreted in the broader context of the American supernatural and its political dimensions. A previous generation of historians simply described the Mormons *as* deluded, taking the antisupernaturalist thinking of critics and newspapers as full explanation for the rise of Mormonism. Fawn Brodie's *No Man Knows My History* borrowed directly from the newspapers, arguing that Smith's "dramatic talent" found outlet "in the cabalistic ritual of rural wizardry, then in the hocus-pocus of the Gold Bible mystery," and finally in the role of prophet of God. In Brodie's view, Smith's machinations were conveniently "free from the tempering influence a more critical audience would have exercised upon it."[12] More recently,

D. Michael Quinn made a similar assumption by taking critics' accusations of Mormon magic and superstition at face value ("in 1829–30, Smith's claims primarily attracted believers in folk magic") rather than reading these critiques as a cultural response to credulity, miracles, and antirepublicanism. When a neighboring minister quipped that John Whitmer's family was "gullible in to the highest degree and even believe in witches," he was not identifying these Mormons as practitioners of the Renaissance high occult any more than references to Ann Lee as a "fortune teller" made her a card reader. He was accusing them of supernaturalism—the false belief in the continued presence of witchcraft and miracles—and, hence, of being a danger to the republic.[13]

By classifying Mormonism and its wonders as unique, historians have made Mormonism an embodiment of a modern/antimodern dichotomy. Mormonism was antimodern, and this rejection of creeping modernity provided the inspiration to those left behind in the transition to capitalism. Quinn argues for Mormon magic as the antithesis to modern reason; Givens and others have argued that the immediacy of response in Mormonism was something modernity left behind.[14] On the contrary: the case for and against Mormonism developed in a culture long accustomed to the arguments of sense evidence and miracle claims. Mormons employed Enlightenment language and discourse, much like other Christians in the early republic, and seamlessly wove miracles and wonders into that discourse. They argued for the Book of Mormon's divinity on the strength of witness attestation—it was, after all, "a marvelous work and a wonder"—and if that were not enough, visions, healings, and exorcisms swirled around the movement. Converts found these evidences convincing.

Parley Pratt put the case for evidence and miracles in a play, *The Dialogue between Mr. Tradition, Reason, and Scriptus.* Mr. Reason embraces the Book of Mormon, for if "the New Testament is true, because miracles were wrought," then Mormons can produce "more than *sixty thousand* who have seen miracles wrought with their own eyes. Multitudes have been healed by the prayer of faith in the name of Jesus, both in the church and out of it, since the year 1830." Indeed, the witnesses for Mormonism were more rational than those of the New Testament; perhaps unintentionally aping David Hume's dismissive comparison of the French Prophets to the New Testament demoniacs, Mr. Reason explains that New Testament evidence came only from the writers, not the witnesses themselves: "Luke testifies that multitudes saw miracles," Mr. Reason says, "but the multitudes have informed us nothing about it."[15] Mormons, meanwhile, had living multitudes who could be interviewed.

From the very beginning, however, Mormonism's public career was tied to the problem of superstition and political order. After all, the first public mention of Mormonism did not come with the Book of Mormon. It came in a newspaper: when Obadiah Dogberry (the pseudonym of Abner Cole) published a selection from the Book of First Nephi in his *Palmyra (NY) Reflector,* the wider public had its first encounter with the Book of Mormon. It was not an unmediated view. While numerous historians have noted this first appearance of the Book of Mormon in print, none have examined that issue of the *Reflector* in its entirety.

The *Reflector* of January 2, 1830, was in fact a typical piece of antisuper-naturalism. Along with the first three pages of 1 Nephi, Dogberry added his own note about the "GOLD BIBLE." It was damning faint praise: "From a part of the first chapter, now before us, and which we this day publish, we cannot discover anything treasonable, or which will have a tendency to subvert our liberties." Thus, upon hearing of a wondrous new bible and a restored religion, Dogberry *expected* that it would be treasonous or subversive to liberty—and he expected his readers to anticipate the same. The immediate reaction to new religious revelation based on miraculous evidence was the expectation of political trouble.

Dogberry had already been schooling his readers in the dangers of witch-craft and claims to the supernatural. Beginning with the December 1829 editions of the *Reflector* (the newspaper's first issues), Dogberry had written a series of articles on a very different false prophet—the "Sabbatai Levi" (or Zevi). Dogberry penned a history of the seventeenth-century Ottoman Jew who proclaimed himself the Messiah and led "deluded and infatuated" followers from as far away as Italy with his miracles. Dogberry entitled this series "Imposters," and proclaimed the Sabbatai Zevi as a charlatan out for personal power. The series on Zevi concluded in the same issue that published the first extracts of the Book of Mormon. Dogberry also penned a satire of the Book of Mormon, written in King James style and ridiculing "Joseph, thou who has been surnamed the *Ignoramous.*" The same issue also reported on a disgruntled Baptist elder of New York State who warned his congregants that "political intriguing should be kept out of the church."[16]

Thus from the very beginning, the public critique of Mormonism was connected to the antisupernaturalist thesis. If there was a "prepared people" when Smith revealed the new gospel to the world, it was perhaps less the future Mormons than the *anti*-Mormons, well-schooled in a thread of popular and political discourse that had already determined that new revelations and miracles were cleverly designed frauds. After the Book of Mormon went to print, the *Reflector* included a discussion of superstition—without reference to the Book of Mormon: "[Superstition] may be extended to those, who, without any evidence, believe that prophecies are still uttered, or miracles are performed. It is also applied to those who believe in witchcraft, omens, etc."[17] It seems likely that Dogberry had the Mormons in mind.

Yet when Dogberry borrowed the arguments against the miraculous, he also borrowed their mistakes; *evidence* was precisely what Mormon missionaries wanted to talk about, and their greatest evidence was the Book of Mormon itself. Mormon preachers emphasized the reality of the Book of Mormon as a sign and a wonder.[18] Missionaries and converts saw the Book of Mormon as a miraculous whole, in Pratt's words, "a sign, a standard, an ensign" of the last days.[19] William McLellin, Stephen Post, Samuel Tyler, and a host of other diarists left Books of Mormon for people to read in the hope they would be converted. Other converts confessed that merely reading the Book of Mormon prompted conversion; Benjamin Heaton and his wife only needed to read 138 pages before they believed the Book of Mormon to be true.[20]

The Book of Mormon is a text saturated in miracles. The narrative within provides a chronicle of divine providence and redemption in the New World. A tribe of Israelites flees the Babylonian captivity and sails to the Americas, where they soon split into competing factions—the followers of Nephi and those of his brother Laman. Their conflict, and the continuing warfare of their descendants, provides the bulk of the record that follows. Miracles play a determinative role in the struggle. In their initial wanderings, Nephi discovers a miraculous artifact: "a round ball, of curious workmanship, and it was of fine brass. And within the ball were two spindles; and one pointed the way whither we should go in the wilderness."[21] This was the liahona, an orb that operated by divine power, "according to the faith, and diligence, and heed, which we did give unto them. And there was also written upon them, a new writing . . . which did give us understanding concerning the ways of the Lord; and it was written and changed from time to time." The liahona guides Nephi to hunting grounds, then across the oceans. When Laman leads a mutiny against Nephi during the voyage, the liahona ceases to function and the Israelite ships founder until Laman and his allies release Nephi, and "behold, I took the compass, and it did work." The Book of Alma later explains the proper interpretation of the liahona; it worked "according to their faith in God; therefore, if they had faith to believe that God could cause that those spindles should point the way they should go, behold, it was done; therefore they had this miracle, and also many other miracles wrought by the power of God."[22] The logic of the liahona was readily apparent: when the Nephites were faithful, miracles worked; when they forgot the Lord, "those marvellous works ceased."[23] Supernatural aid could be expected with faith, and divine objects could be expected to enter into the physical world.

Throughout the Book of Mormon, miracles convince skeptics. Angelic visitations frequently fill this role. Angels protect the Nephite Jacob from apostasy; he is immune to the false preaching of Sherem "for truly I had seen Angels, and they had ministered unto me." Alma converts upon the visitation of an angel whose voice shakes the earth like thunder: "There was nothing save the power of God, that could shake the earth and cause it to tremble." Amulek learns of a holy man by angelic testimony, and "I know he is a holy man, because it was said by an angel of God." Samuel, the righteous Lamanite, preaches to apostatizing Nephites that "the angel said unto me that many shall see greater things than these, to the intent that they might believe that these signs and these wonders should come to pass" and "to the intent that there should be no cause for unbelief among the children of men."[24]

It is a powerful and uncompromising argument on the sufficiency of miracles: once signs and wonders appear, there is *no cause* for disbelief. Thus when Laman and his wicked brothers fall away from the true faith, Nephi asks in exasperation, "How is it ye have forgotten ye have seen an angel of the Lord?" Similarly, a pillar of fire sunders a Lamanite prison to free faithful Nephites, and the Lamanites "saw the heavens open, and angels come down out of heaven—And there were about three hundred souls which saw and heard these things; and they were bid to go forth and marvel not, *neither should they doubt.*" And the Lamanites "were convinced of them, *because of the greatness of the evidences which they had received.*" The peoples of the Book of Mormon and some Christians of the early republic both saw miracles as a form of evidence in religious discourse.[25]

The Book of Mormon offers numerous stories of public supernatural events that cannot be denied. Indeed, the narrative seems to emphasize that everyone could see and hear such things, and that no one, therefore, had any good reason to deny the miracles or the authority they implied. To hear God's word is natural and evident; to fail to see it is to be "blind in their minds," as 3 Nephi puts it.[26] This sufficiency of miracles is most evident when Christ arrives, in 3 Nephi, with correspondingly impressive miracles and evidences. There can be no question as to reliability of witnesses, for Christ shows himself to everyone in the Americas, "all the people of the land did hear these sayings, and did witness of it." Christ allows every Nephite and Lamanite to feel his wounds. Nations of Doubting Thomases *all* receive physical confirmation of the resurrection's reality. The Nephites and Lamanites "did see with their eyes, and did feel with their hands," and therefore "did know of a surety, and did bear record."[27]

Christ teaches the assembled peoples of the New World, then calls for all the sick, lame, blind, deaf, and leprous to be brought before him, and "did heal them every one as they were brought forth to him." Soon thereafter, angels appear in fire in the heavens, and "the multitude did see and hear, and bear record; and they know their record is true, for they all of them did see and hear." Before Christ leaves the earth, he touches each of his twelve disciples, imparting powers unto them, and warns the people: "Wo unto him that shall deny the revelations of the Lord, and that shall say, the Lord no longer worketh by revelation, or by prophecy, or by gifts, or by tongues, or by healings, or by the power of the Holy Ghost; yea, and wo unto him that shall say at that day, that there can be no miracle wrought by Jesus Christ."[28] To deny miracles is to deny Christian truth.

That is, unfortunately, precisely what happens in the remainder of the Book of Mormon. After two hundred years of fellowship, new churches spring up that "did persecute the true church of Christ . . . because of the many miracles which were wrought among them," and therefore "the work of miracles and of healing did cease," leaving Nephites and Lamanites with "sorceries, and witchcrafts, and magics."[29] The collapse of Nephite civilization occurs quickly; in the 1830 edition, the decline and fall occupies fewer than twenty-five of six hundred pages. Though the Nephites had survived cycles of belief and apostasy before, their final downfall is marked by the wholesale removal of the miraculous. Without miracles, there can be no true church. This loss of divine power is not the only difficulty facing the last generation of Nephites, but it is the point on which Moroni—whose warnings conclude the Nephite texts—chooses to make his final homily to the readers he hopes will one day find the plates. Moroni's ultimate message to a fallen humanity is on the importance of and belief in miracles. Those who say "that there are no revelations, nor prophecies, nor gifts, nor healing, nor speaking with tongues, and the interpretation of tongues. Behold I say unto you, he that denieth these things knoweth not the gospel of Christ. . . . Do we not read that God is the same yesterday, today, and forever, and in him there is no variableness neither shadow of changing? And now if ye have imagined up unto yourselves a god who doth vary, and in whom there is shadow of changing, then have ye imagined up unto yourselves a god who is not God of miracles. But behold, I will show unto you a God of miracles.[30]

The link between miracles and surety is not the *only* theme in the Book of Mormon. But the authoritative power of miracles in settling questions of religious truth was one theme of the Book, and of Mormon preaching. McLellin and Pratt convinced a "once strong opposer" to convert to Mormonism by reading to him Alma 9–16, a section replete with miracles.[31] These chapters contain the deposition of Amulek, who explains that his experiences ought to be believed because of the evidences of "marvellous works" testified to by "more than one witness."[32] When converts and missionaries printed citations from the Book of Mormon, they chose passages that highlighted nineteenth-century religious concerns, including the question of whether miracles had ceased. Receiving prominent mention was 2 Nephi 28–30, in which Nephi predicts that a day will come when miracles, hell, and the devil are denied and exhorts the faithful not to listen to such appeals. The troublemakers of the Book of Alma—all silenced by miraculous proofs—also received mention in publications.[33]

It was equally important for faithful Saints to preach about the *coming forth* of the Book of Mormon. The evidences they gave came from the Book of Mormon, but more frequently they were *about* the Book of Mormon. This event was the central miracle of Mormonism; as Givens writes, the "'message' of the Book of Mormon *was* its manner of origin."[34] The Book of Mormon and its arrival were for the early Saints a physical evidence of the reality of divine work. Joseph Smith Jr. explained to the Saints that the Book of Mormon "has sprouted and come forth out of the earth, and righteousness begins to look down from heaven, and God is sending his powers, gifts, and angels to lodge in the branches thereof."[35] The Book of Mormon itself was a miracle.

Further proof of the miracle, for Mormons, came from two other sources outside the text of the plates: the physical evidences of ruins across the American frontier and the reliability of eyewitness accounts. It is in the case of the latter that the Testimony of the Three and Eight Witnesses became all-important. Each copy of the 1830 Book of Mormon was appended by a pair of signed statements testifying to the reality of the plates. (These testimonies now precede the text of each Book of Mormon.) Oliver Cowdery,

David Whitmer, and Martin Harris all declared that they "have seen the plates which contain this record, which is a record of the people of Nephi," and that "an Angel of God came down from heaven, and he brought and laid before our eyes, that we beheld and saw the plates." The Eight Witnesses—four Whitmers, three Smiths, and Hiram Page—added a second testimony, that Smith himself "has shewn us the plates of which hath been spoken, which have the appearance of gold; and as many of the leaves as the said Smith has translated we did handle with our hands; and we also saw the engravings thereon, all of which has the appearance of ancient work, and of curious workmanship."[36] For the converts of the 1830s, the Three and Eight Witnesses added an empirical dimension to the miracle of the golden plates. Readers did not have to take Smith's word for it; each and every copy of the Book of Mormon advertised the evidentialist proof for the miracle of the plates. (Alexander Campbell's *Delusions* made sure to undermine the validity of the Eight Witnesses. Campbell paraphrased the Testimony's claim that the witnesses "handled as many of the brazen or golden leaves as the said Smith translated," to which Campbell derisively replied, "So did I.")[37]

Evidences for the Book of Mormon also appeared in the American landscape—in the hill mounds, burial sites, and artifacts of Native Americans. Philosophers and antiquarians attempted to explain these vast formations; interpretations often alluded to a pre-Columbian civilization somehow distinct from the Native American cultures of their own day. The Euro-American imagination, vested in stadial ideas of civilization, could not accept that "primitive" races like the Native Americans could have built complex structures—or that a civilization that once built cities should abandon them.

If Indians, in the white imagination, could not have built such structures, who had? The early republic did not lack for explanations. Caleb Atwater argued that the ancient tumuli, forts, and skeletons uncovered in the Ohio Country must have originated with some vanished civilization.[38] Ethan Smith's *View of the Hebrews* postulated a Semitic origin of the Native Americans.[39] Lorenzo Dow believed "this western country was once inhabited by a warlike informed people, who had use of mechanical instruments . . . deserted long before the discovery of America by Columbus."[40] Josiah Priest's 1833 *American Antiquities and Discoveries in the West* went through eight printings; it provided exhaustive details of an ancient America regularly visited by Old World civilizations, as when Priest claimed to "have found the remains of an Egyptian colony, or nation, as in the case of the works and catacomb at Lexington [Kentucky, which], is in latitude but five degrees north of Egypt.[41]

Mormons did not invent the assumption of pre-Columbian empires distinct from Native American civilization. It was a part of white American intellectual discourse and, hence, part of the language of religion and history that shaped the American discussion of miracles. These North American remains—the seemingly endless numbers of forgotten dead in burial mounds and barrows—seemed proof of ancient cultures. When Edward Partridge paid homage to an ancient fortification, he found proof of the golden bible: "2 or 3 heaps of stone, one of which had the appearance of being laid up 6 or 8 square. . . . We judged that one or two of these heaps of stone were formerly alters for offering sacrifices for the Lord."[42] When white explorers stumbled upon forgotten cities, the Mormon publication *Evening and Morning Star* declared that the "ancient ruins in Central America" were the cities of the Nephites: "We are glad to see the proof begin to come, of the original or ancient inhabitants of this continent. It is good testimony in favor of the Book of Mormon."[43] George Burket, traveling near St. Louis in 1835, saw "ten or twelve large mounds witch have been thrown up by the Neafites." The experience moved Burket to a religious ecstasy: "I am Lost in Wonder and amazement at the goodness of god in preserving the Words of this People and bringing them forth."[44]

Miracles became the standard from which Mormon proselytizers challenged the existing churches. Orson Hyde's 1836 broadside declared: "When Jesus gave his disciples their last commission to go into all the world to preach the Gospel, he said unto them: 'these signs shall follow them that believe, in my name they shall cast out devils; they shall speak with new tongues; they shall take up serpents . . . they shall lay their hands upon the sick and they shall recover.'" Hyde interpreted the admonition literally: "It appears that this miraculous power did, and ever will continue with *true believers*," and therefore, "How, I ask, can the clergy of this day be of God; and yet deny all miraculous powers?" Hyde's contention in this appeal to the churches of Canada mentioned neither the Book of Mormon nor Joseph Smith but focused almost singularly on the need for restored apostolic miracles to establish the true church.[45]

Hyde was not speaking theoretically. Jared Carter enumerated at least twenty-four healings in his 1832 ministry. Some of the diseases he rebuked were merely "ague," but others included blindness and breast cancer.[46] David Patten, who reported at least ten healings in his undated journal, described his confinement to bed, partially lame because of his "disobedience," until "one evening . . . I prayed that I might be healed and I prayed in faith and the healing power came Down in such a wonderfull manner that the spirit ravished our hearts even I got up and found that I was healed."[47] He then immediately healed his wife.

Healings were the most common apostolic power mentioned. For example, Patten encountered a father "believing the Book of Mormon but had so menny notions of his own." The wife and daughter of the family were ill, however, and said "if they could be healed they would believe." Patten prayed, they were healed, and the family became full church members in obedience to the doctrines and teachings as revealed to Joseph Smith Jr. Orson Pratt reported something similar when, in 1833, he healed a Mrs. Kelsey of "a disease with which she had been afflicted five or six years. She covenanted to obey the gospel if the Lord would heal her. I prayed for and laid my hands upon her in the name of Jesus, and she began to recover, and a few days after was baptized."[48] Multiple similar instances of healing are reported in a swath of the missionary journals and diaries from the 1830s.[49]

Exorcism functioned similarly to healing, establishing—through the defeat of demons—the authority of the church. Smith's first miracle (Smith's own term) after the founding of the church was an exorcism, and the story was repeated widely to Saints and Gentiles alike: "JO's greatest as well as latest miracle," the *Reflector* declared, "is his 'casting out a devil' of uncommon size from a miserable man."[50] Smith's own account of the incident was that Newel Knight was beset by a demon, "his visage and limbs distorted," and Knight begged Smith to cast it out of him. Joseph declared, "If you know that I can, it shall be done." Knight was levitated and tossed about the room, but eventually the demon was cast out. Knight received "the visions of heaven" and an outpouring of prophecy.[51]

Exorcism was not as common as healing, but Mormon missionaries prepared for demons nonetheless. Smith received a revelation that provided practical advice on the subject: "If it be the devil as an angel of light, when you ask him to shake hands he will offer you his hand, and you will not feel anything; you may therefore detect him."[52] Mormons needed to be prepared to meet the devil and his minions. Carter dismissed a demon after several failed attempts, and "in this display of the power of God I had one of the most infalalbe proofs of the devine origin of the above mentioned revelation."[53] Further displays of healing and exorcism followed. In England in 1840, Theodore Turley rebuked a demon that tormented a boy, and was filled with gift of teaching and explained to those around him "the working of the Spirits."[54] Heber C. Kimball, while on mission to England, "was struck with great force by some invisible power and fell senseless on the floor as if I had been shot." He "could distinctly see the evil spirits, who foamed and gnashed their teeth upon us."[55] In Maine, Orson Hyde laid his hands on "Mr. Lawrey, who at times was possessed with the Devil."[56] McLellin was called on to cast out demons four times in March and April 1833.[57] According to Mormon oral tradition, Patten met a pseudo-demon and "very remarkable personage" in 1835. While travelling in Tennessee, he came across Cain—son of Adam, murderer of Abel. Covered with thick hair and as tall standing as Patten was on horseback, Cain declared his mission was to destroy souls, whereupon Patten "rebuked him in the name of the Lord Jesus Christ and by virtue of the Holy Priesthood, and commanded him to go hence, and he immediately departed out of my sight."[58] These were commands in the name of Christ *and the restored church*, and when ordered, demons went. Successful exorcisms by the Saints validated their church as the true authority in the world; the LDS hierarchy proved its divine origin *because* it could cast out demons. The religious logic mirrored the exorcisms of divine right monarchies (though transplanted to a very different context) rather than the rationalized, clockwork universe associated with republican cosmology.

The conflicting cosmologies were readily apparent in anti-Mormon works, which took pains to critique Mormon miracles while lambasting Mormon power. The earliest extended critiques of Mormonism—Alexander Campbell's *Delusions* and E. D. Howe's *Mormonism Unvailed* [sic]—included extensive exposition on and ridicule of the miracles of the Book of Mormon. In the midst of numerous attacks on Mormon behavior and belief, Howe and Campbell repeated the stock phrases of antisupernaturalism and its allusions to the end of democracy.

Alexander Campbell lost a number of his own adherents to the Saints. He returned fire in *Delusions;* the title encapsulated his argument. Like Dogberry, Campbell opened with a discussion of the Sabbatai Zevi; like the false messiah Zevi and the "credulous Jews," the "New York impostor" was simply one in a long line of "diviners, soothsayers, magicians, and all the ministry of idols." Campbell compared Smith to Muhammad, Simon Magus, and Judas. He insinuated that all prophets eventually take up arms and hinted the Mormons might do the same.[59]

Beyond insults, Campbell took great care to enumerate and vilify the Book of Mormon's miracles. He cited the Book of Moroni's argument that "miracles will never cease; because God is the same yesterday, to-day, and forever." Campbell wondered if by extension, God "must always create suns, moons, and stars, every day!!" The liahona was identified and derided: the "compass was only known in Europe about 300 years ago; but Nephi knew all about steam-boats and the compass 2400 years ago." Campbell sardonically asked why all the Nephite people were allowed to touch the wounds of Christ if "none of them had expressed a doubt." These remarks were preface for Campbell's attack on contemporary miracles: "They say that spiritual gifts are to be continued to the end of time," wrote Campbell. He challenged them directly: "Have they wrought any miracles? They have tried, but their faith failed. Can they shew any spiritual gift? Yes, they can mutter Indian, and traffic in new bibles."[60] While he did not only attack Mormon supernatural-ism, miracles stood out to Campbell as *the* Mormon argument that required refutation—an assessment supported by the prominence of miracle-talk in early LDS literature and diaries.

Howe liked Campbell's argument so much, he plagiarized parts of it.[61] When he was not lifting passages, Howe followed Campbell's general line, beginning with the usual condemnations reserved for treasure digging. Smith was "very expert in the arts of necromancy," "well skilled in legerdemain," full of "extreme ignorance and apparent stupidity," with a "low and licentious imagination." Smith's family "commenced making proselytes among the credulous, and lovers of the marvelous," taking advantage of "our worthy fellow citizens [who] have been seduced by the witcheries and mysterious necromancies of Smith and his colleagues." David Whitmer and Martin Harris "were noted in their neighborhood for credulity and a general belief in witches, and perhaps were fit subjects for the juggling arts of Smith." Indeed, some Mormons believed the Book of Mormon, Howe insisted, because of "the ghost stories which he [Smith] related concerning it." The Three Witnesses, to Howe, were simply the first of "that class of people about him, who were willing dupes, and anxious devotees to the marvelous. To establish the truth of any pretension . . . required nothing but some little necromancy."[62]

Howe noted the same miracles Campbell did. He treated the liahona (the "notable ball," Howe called it) as something like a running gag: "'Within the ball were two spindles, and the one pointed the way whither we should go.' Which way the other pointed, we are not told, but probably the way they should not go." Howe mocked the unearthing of the plates as "an important record which had been made by a miracle, kept for ages by a miracle, dug from the ground by a miracle, and translated by a miracle," but when Smith's first 116 translated pages were lost, "even a miracle could not restore it." *Unvailed* described Mormon glossolalia as "mere gibberish, spoken at random and without thought." Howe sardonically requested more miracles, wondering why God could not have provided the Nephites with firearms, or Smith with an absolute knowledge of the future. Howe made no compunction about the argument from miracle: "Miracles will account for any thing, however ridiculous." In arguing against the efficacy of miracles as proof, Howe was not only poking fun; he was responding to a major argument of and for the Book of Mormon.[63]

Howe informed readers that Mormons were the kind of people who would believe in miracles—the dregs of society: "the credulous and the unsuspecting," in "a state of unqualified vassalage . . . poor, and destined so to remain, until they pursue a different course as it related to economy and industry."[64] The oft-cited accusation that Mormons came mostly from the lower classes had its basis in the assumptions of antisupernaturalism; Saints actually obtained converts from a surprisingly diverse group of Americans.[65] Mormons themselves knew this, as did their enemies. The missionary Lorenzo Barnes concluded in 1836 that "this enquiry after truth has not been confined to the lower class of people but all classes have been made partakers more or less."[66]

Thus, what Howe was actually doing with his accusations of Mormon crudity, credulity, and poverty was setting his readers up for the second half of the antisupernatural thesis: that Smith and the Mormon leadership sought power and money via their miracles. Howe missed no opportunity to discuss Smith's pecuniary status; "from almost a state of beggary," he writes, "the Smiths were immediately well furnished with the 'fat of the land' by their fanatical followers, many of whom were wealthy." Indeed, Smith only published the Book of Mormon after "profound calculations were made about the amount of their profits on the sale of such a book." As in most antimiraculous warnings, the desire for money led the imposters to a desire for power. Howe writes that the Mormons "frequently boast of their increasing strength, and that consequently they will soon be enabled to possess themselves of all the secular power of the country." That would mean a Mormonocracy: "Everything will be performed by immediate revelations from God. We shall then have Pope Joseph *the First,* and his hierarchy."[67]

Howe's and Campbell's logic and language appeared in critiques throughout the 1830s. The *Evangelical Magazine and Gospel Advocate* attempted to "check the progress of delusion" by undermining the miracle of Smith's translation by pointing out "that the Book of Mormon was brought to light by the same magic power by which he pretended to tell fortunes, discover hidden treasures, &c."[68] Mormonism had "no redeeming feature" because

"Jo Smith pretends to cast out devils, to give the Holy Ghost by laying on of hands, to heal the sick, &c." (Almost all LDS works referred to the prophet as Joseph; anti-Mormon works repeatedly used the diminutive "Jo" or "Joe.")[69]

Sometimes the accusations against the Mormons displayed a softer touch. The *New Bedford (MA) Mercury* essentially thought them harmless: "The Bible of Mormon cannot survive the present generation. And the next will remember it, only to smile at the credulity of the present."[70] This sort of benign neglect, however, was more often limned with intimations to readers of what impostors would do if given true "religious liberty." Sometimes these warnings could be quite explicit. "The plan," wrote Ezra Booth in a series of newspaper articles, "ingeniously contrived, having for its aim one principal point, viz.: the establishment of a society in Missouri, over which the contrivers of this delusive system, are to possess unlimited and despotic sway."[71] Mormonism was "a deep laid scheme . . . designed to allure the credulous and the unsuspecting, into a state of unqualified vassalage."[72]

In 1833, a committee of more than four hundred non-Mormon (Gentile) residents of Jackson County demanded an end to Mormon settlement there. The committee acted out of the fear—or so they claimed—that "should this population continue to increase they would soon have all the offices in the county in their hands; and that the lives and property of the other citizens would be insecure, under the administration of men who are so ignorant and superstitious as to believe that they have been the subjects of miraculous and supernatural cures, professing to converse with God and Angels—possessing and exercising the gift of divination and unknown tongues." Mormon supernaturalism unfitted them for public service. Should any Mormon achieve elective office, rights of citizenship and property would be forfeit. Lest any reader miss the notion that the Mormons were morally and intellectually incapable of self-rule, the Missourians added a dose of stadial racism; Mormons in Missouri underwent "a gradual falling off of their characters, until they had nearly reached the low condition of the black population."[73]

The LDS propensity to equate Christian leadership and the public good with rule by God's appointed agents, who established their legitimacy by supernatural proofs, did not ease tensions with Gentile critics. Soon after the founding of the church, rumors circulated that Martin Harris had bragged, "Within four years from September 1832, there will not be one wicked person left in the United States; that the righteous will be gathered to Zion, (Missouri) and that there will be no President over these United States after that time."[74] Fourteen years later, Smith ran for president with a claim to

be "emphatically, virtuously, and humanely for a THEODEMOCRACY."[75] Two
months after that, Smith was lynched while in jail on charges of treason.

Like the nativist prophets before them, Mormons sought political answers
to their problems. Almost from the founding of the church, as Mormons
faced repeated charges of delusion, credulity, treason, and tyranny, church
members participated actively in party politics and went to the polls in large
numbers. They had voted en masse for the Democrat, Martin Van Buren,
in the 1836 presidential election but had switched to the Whig candidate,
William Henry Harrison, four years later. Their impact on local politics was
even greater. As the Saints drifted from intended Zion to intended Zion in the
1830s and 1840s, they worked to put their candidates—and sometimes their
members—into office. Saints petitioned state legislatures of Ohio, Missouri,
and Illinois as well as the U.S. Congress. Cowdery served as a delegate to
the Ohio nominating convention in 1835, and Mormons won the Kirtland
township offices in 1836.[76] When Saints' lobbying efforts, spearheaded by
the LDS ally Alexander Doniphan, resulted in the creation of two new Missouri counties specifically for Mormon settlement, the Saints staffed the full
slate of county offices, and John Corrill became the first Mormon elected
to a state legislature. Joseph Smith was the mayor of Nauvoo, Illinois, and
headed its militia. Outside the electoral process, the Saints developed even
more trappings of governmental and institutional power. They built cities
from scratch, and raised militias in Ohio, Missouri, and Illinois. Mormons
even created a paramilitary enforcement agency—the Danites. According to
Quinn, Smith commissioned "theocratic ambassadors to England, France,
Russia, and the Republic of Texas."[77]

The conflicts of Mormonism, however, were not solely between Saints
and Gentiles. Internal squabbles split the church repeatedly in the 1830s,
and when they did, the challengers were deeply imbued with the politics of
the supernatural and the antisupernatural. Seer stones, which had in part
permitted Smith to translate the Book of Mormon, provided a supernatural
power to which Smith (and others) could turn. Smith had long been associated
with the use of seer stones, for which he was mercilessly lampooned by his
enemies. Others, however, defended the accuracy and practical results of his
wonderful stone. In his infamous 1826 trial for being "a disorderly person
and an impostor," Smith had at least one reliable witness to his supernatural
powers. Josiah Stowel testified that he "positively knew that the prisoner
[Smith] could tell, and professed the art of seeing those valuable treasures. . . .
The prisoner had told by means of this stone where a Mr. Bacon had buried

money." Nevertheless, with five other witnesses testifying to "a deception so palpable," the court convicted Smith.[78]

Smith was not the only Mormon with a seer stone. Newel Knight's auto-biography mentioned that Hiram Page "had managed to get up some dis-sension of feeling among the brethren by giving revelations . . . through the medium of a stone he possessed." Page, apparently, had demonstrated his own seer-stone abilities and "had quite a roll of papers full of these revelations, and many in the Church were led astray by them. Even Oliver Cowdery and the Whitmer family had given heed to them."[79] Shortly thereafter, Smith received and transmitted a revelation that insisted that "no one shall be appointed to receive commandments and revelations in this church, excepting my servant Joseph." More specifically, Cowdery was ordered to "take thy brother Hiram" and "tell him that those things which he hath written from that stone are not of me, and that satan deceiveth him." Page (and presumably others) could still teach and preach, but only "by wisdom"; Smith alone could speak by commandment. Thus, while numerous people in the church experienced and performed miracles, only Smith received revelations; miracles validated the authority of the church Smith founded, and revelations validated Smith's authority in the church.[80] Establishing the principle that limited revelation to the president of the church alone assured that all miracles performed in the name of the Mormon church would also support Smith as the prophet and restored font of divine instruction. Ubiquitous miracles performed by multiple Mormons established the divine warrant for a single head of a restored church.

At least, that was the theory. Beginning in 1834, Smith faced serious challenges to his primacy as revelator to the true church. Smith's efforts in that year to redeem the beleaguered Missouri Saints—he led the Zion's Camp militia from Kirtland to Far West—collapsed in disaster. Smith failed to prevent the expulsion of the Saints from Jackson County and lost several men to a cholera epidemic. Murmurings against the Prophet echoed back in Ohio. Smith recorded the epitaphs against him in Kirtland: "Tyrant—Pope— King—Usurper—Abuser of Men—Angel—False Prophet—Prophesying lies in the name of the Lord—Taking consecrated monies," accusations that recalled the antisupernatural arguments of Howe and Dogberry. Smith was placed before an ecclesiastical court but was eventually exonerated.[81]

The crisis was marked by further misunderstanding about Mormon mira-cles: Did wondrous powers validate the wonder-worker, or the church itself? Almost immediately after Zion's Camp, the Church Council at Far West reiterated that miracles *alone* were not authoritative. A breakaway group of Mormons that had been speaking and interpreting in tongues and, on that authority, consecrating priests challenged "the heads of the Church . . . to come down and receive the gifts as they did." The Council determined such things were of the devil; the dissenters acquiesced.[82] Gifts were still possible, but they had to be done in the name of the institutionalizing church.

In 1837, some Kirtland Mormons put faith in two separate children who prophesied by means of a stone. James Colin Brewster saw Moroni and insisted that the High Council should adopt "a plan for better organization of the Church in temporal affairs" based on the validity of his evidence from the stone.[83] Brewster and his parents were disfellowshipped. Another Kirtland seer stone was used by a Mormon girl who could see into Missouri from Ohio: "This girl sees by the help of a stone. She told me she saw a seer's stone for me, it was a small blue stone with a hole in one corner . . . not far from the lake shore a little west of Buffalo." Lucy Mack Smith gave an intriguing suggestion that later that year, "a certain young woman, who was living at David Whitmer's, uttered a prophecy, which she said was given her, by looking through a black stone." The unnamed woman declared that Joseph Smith was in transgression and would soon be replaced by Whitmer or Martin Harris. The rise of such competing miracles took on particular valence as Smith struggled with the financial crisis of 1837, in which his own bank collapsed. Amid these economic woes, the unnamed woman became "an object of great attention among those who were disaffected," including Carter, Whitmer, and Williams. Carter repented when he was struck "with a violent pain in his eyes" and subsequently healed by the Lord, another example of belief and obedience by way of miracle. The others, however, "continued obstinate" and the woman "would dance over the floor, boasting of her power."[84] The woman does not recur in Lucy Smith's memoir, but Whitmer and Williams were charged by Brigham Young with plotting against Smith, and the High Council disfellowshipped Whitmer in 1838.[85]

John Corrill turned the full brunt of an antisupernatural attack upon Smith. Corrill joined the church in 1831 after studying the Book of Mormon but worried about too great a faith in miraculous evidence. Exercises could be diabolical, after all, and as early as 1832 Corrill accused Smith of creeping monarchism.[86] Ultimately, Corrill rejected the supernatural powers of the church, and thus, the leadership of Smith; he finished his own history of the church with strong republican rhetoric: "I had rather enjoy liberty in Hell than suffer bondage in Heaven."[87] Corrill was excommunicated in 1839.

The struggles in the waning days of Kirtland and Far West were political, ecclesiological, and supernatural battles. A church based on miracles and revelations was thrown into schism, and various parties within that church claimed supernatural justification for their leadership. In the midst of the 1837 crisis, Smith received a revelation rebuking the dissenters: "Exalt not yourselves; rebel not against my servant Joseph; for verily I say unto you, I am with him, and my hand shall be over him; and the keys which I have given unto him, and also to youward, shall not be taken from him till I come."[88] The choice was no longer about reforming the LDS church, but about leaving it. Several Saints, including Martin Harris, went. Others humbled themselves and were forgiven.

It is difficult to ascertain how many believers followed the competing miracles; at least 500 Saints remained in Kirtland in 1840s, maintaining a strained relationship with the church at Nauvoo.[89] A large majority of Mormons, however, remained loyal to Smith, and it may well have been his organizational savvy that ensured his continued leadership of the Saints. Alternatively, it may be that Smith simply retained, and had always retained, the goodwill of most of the Saints; that when they committed to the church, they committed to the authority of the new signs that validated the new prophet. "What will the Lord have to do with his church," wrote Mary Fielding in the midst of the Kirtland leadership crisis, "before it will submit to be governed by the Head[?]"[90]

Smith did not *only* have supernatural power, of course. He was an astute and canny leader with a variety of political tools at his disposal; with the advent of the Danites, those tools began to include coercion and force. The origin and extent of the Danite movement and its activities are a subject of historical debate.[91] The institution emerged after the 1838 excommunications of David Whitmer and Oliver Cowdery; it was probably the brainchild of Sampson Avard, a relative newcomer to the elite of the LDS church, but it was jointly administered by Avard, Rigdon, and several others, possibly including Smith himself.[92] The Danite purpose was to drive the perennial dissenters from Missouri. In a strange twist, Rigdon adopted one of the standard tropes of antisupernaturalism: he accused the dissenters of civil crimes rather than heterodox theology. The "Note of Warning" that Rigdon and the Danites sent to leading dissenters justified their actions based on a danger to the public: "You are, at this very time, engaged with a gang of counterfeiters, coiners, and blacklegs. . . . If we suffer you to continue, we may expect, and that speedily, to find a general system of stealing, counterfeiting, cheating and burning of property," and therefore, "we will out you from the county of Caldwell, so help us God!" Coercion could be justified to protect the public from crime rather than heterodoxy.[93]

Most historians agree that Rigdon made the situation irrevocably worse on July 4, 1838, when he gave an oration at Far West in defense of religious freedom. Most of the content of the speech was fairly typical for such a performance: "Our country and its institutions, are written on the tablet of our hearts." Rigdon even agreed with the antisupernaturalists that "it is on the virtue of the people, that depends the existence of the government."[94] Nor was his religious interpretation of the American Revolution—a divinely appointed war that was "preparatory to the great work which he had designed to accomplish in the last days"—far removed from traditional nineteenth-century Protestant interpretations.[95] Yet as both Mormons and Gentiles listened, Rigdon delved into a disastrous turn of phrase.

"We have not only when smitten on one cheek turned the other, but we have done it . . . until we are wearied of being smitten," Rigdon said. More importantly, "from this day and this hour, we will suffer it no more." Rigdon then warned "all men . . . to come on us no more forever," and threatened that for any "mob that comes on us to disturb us; it shall be between us and them a *war of extermination* . . . for we will carry the war to their own houses, and their own families, and one party or the other shall be utterly destroyed." In just a few months, Rigdon's own words would be visited horribly upon the Mormons in Lilburn Boggs's extermination order.[96]

The Mormon faithful seemed to like the speech; John Corrill noted that several other sermons of similar tone and intensity circulated among the Missouri Mormons.[97] The speech was, in fact, a kind of declaration of independence; the LDS membership, through Rigdon, "proclaim[ing] our liberty this day as did our fathers." The Saints "will never be the aggressors," but they would "claim our own rights," and Missouri could do likewise, if it left them alone.[98] Smith gave it his official imprimatur, noting especially that Mormons should not "be mob[b]ed any more without taking vengeance."[99] Combined with the development of the Danites, the removal of dissenting elements, the claiming of county offices, and the laying of the cornerstone of the Far West Temple, the Saints of Caldwell and Daviess Counties possessed numerous characteristics of an incipient government and nation.[100]

Outside the Mormon fold, the speech had disastrous consequences. Rigdon's martial and reactionary paragraphs were reprinted in the Gentile press; if anyone had missed it, the speech circulated in pamphlet form and in newspapers over the next few weeks. "There were one or two sentences," Corrill wrote dryly, "to which considerable exception was taken by the people of other counties."[101] A resident of Clay County referred to the speech as "containing the essence of, if not treason itself."[102] The *Quincy (IL) Whig* summarized Rigdon this way: "He declared they would 'carry war and extermination' to all who would oppose them in their wild career."[103] Another newspaper claimed "the Mormons are desperate, and rendered more so by the fanatical spirit infused into them by the arch-deceiver Jo Smith." Given that, the paper then turned Rigdon's words back upon him: "If this war should break out, it must be a war of extermination."[104] Yet the objections, while reacting to an immediate military threat, also underscored Rigdon's broader message of political autonomy—and rejected it wholesale. Even in slaveholding Missouri, a tyrant anywhere in the United States was a threat to liberty across the United States. There could be no *imperium in imperio*.

Tensions in Missouri came to a head on election day. A balloting location in Gallatin, Missouri, became the site of a scuffle between Mormons and Gentiles on August 6, 1838, probably precipitated by the Whig candidate William Penniston. As John D. Lee recalled it, the riot came when Mormons defended their belief in miracles: "A drunken brute by the name of Weldon" approached the Mormons at the polls and asked, "Do you Mormons believe in healing the sick by laying on of hands, speaking in tongues, and casting out devils?" When a Mormon answered in the affirmative, Weldon replied, "You are a d—d liar. Joseph Smith is a d—d imposter." Then Weldon attacked.[105] The melee soon became general. No one was killed, but the Mormon community heard rumors of a massacre and accordingly brought its militia to bear on the situation. On August 8, a company of Danites forced Judge Adam Black to sign an affidavit that he would uphold the laws of the State of Missouri. A few days after that, arrest warrants were issued for Smith and Rigdon. The two Mormons refused to be served. According to the Scottish immigrant Douglas Miln, that meant that "the Mormons declared war, & took the field in open & armed defiance of the laws of the State."[106]

There was little doubt in the Gentile mind that the potential Mormon tyranny was turning into the real thing; the *Missouri Republican* declared the Mormon "object was a kingly government."[107] Another paper informed readers that Mormons "can muster from 1000 to 1500 fighting men; and of that degraded and ignorant class, who will implicitly obey the will of their leaders." A public meeting of Ray County, the paper further reported, had declared the Mormons "highly insurrectionary and unlawful" and "entirely revolutionary in their feelings and institutions."[108] The *New York Spectator* claimed Smith had a power "as absolute over this deluded people, as the Emperor's of Russia over his lowest serfs," and that the leadership founded its power "upon the superstition of ignorant men." The Mormons were "the most dangerous and formidable set of disorganizers that ever set up the standard of revolt in any country; and no time should be lost in taking effectual measures to defeat their nefarious schemes."[109]

The state militia—commanded in part by Gentiles formerly employed as LDS lawyers, David Rice Atchison and Alexander Doniphan—was mustered out. Smith and Avard armed their own forces. Smith never precisely declared independence, but he did insist that the laws of the state were unfairly administered and that the Saints would protect their rights; in addition, "God will send angels to our deliverance, and we can conquer 10,000 as easily as ten."[110]

October 1838 lives in infamy in Mormon history. Within two weeks, Mormon armies had sacked the city of Gallatin, state militia clashed with Mormon forces at the Battle of Crooked River, and Missouri governor Lilburn Boggs had issued the "extermination order," which told three generals and 1,300 men to move against the Mormons, for "the Mormons must be treated as enemies, and must be exterminated or driven from the state if necessary for the public peace."[111] Three days later, eighteen Mormon noncombatants were slaughtered at the Haun's Mill Massacre.

The next day, October 31, Gen. Samuel D. Lucas sent word from his army near Far West and requested Smith's surrender. On November 1, Far West capitulated. Mormons surrendering were greeted by Gen. John B. Clark with a lecture on republicanism and superstition: "[I] invoke *that Great Spirit, the Unknown God* to rest upon you, and make you sufficiently intelligent to break that chain of superstition, and liberate you from the fetters of fanaticism with which you are now bound—that you no longer worship a man."[112] Mormonism was not the problem; it was merely one facet of the problem of superstition. Clark's report to the governor confirmed that the Mormon war had been "an insurrection of no ordinary character. It had for its object *Dominion,* and the ultimate subjugation of this State and the Union."[113] Smith was sent to prison, and the Saints were exiled to the swampy land north of Quincy, Illinois, where they would attempt for a third time to build their Zion.

This sketch is not a comprehensive account of Mormonism from 1830 to 1838, but it is an account of the ways in which supernatural and miraculous claims built that faith tradition and its institutions in its first decade. The

Saints were not the only group to receive revelations, speak in tongues, or perform miracles in the early republic. They were the only one of those groups to survive and build a worldwide church of millions. (The religions of Kenekuk and Handsome Lake continue as smaller, primarily ethnic faiths.) This commonality, therefore, does not directly explain their success (though it does explain why converts found their approach and miracles convincing), but it does explain the political and military response from Gentile hands.

The Mormon claim to miracles and other supernatural powers triggered an autonomic response in the American intellectual and religious body politic; it was a refrain Americans had heard before and that they were trained to take seriously as a potential *imperium in imperio* and threat to the well-being of the community and republic. Thus, it was not that Mormons voted as a bloc, or lived as a centralized community, or insisted on protecting their religious liberty. Rather, it was that the language and logic of the republican antisupernatural had prepared Americans to associate miracle-mongering with tyrannical behavior, and the Latter-day Saints behaved in a manner close enough to the expectations to warrant threats, and when those failed, force. The question the "brute" Weldon brought to the polls was not, "For whom will you vote?" but, "Do you believe in miracles?" The Mormons did not create the antimiraculous in America; they walked right into it.

SEVEN

The Sects That Weren't

Pity William and Elizabeth Babcock. For a few years at the eastern edge of Vermont, they believed they had discovered a direct conduit to God through angelic visitations, healings, and other supernatural events—a rational faith, they believed, validated by evidence. Yet despite several years of intensive ministry guided by angelic visitations, their acknowledged membership never grew much beyond fifty. The movement collapsed within a decade.[1]

The "Babcockists"—the church never did get its own name—had supernatural events in abundance. More than two hundred communiqués from an angel came to earth through Elizabeth and a handful of other women. The Babcocks dreamed of a world without doctrinal disputes, a world where "God would direct his Children in their temporal business, every particular of which ought to be enquired of . . . & the world seeing them prosper would be convinced." Christians need no longer puzzle over theology or ecclesiology, William believed; they could simply ask God directly and receive heavenly answers through the angel. Before instituting such a church, of course, the Babcocks "referred the matter to the decision of the Angel." They wrote up a declaration of faith in January 1810. The angel blessed them with manifestations the following week.[2]

The early republican understanding of fact, evidence, and the supernatural encouraged the rise of miracle claims and the churches they inspired, but not every claimant to miracles built a lasting edifice. All that now remains of the Babcocks' mayfly religion is a sheaf of sermons and a yellowing journal in the American Antiquarian Society. Jemima Wilkinson's papers likewise consist of a handful of letters, legal documents, and sidelong references in diaries and memoirs. Jacob Cochran, Abel Sargent, Jacob Osgood, and a host of others left even fainter traces in the historical record. Yet these minor prophets demonstrate the ubiquity of miraculous claims and their language of facticity and witness testimony; they also suggest the persistence—and success—of antisupernaturalism. Claims to miracles, healings, tongues, and exorcisms did not just occur among successful sects or those that survived into the twentieth century. Indeed, the disappearance of these sects that weren't may well have made the Mormons seem more anomalous in the twentieth century, obscuring the supernaturalism of the early republic.

The Babcockists, for example, looked a lot like the early Shakers or Mormons. Their origins were partially recorded by William Babcock himself. He began as a Freewill Baptist with perpetual worries about deism: "It is astonishing & lamentable how dreadfully this error has increased," he wrote. Indeed, in August 1801 "for a few moments I disbelieved the whole Christian System. . . . Instantly retired & prayed that this Deistic temptation might be taken from me."[3] His objection to deism probably derived from his belief in the supernatural. Deists lived in a clockwork universe; Babcock did not: "I have never read, nor shall I ever read; that God has recalled any of the powers & Gifts, given to the Church." Only "want of faith" kept gifts away. In 1801, he wrote that "evidences [of God's revelation] are necessary to be continued whilst man continues upon Earth." By 1803, Babcock received those evidences; he met a "Dr. Price" who possessed "the Secret of power of removing pain by laying on his hands." Price healed Babcock's wrist. Later, Babcock himself developed the power "to remove pain." In a different encounter with the supernatural, Babcock and a companion saw "a very bright shining light, exceedingly bright," burning in the woods as though it were "the chamber of some house," though "there was no house nearer than the meetinghouse." When they passed, the light vanished.[4]

When William met Elizabeth in 1805, he was therefore well-versed in supernatural powers. Yet he nevertheless subjected Elizabeth's angel to a series of tests. He prayed to God to reveal to Elizabeth, through the angel, "some exercise of my mind past," since "the morning exercises of my mind, are unknown to every mortal. If God should please to answer it would establish my faith beyond controversion." He did not record the result of that experiment, but two days later prepared another test. The angel "gave imperfect answers." Elizabeth explained that "if she had obeyed the Spirit, she should have had full answers."[5]

The ultimate results of this Baconian effort are unknown; William ceased to make diary records at this juncture, perhaps because it was around this time he became drunk and slept with "MB" outside of marriage. When he resumed entries in 1808, William and Elizabeth had married, and a slew of supernatural events whirled about the new movement. The angel continued his visits, in various guises. One night Elizabeth "saw the Angel come to the door, the light of his Glory filled the room." At other times, Elizabeth merely spoke in her sleep while someone else took dictation. Once the angel directed Elizabeth to address Daniel Morse directly, and "the Lord struck him with his power & his soul was converted in the course of the night." The angel appeared and converted a man in Haverhill through no act of the Babcocks; they only heard about this wonder through a letter. Trueworthy Dudley found herself "afflicted with the Devil and waked by him several times." She overcame the evil one, and within a month she, too, could talk to the angel.[6]

The angel directed worship, defined the issue of silent prayer, confirmed that meetings should end with a blessing, provided missionaries with itineraries, and established the form of communion (every other month). When a question arose about whether "Judas was present at washing of feet, but absent at the institution of the Lords supper," the angel chimed in to set the matter straight. The angel kept the church in Springfield aware of the doings of the branch in Fishersfield. It instructed the faithful concerning travel (Babcock wondered why the angel allowed him "to carry my Books & Clothes out of this Country last winter to Barrington"), communication ("by Sister Betsy's manifestation I learnt brother Otis had delivered my letters"), and real estate ("Another manifestation respecting buying br Spencer's farm"). The angel could even be involved in the most commonplace of events, as when Babcock wrote that it "directed me to take an emetic. . . . I prayed for the Angel, he came & directed me to take it, a teaspoonful every hour until it operated."[7]

In 1811, however, Babcock's journal ended, and soon the sect vanished as well. By 1816, William and Elizabeth had left for Barrington—where the angel had once told them never to settle. A number of problems beset the group. Several women learned to converse with the angel; it is possible that with more interpreters, the angel's voice became muddied. An angelic prophecy about a son for the Babcocks came true when Elizabeth gave birth to a boy in 1810. Dancing quickly turned to mourning; the boy died despite the angel's promise he would survive. A failed prophecy—the supernatural proved false—may have functioned as a negative proof, or as proof that the voices were demonic and not celestial. Alternatively, interest may have simply waned, given the slow pace of conversion. The move to Barrington may have disrupted denominational organization. Or perhaps the angel told them to disband.[8]

Several other wonder-working sects took similar passage to serene obscurity. The fiery Osgoodites—founded by Jacob Osgood in the first decade of the nineteenth century—offered manifold miracles and stinging jeremiads. Osgood and his followers were pacifists, and his failure to serve in the militia put him in prison from 1820 to 1821, where he wrote an autobiography justifying "that faith which was delivered to the saints; to heal the sick by laying on of hands, which made the hypocrites awful mad." Osgood once changed the weather through prayer alone, cured disease, and circulated stories about the providential deaths of opponents of Osgoodism. "We believe in God's power to be above all," went their creed, and they openly challenged state laws about militia service, alcohol consumption, and even spending bills.[9] Yet the Osgoodites sputtered after Osgood's death in 1844, and by 1890 they were extinct.

Nor were the Babcocks alone in establishing a church in which angelic communication would answer all theological questions. Abel Sargent's Halcyon Church emerged from Universalism; Sargent "held converse with angels, and . . . was made the medium of communication to the world." Around 1812, Sargent travelled through Ohio with twelve apostles, "mostly women, preaching and pretending to raise the dead." In his memoir of 1853, James Finley classed the Halcyon Church as one of the "new isms that followed" the Cane Ridge revivals, along with someone dubbed "Elder Farnum" who also "pretended to have received the spirit of immediate inspiration, and raised a party called the 'screaming children.'" Sargent, too, vanished from the historical record, but not before Peter Cartwright claimed to have caught him using a cigar and flash powder to provide ersatz evidence of an angelic arrival.[10]

Like the other wonder-workers of the early republic, the Babcocks were bound up in antisupernaturalist biases of the nineteenth century and the realist fallacies of later historians. The Baptist scribe I. D. Stewart dismissed the incident as the "angel delusion." It was a delusion, Stewart explained, because "women claimed to have interviews with angels, and a few men became the[ir] unfortunate dupes."[11] The only modern historical treatment of the movement dismisses the angelic outbursts as "spiritual fantasies" intended as negotiations around the early republic's shifting economic and gender roles. It also links the angels to William's "arrested emotional and sexual development." The historians write that in the midst of preaching,

William "stopped and walked to the opposite side of the room & kissed a woman" because "the woman desired it and I felt a duty to gratify her."[12]

Only that kiss never happened. As Babcock clearly noted, the tale was "invented & published in that neighborhood by a brother to Capt Newell of this town." The randy preacher was a rumor, but Babcock did not despair: "May God have mercy upon all of them, both relator and audience."[13] Once again, historians have based their understanding of a wonder-working sect by adopting the innuendos of antisupernaturalists as fact rather than by evaluating the words and experiences of the wonder-workers themselves. By explaining the supernaturalism of Babcock (and his wife) as an outgrowth of sexual frustration, this argument repeats the central problem of the historiography of the American supernatural: assuming that because the supernatural has no referent in the real world (it is a "fantasy"), it must be explained by something other than belief.[14]

The Babcockist case followed the precise contours of the antebellum American supernatural, and not any generalized "stubborn . . . older ways of seeing and knowing God" that refused to "yield to . . . scientific and intellectual advances."[15] William laid out a defense of the continuation of miracles and expressed his belief that such things amounted to proofs of God's message. Moreover, Babcockist theology foreshadowed the Mormon practice of dialogic revelation. The angel answered questions and solved points of doctrine, often as soon as the question was asked. "We kneeled & prayed God to send his angel," Babcock wrote in 1810, "which he immediately did."[16] This supernatural give-and-take does not suggest any direct connections between the Babcocks in 1811 and the Smith family in 1830; rather, it demonstrates the pervasiveness of supernatural activity in the early republic. One religion practicing dialogic revelation might be an anomaly; two groups is a pattern. The supernaturalism of early America is perhaps best exemplified not by Mormons or nativists but by the lesser prophets, particularly Jemima Wilkinson and Jacob Cochran.

Wilkinson began her ministry in spectacular fashion, announcing in the midst of the American Revolution that she had died and another spirit had risen in her body. She was Wilkinson no longer; she had become the Public Universal Friend. Under this moniker she gathered a church of more than four hundred, with branches in four states. Like her Shaker contemporaries, Wilkinson sought to construct a communal village out of what she perceived as wilderness—the Iroquois country of the early republic. Her experiment, the city of "Jerusalem," lasted until her death. Predating the Mormons and the public ministry of Ann Lee, Wilkinson and her city of refuge became the first wonder-working sect of the new republic.

Wilkinson has not inspired a great deal of historiographical attention. Scholars have primarily seen Wilkinson as a counterpoint to Ann Lee; it is a comparison that rarely favors Wilkinson. Wilkinson's new Jerusalem lasted more than twenty years, three times as long as Brook Farm, but the latter experiment has more than three hundred articles to its credit; Jerusalem barely has any.[17] Historians have shown more interest in Wilkinson's creative reworking of gender than in her church. Yet Wilkinsonians (or the Universal Friends, as they dubbed themselves), despite their obscurity, provide a crucial case study. The prophetic and supernatural claims of the Wilkinsonians preceded all their contemporaries, but within a generation, the movement lost its early fervor and perhaps its supernaturalism as well.[18]

Wilkinson was born (the first time) in Cumberland, Rhode Island, in 1758. Raised as a Quaker, she and her sister were both disowned by the local meeting—Jemima for failure to attend services, and her sister Patience for having a child out of wedlock. Whether the latter prompted the former is unknown. Whatever the source of her dispute with Quakerism, Wilkinson soon found a better way to heaven. Two months after her excommunication, in October 1776, Wilkinson fell ill with a fever. A description of that event, penned either by Wilkinson or one of her followers, recalled "this truly interesting and great event": Wilkinson, "on the 2d Day of her illness . . . appear'd to meet the Shock of Death." Dead to the world, perhaps, but Wilkinson saw the heavens open, and archangels descending, "saying, Room, Room, Room, in the many Mansions of eternal glory for Thee and for everyone."[19]

What happened next changed the vision into a physical miracle, for the angels informed Wilkinson that the "Spirit of Life from God . . . was waiting to assume the Body which God had prepared for the Spirit to dwell in." Wilkinson was amenable: "Here I am," she told the angel, "send me." In this way, Jemima Wilkinson died. Something else rose in her place: "Between the hour of nine & ten in the morning dropt the dying flesh & yielded up the ghost. And according to the declaration of the Angels,—the Spirit took full possession of the Body it now animates."[20]

It was not technically a resurrection. Jemima Wilkinson had died; what returned was some kind of heavenly spirit (the Public Universal Friend, or P.U.F., as Wilkinson herself abbreviated it). The Friend was divine, though not immortal. Indeed, one of the clearest explanations of her nature came in her last will and testament, which suggests the Friend had no illusions about her mortal frame: "The Universal Friend of Jerusalem . . . in the year one thousand seven hundred and seventy six was called Jemima Wilkinson and ever since that time the UNIVERSAL FRIEND a new name which the Lord hath named."[21] An investigator in 1791 put it more succinctly: "She sets forth that she is sent by Jesus Christ, and enlightened by his spirit to convert mankind."[22]

The Friend, however, sometimes alluded to being something more than a mere messenger. She sometimes referred to herself as "I am that I am." In Exodus 3:14, those words come from the burning bush. Wilkinson's use of the term was no less fearsome. When a critic chastised her masculine garb, Wilkinson replied, "I am not accountable to mortals, I am that I am." When Ezra Stiles was gauche enough to ask her age, Wilkinson explained, "If thou askest the spiritual part of me, I am that I am."[23] Wilkinson's followers also sometimes blurred the distinction between the spirit of the Friend and the spirit of God; Ruth Spencer wrote penitently to Wilkinson, "Let not my unworthiness turn back the source of mercy and boundless grace that flow from the goodness of thine own *Self* or *Nature*."[24] Abner Brownell, the Friend's most notable apostate, accused her of making a personal "Allusion to the Second Person of the Trinity."[25] It is possible that Wilkinson herself did not fully understand her exact nature; she and her followers alternately conceived and spoke of the Friend as divine, as a prophetess, or as a Christ-spirit who lived inside of Wilkinson. Newspapers rarely worried about such theological niceties; Wilkinson was "the pretended *Messiah*" of a "deluded religious sect" who "professes that she is our Lord and Saviour Jesus Christ come again into the world, a second time."[26]

The resurrection was not Wilkinson's only foray into the supernatural. Though later followers disagreed about the extent of Wilkinson's supernaturalism, her ministry included miracles, particularly her "foretelling of future Events, and pretended Gift of Healing," according to Brownell.[27] A 1798 visitor wrote of Wilkinson's claims to "many mighty miracles."[28] In 1819, in Jerusalem, smoke obscured the sun for twelve hours in a New York version of the Dark Day.[29] Ezra Stiles visited Wilkinson and some of her converts—including the prominent judge William Potter and his daughter Alice Hazard. Stiles understood that after Hazard joined the church, she "cast out seven Devils from her brother."[30] Brownell saw the Friend cure a madman, an event that caused the "great noise of a miracle." Brownell later saw the afflicted man slip back into insanity, an event that must have aggravated his increasing disbelief in the Friend. Yet even Brownell admitted amazement at the story of a women who brought her newborn to see the Friend, walking through twelve miles of snowstorm. When both mother and babe arrived unharmed, "this was call'd a miracle," Brownell wrote, "and I must confess it seem'd wonderful that she liv'd through it."[31]

Brownell confirmed that Wilkinson's prophecies and healings brought conversions. Those healed spread the faith, according to Brownell; they would "stir and ride about, it would seem to make a sudden Alteration with them, and they would get pretty well, soon, and then there would be a great Report of a Miracle's being done, which would be much nois'd abroad."[32] Supernatural confirmations followed the believers; one Universal Friend became ill and prayed for relief, whereupon she was granted a visionary "Prospect of a most Beautifull City which appeared before me day and night for some days." She credited the vision with her recovery, "great Evidence that I was on my way and in Faver with the Lord." Moreover, she wrote, everyone would one day "have that Evidence Enoch had"—that is, bodily assumption—as confirmation of their faith.[33] Even David Hudson's yellow biography of Wilkinson included a believer's confession that miracles formed the basis of faith: "The Universal Friend has wrought thirteen miracles, which I have seen with my own eyes, curing the lame. . . . I am therefore satisfied of the divine character of that person."[34] Hudson's commentary included the story as a counterpoint to the same believer's later apostasy, but the words echo the declaration of Universal Friend Sarah Niles, who rejoiced that the movement had "power . . . sufficient to cause the dumb to speak, the deaf to hear & the dead to be raised."[35]

The Friend's supernatural transformation in 1776 gave her another kind of power, by rendering her genderless. "She is not supposed to be of either sex," reported the *American Museum*. "Her followers," the *Museum* explained, "do not admit she is a woman, as a female Messiah appears an incongruity."[36] Historians have shown great interest in the complexities of gender and performance in the career of the P.U.F. Wilkinson appeared in masculine garb with a masculine hairstyle. An 1812 diarist noted, "When I first met Jemima Wilkinson, I was impressed with the idea that I saw a man."[37] Another writer remembered the P.U.F. preaching "with a masculine-feminine tone of voice, or kind of croak, unearthly and sepulchral."[38] The historian Catherine Brekus has noted that this unsexing of the Friend was not precisely a spiritual hermaphroditism; Wilkinson's "genderlessness" was an assumption of masculine aspects. Thus, "even as Wilkinson freed women to testify and preach in public, she never justified their right to speak as *women. . . .* Wilkinson's denial of gender was actually only a denial of the *female* aspects of gender." This masculine genderlessness, Brekus suggests, allowed Wilkinson to preach in public with much less controversy than other female preachers of postrevolutionary America. (Her most prominent female disciples adopted a similar dress and demeanor.) This assumed masculinity was in turn made possible by supernatural claims—after all, she was not Jemima Wilkinson but a spirit (or a god) called the P.U.F.[39]

Yet while contemporary critics mocked Wilkinson's masculine manners, they also mocked her as a religious counterfeiter, versed in imposture and covetous of power. A rival Rhode Island minister called her "Jemimy Wilkinson the Imposter with the number of Deluded Creatures that go about with her."[40] A former believer said she was "ambitious, troublesome, and litigious" and had "pretended to faint" and to have risen again only because she was "aspiring to more power."[41] As the sect grew in Pennsylvania (following several preaching tours), Philadelphia's *Freeman's Journal* attacked the Universal Friends as "villainous impostors" and the local Wilkinsonian prelate, James Parker, as a man whose face concealed "the cunning which lies hid in his heart."[42] Wilkinson was "the undaunted champion of a diabolical system" and only by being "viewed as a fanatic" had she escaped "the vengeance of an indignant and insulted public."[43] Another paper declared, "Had Jemima Wilkinson made her appearance a century or two ago, she would then have been capitally punished."[44]

Two years after Wilkinson's death in 1819, David Hudson wrote his famed biography, *Memoir of Jemima Wilkinson.* That work has been roundly criticized by historians for its many inaccuracies, but it was not really intended as a work of history; it was a theological case against false prophets. Hudson's introduction lays out the case for Christianity and bemoans that charlatans, "exciting the wonders of the credulous," damaged the reputation of the true church. He therefore wrote the book as a chapter in a much longer "account of enthusiasm, delusion, and imposture" that comprised the history of wonder-working cheats. In short, it was an entry in the annals of early republican antisupernaturalism, the biography of an impostor.[45]

Wilkinson, in Hudson's account, grew up a "fine blooming girl" who used "flattery, persuasion, and pretences of ill health" to get what she wanted as a child. She grew up without the "obedience, industry and benevolence" that characterized the Quakers. Her presumed illness came about through "strong mental delusion"; her resurrection was slapdash fakery. Hudson accused Wilkinson of secretly manipulating bed-curtains with her feet and then claiming the movements were supernatural signets of approbation. Wilkinson, he wrote, rose not from the dead but "from the—BED."[46] After her resurrection, she immediately began "the impositions which she attempted to practice in working miracles, healing the sick, and raising the dead." She produced "eye and ear witnesses" to such wonders, who "were as bold in propagating these extravagant absurdities as their new friends were credulous in receiving them."[47]

Wilkinson's miracles, Hudson wrote, were "the most impolitic of all her pretensions," since they provided a means by which believers could test her supernatural bona fides. Hudson likely invented Jemima Wilkinson's most famous miracle of all—her attempt to walk on water. Wilkinson likely never tried any such thing, but as tales of imposture go, it was a whopper. Despite her earlier successes in faking miracles (according to Hudson), the Friend was nervous about trying this one. But as Hudson told the story, "some of her followers also felt a strong desire to see her give some evidence of the truth of her assertions concerning herself," both to increase their own faith and to "answer the reasons and arguments made use of by their enemies." Wilkinson, "finding herself thus beset on all hands, was at length compelled to undertake the hazardous experiment." The P.U.F. turned to "the resources of her cunning mind," and at water's edge, informed the crowd of believers and skeptics alike "that if they had faith to believe that she could perform the works of the Lord, they might rest satisfied . . . and as to those who did not believe, they are 'an evil generation: they seek a sign; and there shall no sign be given.'" Thus she escaped the need to walk atop the river. Her enemies made the story "the subject of mirth and ridicule," while her deluded followers had "no doubt" she could "perform such a miracle as would satisfy them all."[48] Whether Hudson invented the story or cribbed it from uncredited oral sources, it quickly became a standard piece of the posthumous evaluation of Wilkinson. (Herbert Wisbey concluded the story was fabricated in his 1964 scholarly biography of the P.U.F.) In 1830, Portland, Maine's *Eastern Argus* called her a "Prudent Impostor" for sidestepping the miracle.[49] An 1829 paper called her "this petticoated mis-leader of a band of lunatics" and scoffed at her purported water-walking mishap.[50]

Hudson's tale of failed water-walking fit the antisupernatural paradigm perfectly. If Wilkinson was truly commissioned from God, she could perform miracles and that would settle the issue. Since miracles did not exist, she could not perform one, and her failure served as evidence of imposture practiced on "the ignorance, credulity, and stupidity of these deluded people."[51] Miracles

THE SECTS THAT WEREN'T 171

were a proof to Hudson—but since he believed they were over, he could use them as a definitive test against impostors. His *History* also contended that once miracles—and Wilkinsonianism—were accepted, autocracy followed: "Such was the unrelenting and tyrannical temper of this destroyer of human happiness, and so strong the delusion which she had already fastened upon her too credulous people, that few of her devoted followers dared to disobey her unhallowed mandates."[52]

Hudson blamed Wilkinson for a litany of antirepublican traits, including a "propensity to dictation and rule," "contempt of industry," and "insatiable ambition for parade, superiority and dictation."[53] Other critics charged she turned followers into servants; the Universal Friend often took refuge in her adherents' homes, requesting the best rooms and servants to wait on her ("they think it a great privilege for them to be so favoured").[54] Brownell's tract took a similar view: the Friend's "cunning Craftiness" deceived "many simple Women."[55] Indeed, part of the Friend's appeal, according to Brownell, was that "women especially . . . could not seem to contain themselves to act rationally and decently" and would "fall down prostrate before her." She was simply waiting, Brownell warned, for people to become "zealous and to set as much by her and the religion she is endeavoring to propagate as ever the Turks did by Mahomet."[56]

The remarkable story of the P.U.F. and her supernatural gifts seems to have taken the place of theological innovation among the Friends.[57] Her interpretations could charitably be called bland: "Try to be on the Lords side," she wrote to a communicant, "Do justly love mercy and walk humbly with the Lord."[58] Her teachings emphasized thankfulness and good works as the responsible form of worship. Her published volume of 1784, *The Universal Friend's Advice,* admonished readers to live peaceably, worship God, and avoid contention. Her second book was plagiarized from a Quaker volume.[59] Innovation was not part of Wilkinson's gospel. (Other wonder-workers in the early republic also failed to achieve theological originality; the lone surviving letter from Jacob Osgood reveals fairly generic Protestantism. He advised his brother to confess his sins: "be faithful to god . . . and you will rain [reign] with him.")[60]

Critics described the sermons and admonishments of the Friend as confused jumbles, "unpleasantly parenetic and didactic" and "abounding with scripture phraseology applied somewhat at random."[61] When Ezra Stiles met her in person, he admitted "she said many pious good Things" but also found she gave "many Texts repeated without Connexions."[62] Yet another visitor found her "command of the contents of the bible . . . surprising. She used few expressions which could not be found in the sacred book." Yet that familiarity turned into "a confused mass of scriptural quotations" whose obscurity "sometimes was impenetrable."[63]

If Wilkinson borrowed her theology, she produced a novel ecclesiology. She seems to have intended to pass leadership to prophets like herself; she would not be the only genderless prophet in the movement. She anointed others, including Alice Hazard and Sarah Richards, as prophets in their own right. These vice-regents mimicked the masculine hair and dress of the P.U.F. and gave their own prophecies. Indeed, later sources suggest that Richards had been inhabited by the biblical visionary Daniel just as Wilkinson was inhabited by Christ.[64] It is not clear how Wilkinson expected this cascading structure of prophecy to work; perhaps if the Christ spirit lived in Wilkinson, and Richards merely housed Daniel, Wilkinson could anticipate all revelatory activity from her subordinate to conform to her own proclamations. This effort to extend her prophetic calling to a second circle of leaders represented a novel solution to the problems of administration and the extension of supernatural power. While the second-tier prophets had warrant to receive supernatural visitations, they were also sent out to establish and lead new branches of the church, which they did with varying levels of success. Parker (possibly denominated as Elijah) was sent to lead the Pennsylvania congregation. That was a mistake, apparently; he soon wore out his welcome and was replaced by Richards.[65]

By 1788, the Universal Friends appeared to be on their way to becoming an ecclesiastically unique but theologically pedestrian sect. Yet that is when Wilkinson began thinking of building "a peaceable habitation for me & my friends to dwell somewhere."[66] She may have been thinking of the Shakers, who had begun formally establishing their communities around the same time. Yet although Wilkinson was often compared to (and confused with) Ann Lee, the two never met. Another possible inspiration was the German perfectionist community at Ephrata; one of her Pennsylvania followers had close connections there.[67]

The promise of cheap land might have been the strongest inducement to move west. In 1788, the Iroquois country was fast becoming white territory. The federal government, private speculators, and multiple state governments all claimed jurisdiction on the basis of fraudulent treaties with the Six Nations and other tribes; the same white land hunger and perfidy that brought

Indians into Handsome Lake's movement also brought Jemima Wilkinson's followers onto former Indian land. The P.U.F. sent her brother Jeptha and Ezekial Shearman into the land to assess its potential. Like Moses's spies in the land of Canaan, they came back with mixed reports. Wilkinson went ahead anyway, sending an advance guard of settlers to Seneca Lake in 1788. She relied on Parker to organize the purchase, but he proved no match for the complicated legal and political maneuverings that comprised the process of white "extinguishment" of Indian land. Parker's first purchase was part of a widespread fraud later invalidated by the New York legislature; his next purchase (named "the Gore") was more sound, but the settlers did not pay attention to the intricacies of the title and discovered after the fact that they had built their settlement just east of the land they owned. Further plans to share the financial burden of resettlement among all the Friends foundered on Parker's mismanagement. Wilkinson removed Parker from authority in 1791.[68]

It was that same year that Wilkinson herself finally moved to the settlement. It is not clear why she delayed coming, but certainly the "gripeing & grinding worldly-mindedness with Pittyful Shifts of low Policy" among the settlers that Parker encountered (and perhaps exacerbated) probably influenced her decision.[69] Almost as soon as she arrived, the community made plans to move again—perhaps to Canada, or to another patch of Iroquois land in the same vicinity purchased by two wealthy Friends, which eventually took the name "Jerusalem." After much squabbling, the P.U.F. moved from the Gore to Jerusalem in 1794.[70]

But the years of indecision took their toll. Parker, reduced in authority, eventually drifted away from the sect. So, too, did Abraham Dayton, who had purchased (and moved to) land in Canada that Wilkinson passed over for her refuge. Worse, the death of Sarah Richards cast a pall over the movement and intensified its juridical troubles. All of Wilkinson's property was legally held by Richards (so that the Friend could literally own nothing). Though Richards willed her property to Rachel Malin, another Universal Friend, that will had not been drawn up by a lawyer; repeated challenges by secular speculators involved the sect in perpetual litigation.[71]

Historians have connected the February 1794 move to Jerusalem with the sect's ultimate decline, but it is possible that the move improved the Friends' fortunes. Visitors to the place found it an ideal spot for a prophetess. A Quaker missionary described the newly settled Jerusalem as a "sequestered, romantic place, suited to her genius."[72] An 1812 visitor similarly found the Friend's neighborhood "uncommonly beautiful, and fit to nourish the enthusiasm of its inhabitants."[73] The U.S. census bore out those observations: A visitor had counted sixty families at the Gore in 1791, but the census takers at Jerusalem in 1800 found more than 1,100 people living there.[74]

That is a remarkable number. A thousand residents made Wilkinson's Jerusalem nearly twice as large as the largest Shaker settlement, and it would have compared favorably to the Latter-day Saint settlements in Kirtland and Independence in the 1830s. The Shakers and Mormons, of course, had multiple villages, so as a whole Wilkinson's movement was smaller. Moreover, not every resident of Jerusalem was a devoted Universal Friend; Scott Larson suggests that Wilkinson had 260 followers at Jerusalem's height. Benjamin Shaw visited Jerusalem in 1798 and distinguished between "certain Disciples which believed on her" and "the Inhabitants of Jerusalem, whom she had deceived with her enticing words." Obviously some residents of Jerusalem did not join the sect. Even so, Wilkinson appeared to be making inroads.[75] Historians have missed this Wilkinsonian renaissance, perhaps because they have been influenced by the repeated insistence of anti-Wilkinsonians that her influence was in decline—or by William Savery's misogynist description of Jerusalem as "several hovels adjacent, which are the residences of women who have forsaken husband and children; and also of men who have left their families, to become what they now literally are, hewers of wood and drawers of water to an artful and designing woman."[76]

Thus by 1800, Wilkinson was primed to become a serious figure in American religious history rather than an interesting footnote. Yet just at that moment, the movement began to crumble; by 1810, Jerusalem claimed only 450 residents. Many historians have cited her continued legal troubles—as usual, involving land. One prominent follower quit the group to pursue real estate profits by selling off his share of the Gore.[77] More problematic were the uncertainties in Richards's will, and the fact that Wilkinson had never formally organized or incorporated her church. Land jobbers connected by marriage to the Universal Friends brought Wilkinson and the Friends to court to seek their ejectment from Jerusalem.

One of the lawyers associated with the jobbers was David Hudson. Thus, his History—written after Wilkinson was dead but before the case was decided—was not merely an intellectual exercise but also part of a specific legal and political campaign to open her lands to private enterprise. Wonder-workers were either insane or tyrants, Hudson wrote, and the state therefore ought to remove them—just as it had removed the native prophets in Indiana and Alabama, and as it would move the prophets in Mormon country.[78]

A series of depositions, taken in 1813, illuminates the decline of the Universal Friends. Intended to collect evidence about land ownership in Jerusalem, the depositions also inquired of their subjects whether and when they had joined or left Wilkinson's church. Benedict Robinson testified that that he "formerly did belong to the said society so far as he regularly attended the meetings thereof. But whether he was a regular member of said society he does not know as he does not now recollect what was deemed necessary to become a member of said Society." He had stopped going to meetings at some point between 1801 and 1803, due to "disputes with members of the said Society and with Jemima Wilkinson herself, although he was "now friendly to the said Society." Similarly, Parmele Barnes admitted that "he did formerly belong to the Society of Universal Friends, and has withdrawn himself there from because he believes in another doctrine." Sherman, the former scout, left because "he disapproved their practice."[79] When William Carter left to join the Shakers, he wrote to the P.U.F. that "I have been considering the much conversation that we had together about the way of God."[80] These comments suggest that theological and doctrinal issues divided the Wilkinsonians rather than economics or "skepticism" about the P.U.F.

It is not clear how theological divisions began to work on the Universal Friends—especially since their theology was so typically Protestant—but it does appear that once ensconced in Jerusalem, the Friend took a very mild position on church discipline, maintaining relationships even with those who left the movement. Such a view would be consistent with her theological haziness; if indeed she preached a general New Light Protestantism connected to her resurrection, then perhaps in her later years she worried more about the Protestantism and less about her own particular sacred mission. If she could make people seek salvation with God without joining her movement, perhaps that was enough. Such a shift would also be consistent with the general decline of supernatural claims surrounding the movement in the latter years; one follower wrote in 1840 that she had resided with the Friend from 1790 to 1797 and that "in her public discourses and private conversations she disclaimed all pretensions to miraculous gifts."[81] A visitor to Jerusalem made several trips to Wilkinson's sickbed in her latter years, trying to "form a correct idea of her doctrines," but it was still "no easy task."[82] If there were fewer miracles, perhaps followers went to prophets who did perform miracles (as Carter went to the Shakers). In 1799, James Parker (now elevated to local judge) had Wilkinson arrested on charges of blasphemy. Yet Wilkinson was not convicted and, in fact, was invited to give a sermon to the court. Such efforts suggest a more prosaic P.U.F. than the resurrected Friend of 1776. If Wilkinsonianism moved toward generic Protestantism between 1800 and 1819, then fewer miracles and wonder-workings might be expected. Perhaps Wilkinson decided she did not want to found a new religion, after all.

Or the cause of the decline may be the most prosaic of all: Wilkinson died and left no clear successor. She had ample warning; she had been ill since 1816. (Local newspapers cited dropsy as her affliction.) The last year of her life she rarely left her room but continued meeting followers and preaching to visitors from her sickbed. In the early morning of July 1, 1819, the P.U.F. died; crowds lined the roads for her funeral four days later.[83]

Despite her illness, no subsequent leader emerged to take her place. Rachel and Margaret Malin maintained her house; James Brown Jr. took care of business matters for the society. New arrivals attempted to revive the sect; according to a much later local history, two men arrived in the 1830s and "claimed to give fresh inspiration of the Friend's doctrine," but the attempt apparently did not pay off. The legal battles continued, with pieces of the Friends' territory passing to nonmembers by fiat or sale. One writer found that a decade after the Friend's death, Jerusalem was the province of a doddering "aunt" and her "twenty fawn colored cats."[84]

Most newspapers carried reports of her death, usually dressed in terminology familiar to antisupernaturalist harangues. Wilkinson was a "consummate and successful impostor" who "by the donations of her followers . . . lived in a luxurious & expensive manner." Then Hudson's spurious biography appeared, and the legends of her water-walking began passing through the newspapers.[85] Wilkinson was soon so familiar to the American reading public that she became a reference point of choice for those who wished to criticize Mormons, "as gross impostors," wrote the *Painesville (OH) Telegraph* in 1831, "as was Jemima Wilkinson."[86]

Jemima Wilkinson became a byword for those who hated modern miracles; perhaps more than anyone else in the early republic, her name and her claims were cited as a reason *not* to believe. Even after her death, critics pointed to Wilkinson as the *ne plus ultra* of imposture and credulity. David Young's 1826 essay on the Morristown ghost hoax cited "the delusion of Jemima Wilkinson" as "proof that mankind are naturally prone to credit every thing." Quitman bemoaned in 1810 "to what extravagancies *human reason* may proceed, in the instance of Jemima Wilkenson and a number of enthusiasts, whose wild flights we daily witness." The *Rochester (NY) Gem* famously dismissed the Book of Mormon as "Jemima Wilkinson-ism." She was the first, and she bore the brunt of the early republic's withering gaze.[87]

Jacob Cochran's religion, meanwhile, received more than looks. The Cochranites are barely recognized by modern historians, yet an observer in 1817 might well have guessed that they, and not Shakers or Wilkinsonians, would be the sect most remembered by posterity. Cochran and his religion burned across Maine's religious firmament in three fiery years, preaching a new age of miracles and the restoration of apostolic Christianity. When fears of the connection between miracles and tyranny emerged, the state stepped in. Massachusetts convicted Cochran on charges of lewdness in 1819. Cochran fled, and the movement collapsed.

Cochranites left few source materials behind by which to judge them. Cochran wrote nothing defending or explaining his teaching. Nineteenth-century sources tend to come from the sect's enemies, and those are "marred by sanctimonious prejudice and a reliance upon oral history that is more gossip than history," according one of Cochranism's few historians.[88] Re-creating the religion from such materials is tenuous at best; the few authors who have tried to capture the essence of Cochranism have usually done so by importing elements from other religions—making Cochranites out to be proto-Mormons or paleo-Oneidans.[89] The connection to other sects of the new republic, however, derives less from doctrines (the Cochranites seem to have had their own peculiar teachings) and more from their common use of the supernatural as an element of worship, preaching, and proselytizing. Like the more successful supernaturalists of the early United States, Cochranites saw the return of supernatural power as rational evidence and justification for their new faith, and for a short time, they were wildly successful; even the movement's most pointed critic cited the possibility that two thousand New Englanders had joined the movement.

Jacob Cochran was born in Enfield, New Hampshire, in 1782. He possibly earned his living as a soldier, grocer, or schoolteacher.[90] Like many Yankees in the early republic, he drifted from place to place, eventually bringing his family to Saco, Maine, by 1816.[91] Cochran's arrival coincided with a period of Freewill Baptist growth and revival on the Maine coast.[92] Cochran might have been part of that revival; "He came making great pretensions to religion," according to a report issued after his 1819 arrest, "in the guise of a Freewill

Baptist."[93] Cochran preached at Freewill Baptist meetings, sometimes along-side the legendary preacher Clement Phinney. Yet by 1816, Cochran had left the Baptists and been "ordained by private brethren."[94]

One reason for the rupture might have been that Cochran had come to believe that miraculous powers still existed in this world—and that he could exercise them. His church claimed "the power of healing the sick, raising the dead, and casting out devils—all of which, they said, had been literally performed among them," according to Ephraim Stinchfield, who investigated Cochran and penned a rancorous commentary on what he found. Cochran "made uncommonly high pretensions of a miraculous power vested in him, equal, if not superior, to the *apostolic.*" Discussions of the powers Cochranites claimed run through almost all the commentaries about them. Cochran could cause penitent followers to collapse with a touch. At his trial, the prosecutor queried as to whether "Cochrane performed a miracle, by raising your daughter?" (The respondent avoided the question.) Cochran attempted at least one exorcism, and the prosecuting attorney in the 1819 trial went to great lengths to show that "innocent people . . . have had the credulity to believe him capable of working miracles."[95]

Given that virtually no Cochranites recorded their own accounts, it is not possible to determine if Cochranites took these miracles as validation for new practices. There were, however, distinctive practices. Cochran reinstituted anointing followers with oil; he held a passover feast, and included an article in the church covenants that their proceedings were to be kept secret from outsiders, "for the secrets of the Lord are with those that love him," according to one apostate, although another devotee added "they were not bound to keep any thing hid that was wickedness."[96] Cochran also added elements that echoed Shaker practice; at the passover feast, men and women would march separately to the table, and his worship service featured "great agitations," which sometimes were meant to represent reaping and winnowing. (Shaker dances were often similarly described.) Stinchfield also suggested that Cochran had an "original purpose of having *all things in common*"; this plan did not pan out.[97]

As with the Wilkinsonians, the changes came primarily in practice rather than in theology. Stinchfield called Cochran's preaching "a mass of incoherent, undigested stuff"; indeed, the only theological points on which Cochranites seemed to insist were the continuation of miracles and an imminent millennium. If their preaching lacked originality, however, it excelled in passion; even Stinchfield had to remark that Cochran had "good words and fair speeches." Cochranite sermons did not come from Cochran alone; in just three years he had congregations and ministers across southern Maine—in Saco, Kennebunk, Portland, and elsewhere.[98]

Cochran also mimicked Shakers in his attempt to rework the marriage contract, and this tenet proved to be his undoing. Critics and followers alike agreed that Cochran denounced marriage in favor of Paul's advocacy of the celibate life; at the trial, numerous followers testified that "it was better for young people not to marry," that the "scriptures forbid marriage," and that "christians ought not to marry." One young Cochranite, Aaron Libbey, explained that Cochran had encouraged him to dissolve his engagement; Cochran's lawyers hastily suggested that the fiancée was "a girl of bad character" and Cochran had saved Libbey from being "ensnared."[99]

Few others took such a charitable view. Stinchfield called the doctrine "the *mystery of iniquity*" and assumed that Cochran had assigned new spiritual wives and husbands to his followers, and that Cochran himself had freely exploited his female followers for sexual gratification.[100] The tales of Cochran's "horrid enormities," "lascivious behavior," and "all manner of iniquity" were traded in the newspapers.[101] "His process was to gull a few men," went one report, "then to seduce women."[102] Stories about Cochran were so thick on the ground that even George Wallingford—one of Cochran's own lawyers—told the jury that "I came to this town . . . with an indiscernible indignation against the defendant."[103]

Was Cochran exchanging spouses as part of his new religion? It is certainly possible; the prosecution brought forth several apostates who claimed it had likely happened at least once. Yet the defense deposed other witnesses who said no such things had ever happened; Cochran had ministered to—and healed—sick women at their bedsides through prayer and power, and this miraculous course had been misinterpreted, they claimed.

The charge of sexual misconduct, of course, was a standard piece of the campaign against the supernatural, the same deployed against Shakers, Mormons, and Babcockists. Accounts of Cochran and the Cochranites included the standard language: Cochran was "the notorious religious impostor," his followers "a few wretches like himself."[104] Stinchfield referred to the sect as Cochran, "this arch-deceiver," and "his stupid followers." Stinchfield also referred to the religion as "quackery" and "religious deception" perpetrated by "an impostor or religious juggler."[105] A solicitor gave the jury this assessment of the gathered Cochranites: "Their appearance indicates that they are not rational."[106]

Stinchfield fully developed the other themes of antisupernaturalism, particularly the notion that all impostors sought personal political power. "Those who are in close communion with him are bound to obey him," Stinchfield declared. Cochran "expects to have the United States, [in] the present season, under his control!" Indeed, "he looks forward to universal domination." Like Shakers and Mormons, Cochranites also came under the charge of secret plans to demolish American democracy, despite the fact that Cochranism was a much smaller religion. Thus, charges that any set of wonder-workers were antirepublican probably did not derive from careful inspection of their political motives but from a political ideology that assumed miracles meant tyranny.[107]

While the state tried Cochran for lewdness and adultery, it did not limit itself to attacking the sexual proclivities of the sect. It inquired whether Cochran attempted to perform miracles, and it repeatedly questioned Cochranite witnesses whether they had not signed a covenant that bound them to secrecy. The lead prosecutor, Daniel Davis, flatly told the jury that no Cochranite testimony could be accepted: "They are all of them under his coercion, and the strongest bonds of delusion" and "subject to his control, marshaled and drilled in his service." All Cochranites could manage was "submission to the will of their leader," and therefore, "What shall we say of the wretch who has deluded them? Shall he be permitted to go unpunished?" Davis did mention the crime of adultery, but he specifically asked the jury to punish Cochran for leading a group of wonder-workers. After all, Davis later added, "We have no dispensation to establish a new religion."[108]

In other words, because a new religion was *theologically* impossible, the state could hold Cochran politically and legally responsible. Such a formulation was only possible if the jury also believed that new miracles inherently indicated a moral turpitude that put the community at risk from internal rot or cabalistic treason. Given the extent of the prosecution's ability to prove Cochran's moral failings—or at least, his refusal to recognize the standing marriage covenants—the defense attorneys opted to tackle the antisupernatural thesis instead. "In his worship of God," Wallingford argued, Cochran "has as strong a claim to protection as any of us, and no voice is to be raised against him, because his system differs from ours." His message to the jury also avoided the purported question of adultery: "If you are to try Cochrane by common report, you will convict him. If you try him by law and the evidence you will acquit him."[109]

The jury chose the former. Initially, the trial ended in deadlock—the recalcitrant juror was accused by newspapers of being a Cochranite—but the state quickly moved to a second trial involving a separate case of lewd behavior.[110] The jury convicted, and while they deliberated, Cochran escaped, "cheating the state prison of a *pious* labourer," snickered one newspaper.[111] Newspapers circulated descriptions of the miraculous preacher, and Cochran was eventually discovered. He served eighteen days of solitary confinement and four years at hard labor; upon his release, he vanished. In his absence, Cochran's nascent religion struggled and then faded away. When Daniel Graham wrote a biography of Clement Phinney in 1851, he found a handful of followers remaining, scattered through Saco and its vicinity. They would "occasionally meet to cheer their spirits by a religious dance, so as to enable themselves to better endure the ills of their sad pilgrimage."[112]

In 1895, G. T. Ridlon extended the life of Cochranism through the Latter-day Saints; he suggested that the Mormons found many converts in coastal Maine in 1832, and condemned Cochranism for the Latter-day harvest. Maine Mormons "had been washed from their moral and rational moorings by the tidal-wave let loose on the community by Jacob."[113] Some later historians have followed Ridlon's lead.[114] The sects are similar, at least on a cursory level; both Cochranites and Mormons believed in divine healing and other apostolic gifts, and both sought to transform the institution of marriage in accordance with a new dispensation. Ridlon's central contention, however, is that both groups were noxious afflictions: "Cochranite grasshoppers, followed by Mormon locusts."[115] The Mormon writer Orson Hyde took a missionary tour of Maine in 1832, where he discovered a handful of Cochranites hanging on—and practicing spiritual wifery. The Cochranites were actually a hindrance to Hyde; one potential convert informed him that people would not likely accept Mormonism even "if it were true because of Cochran's description."[116]

Cochranism and Mormonism had outward similarities, but that does not mean that the former gave rise to the latter. Rather, both movements drew from the same theological and cultural predilections in the early republic: a reliance on personal experience and witness testimony, the confirming power of miracles, and the legal and social backlash of the antimiraculous. Cochranism did not lead to Mormonism; they both grew from the same soil. Cochranism and Mormonism were distinct outgrowths of the same miracle beliefs so prevalent throughout the young republic. In the case of Cochranism, however, state efforts to stamp out the belief succeeded. Whereas Joseph Smith Jr. weathered his initial trials, Cochran served out a withering sentence.

State efforts to scuttle the religion worked, and the brief but intense meteor of Cochranism flamed out. State action, and not theology or practice, ended this particular iteration of the American supernatural.

The minor prophets flourished for a moment and were gone. Wilkinson, the Babcocks, Cochran, Osgood, Sargent, and others wielded supernatural powers detailed by sense evidence, but for various reasons—legal imbroglios, skipping bail, or simple disinterest—could not maintain their edifices as did Handsome Lake or Joseph Smith. Miracles were so common, it seems, that merely appealing to them was not enough.

The disappearance of these manifold but tiny sects may well have aided the broader disappearance of the antebellum supernatural from nineteenth-century historiography. While miraculous sects and leaders crisscrossed the country, their influence and the continued claims to miraculous powers could not be avoided—thus, the repeated return to Wilkinson as the example of credulity. When these sects faded without leaving institutional edifices, and when the nativists were buried under a dismissive banner of "Indian religion," only the Shakers and Mormons remained—then only the Mormons. As sects that practiced the modern supernatural vanished, what had once been a broad discussion of "delusion" and "superstition" became a discussion of Mormonism. Thus, the Latter-day Saints came to stand in for all the supernaturalism of the early republic, as the embodiment of everything strange, and the peculiar antebellum problem of the supernatural became effaced—or rather, foisted upon the Saints in their mountain fastness. Thomas Campbell's 1831 letter denouncing Mormonism compared them to the Shakers, Wilkinsonians, French Prophets, and other "impostors"; by the end of the century, Leonard Bacon's *History of American Christianity* spoke of Mormonism alone as "distinctly American . . . singularly dramatic," and therefore "only incidentally . . . connected with the history of American Christianity."[117] The death of the minor prophets erased the memory of the American season of the supernatural in the days before the Civil War. The supernaturalists became museum pieces examined only occasionally, and the religious history of the early republic became a story of evangelicals against rationalists. Like Wilkinson, the Babcocks, and Cochran, the memory of supernaturalism (and the crises it caused) faded away.

Conclusion
Liberty and Theology

Two revolutionary acts of violence bookend this study. In 1775 and 1838, citizen militias clashed with state-sanctioned armies bent on enforcing the law. Both times, the militias lost, forced back with losses and civilian casualties. In the wake of violence, the partisans of the militias fulminated about liberty and self-defense: such "scenes of desolation would be a reproach to the perpetrators, even if committed by the most barbarous nations. . . . And all this because these colonies will not submit to the iron yoke of arbitrary power," in the words of a pamphleteer. A captive from one action wrote, "Instead of being treated with that respect which is due from one citizen to another, we were taken as prisoners of war, and were treated with the utmost contempt." The language of the state-sponsored armies, by contrast, concerned liberty and rationality. The rebels were "entirely revolutionary in their feelings and institutions," led by a man with power "as absolute over this deluded people, as the Emperor's of Russia over his lowest serfs." It was difficult to stop the soldiers, wrote one officer, from "further slaughter of those deluded people." One of the battles was Lexington and Concord; the other was the Haun's Mill Massacre.[1]

I do not mean to make direct parallels between the Mormon militias and the American rebels or between the British army regulars and Missouri's anti-Mormon forces. Yet the language of rights, authority, and delusion united these violent encounters. Everyone feared arbitrary authority—whether from king, elected governor, or mob twisted by delusive ideas. In each case, the threat was not merely local: the Mormon war had been "an insurrection of no ordinary character," wrote General Clark. "It had for its object *Dominion*, and the ultimate subjugation of this State and the Union."[2]

Patriot rebels launched a revolution; the Mormons capitulated. These battles suggest the fraught relationship among the concepts that historians bequeath upon the era. Liberty required rationality, and religious faith required liberty, making the problem of rationality and religion fundamentally a political question as well. "Rational" faiths could all combine in the defense of liberty; "delusions" could not. This kind of logic provided a useful constitutional glue among scores of Protestant sects in the early republic and gave to future generations the mistaken notion that starry-eyed religious freedom emerged full-grown from the Revolution. Haun's Mill, Prophetstown, and Turtle Creek suggest otherwise. The miracle workers of the early republic forced the issue.[3]

In modern political and historiographical debates, the moral dimension of republicanism is too easily conflated with religion itself. John Adams's claim that "authority in magistrates and obedience of citizens" derived from "reason, morality, and the Christian religion" was neither a profession of faith nor a call for establishment; rather, Adams was pointing out that the United States was "founded on the natural authority of the people alone, without a pretence of miracle or mystery." The miraculous was the enemy of the people.[4]

Defining republicanism through virtue rather than through confession aligned with broad Enlightenment epistemologies; it also possessed clear political benefits that allowed Congregationalist Massachusetts to coexist with disestablished Virginia in a single political union. Quakers, deists, Presbyterians, Baptists, and even (on occasion) Jews could unite under such a banner. Those who could not believe in the cessation of miracles, however, were suspect. The nature of republicanism had a theological presupposition about the supernatural—rather than a creed, denomination, or generalized "Christianity"—as a constitutive part of its nature. The religious politics of the Founding were about theology, not identity.

Yet if Enlightenment assumptions about proofs and sense evidence established the groundwork for clockwork republicanism, they also set the stage for a resurgence of miracles. As the supernatural declined (fitfully), a host of violations of a regular natural order became promoted from preternatural to miraculous, while miracles became all the more important as divine signs. In the search for surety, miracle accounts sought sense evidence and eyewitness testimony. Shakers, Babcockists, Mormons, conjurers, Wilkinsonians, and nativists rose to take their unusual place in the Enlightenment cosmos and triggered the crises inherent in the very fabric of the republican settlements of church, state, and virtue.

The republican debate on miracles, magic, and the supernatural was therefore fundamental to the construction of religious freedom in the early republic. Questions of religious liberty turned on issues of political expediency but also on precise questions of theology and epistemology. Emphasizing this distinction offers a new historiographical light in which to consider radical sectarianism in America, as well as ways to reconsider continued supernatural practices and beliefs in white, Indian, and African American practice. It should fundamentally annul any automatic assumption of a cessation of supernatural beliefs or the easy classification of religious struggles in the early republic as faith versus reason or rationality against superstition.

The political problem of miracles in the early republic should also trouble the contentious twenty-first-century struggles over church and state. Winnifred Sullivan has recently described full religious freedom as an "impossibility," since religious freedom depends on a priori definitions of religion, and this "rationalization . . . asks the government to be the arbiter of religious orthodoxy." Sullivan finds this outlook disquieting, along with the fact that any American judge would "describe a four-day trial as 'talking theology all day,'" even when that trial was about legal definitions of religion.[5] Yet in a sense, theology was implicit in the republican division of church and state itself. The idea of removing church from state as a political measure was not meant as a protection for folk beliefs such as magic and fortune-telling. It was meant to protect moral and rational religious practice—from deists and Unitarians to Baptists and even Quakers—all of whom could be counted on to make rational decisions about the state, free of delusion or beliefs in direct divine interference. The act of separation itself was limned with a certain kind of religious value. Wonder-workers did not deserve protection; indeed, they deserved persecution—for the sake of the state if not the church.

Ongoing efforts to reclaim the "Christian" nature of the early republic ought to examine the problem of the supernatural as well. Certain wings of the modern evangelical movement have long insisted that the "Christian heritage" of the American Founding entitles them "by divine imperative to 'take their place at the table,'" as David Sehat writes.[6] Modern evangelicalism is much more attuned to the presence of miracles and the supernatural in modern life than were most Protestant varietals of the early republic. President George W. Bush famously invoked the "wonderworking power in the goodness and idealism and faith of the American people." U.S. Senator Tim Scott has an unofficial "prayer team" organized via his website who pray, among other things, "that the Lord will send his angels to protect and be encamped around Tim, his family, and staff members."[7] Contemporary evangelicals—broadly speaking—expect the touch of the supernatural in their lives, in ways small and great. This transformation of American Christianity has long-term origins, and I neither advocate nor condemn it here. Yet personal experience of miracles and wonder-working power were, in the days of the early republic, often identified as a sure sign of charlatanry. Belief in a modern supernatural was precisely what Adams, Jefferson, and a host of early American demonologists condemned as dangerous to democracy. Of course, those same demonologies often engaged in racist stereotypes and misogynist rants to make their points, so we need to be very careful in how we apply these lessons. Nevertheless, the fact that the Founders preferred a certain kind of theology about the supernatural that is not generally in accord with modern evangelical Christianity should give pause to those who blithely praise the Founders as "religious men."

Both the case for an absolute religious freedom, untouched by politics, and the case for a Christian Founding in some ways rely on the interpretation of early American faith as rationality versus religion. By assuming the church-state arrangements of the early republic were variants on this presumed eternal struggle, current debates about separation become mere assertions that either rationality or religion is the surest security for liberty, and therefore the rational/religious Founders were right. If, however, miracle workers mined the same rationalist Enlightenment discourses to defend their own beliefs in a renewed supernatural and *still* faced political censure, then the religious politics of the early nation were about finding broad agreements on republican religious practice—differentiating not between rationality and religion but between *kinds* of religion. Haun's Mill was a consequence of this differentiation.

None of this should diminish the achievement of the Founding generations in establishing a baseline of religious toleration far beyond anything then attempted in the West. Yet in any state embracing religious freedom, there are always questions of degrees. The Founders still saw religion as a constitutive part of the state: moral, virtuous, and rational—not superstitious and not miraculous. It was not that *any* religion would qualify or even that *any* Christianity would qualify. In that sense, liberals are wrong about a secular state; conservatives are wrong if they assume the Founders would embrace their religions of personal revelation. Questions about religion and the Founding, considered in the light of miracles and wonders, should therefore remove our discussions from the battles over identity and take us into the realm of theology. Distinctions about church and state are by definition theological as well as political.

Whittier identified one of the fundamental problems of Christian liberty in his demonology, *The Supernaturalism of New England:* If Christianity gave people liberty, how could the church of Christ have existed for so many centuries before becoming allied to democracy? For Whittier, the answer was superstition: "For long weary centuries the millions of professed Christians stooped, awe stricken, under the yoke of spiritual and temporal despotism. . . . Superstition, in alliance with Tyranny, had filled their upward pathway to Freedom with Shapes of Terror." This was the danger of superstition, and he saw it when upstanding citizens of Poplin, New Hampshire, upon hearing of the dreams of a "wise woman" in the 1840s, headed out to dig for treasure, "delving in grim earnest, breaking the frozen earth, uprooting swamp-maples and hemlocks" until the "snows of December put an end to their labors." Liberty and religion were not questions that existed exclusively in Baptist revivals, or in the pens of Founders, or in the treatises and sermons of abolitionists. They lived, too, among witches, sectarians, miraculous healers, angels, and treasure diggers, who embraced their liberty, followed sense evidence, listened to witnesses, and left behind great holes and traces in the early republic that historians have not yet seen. But Whittier and his fellow Americans did see it: "The yawning excavation still remains, a silent but somewhat expressive commentary upon the 'Age of Progress.'"[8]

Notes

Introduction

1. McNemar, *The Kentucky Revival*, 68.

2. Whittier, *Supernaturalism*, 3.

3. Bayley, *A Narrative*, 10–11.

4. P. Edward Peareson to Thomas Cooper, 4/26/1837, in *The Statutes at Large of South Carolina*, 743; *South Carolina Gazette* (Columbia), 11/10/1792.

5. William Plumer, "The Shakers at Harvard, Massachusetts," ed. F. B. Sanborn, *New England Magazine* 22 (1900): 306. Plumer wrote the article in 1782.

6. *Life of John Colby, Preacher of the Gospel* (Lowell, MA, 1815), 47–48. See also the similar events in *An Account of the Singular Case of Rachel Baker the Celebrated Somniloquist, or Sleeping Preacher* (New York, 1815).

7. *Times and Seasons*, 1/1/1844, vol. 5, no. 1.

8. D. M. Dewey, *History of the Strange Sounds or Rappings* (Rochester: D. M. Dewey, 1850), 78. The story of the turnip is filed under the "Additional Facts" section in this second 1850 version.

9. Spencer Fluhman called for such a comparative history of new American religions and their adversaries in his study of anti-Mormonism (see Fluhman, *Anti-Mormonism*, 19). Jonathan Barry's recommendation to treat each case of witchcraft (or here, miracles) as its own microhistory has also influenced my approach, though what I chronicle here are more akin to case studies (Barry, *Witchcraft and Demonology in South-West England* [New York: Palgrave, 2012], 256–57).

10. Clark, *Thinking*, 2–3. The story of diabolic flatulence "like a blue mist" comes from Würzburg in 1590 (Lyndal Roper, *Witch Craze: Terror and Fantasy in Baroque Germany* [New Haven: Yale University Press, 2004], 82). The nest of human genitals was famously cited by Heinrich Kramer (*The Hammer of Witches*, trans. Christopher S. Mackay [Cambridge: Cambridge University Press, 2009], 328).

11. Among many similar approaches, see Diane Purkiss, *The Witch in History* (New York: Routledge, 1996); and Marion Gibson, *Reading Witchcraft* (New York: Routledge, 1999).

12. Clark, *Thinking*, 2–3.

13. Ibid., 3–10. Following Saussure (and others), Clark denied that ideas must have referents in the real world. If language is an open system, wherein people find objects in the real world and then assign names and words to them, the notion that language must have some "correspondence with reality" would be true. If language is, however, a coherent system unto itself with its own truth-making apparatus, such a correspondence is not a necessity; indeed, it is an impossibility. The linguistic turn contends that language comprises reality rather than passively describing it. Insisting that events as described in the sources must have some real-world origin thus becomes the "referential fallacy." The "language of witchcraft was unreadable, because signifier and signified combined to produce a sign that—to the modern mind—meant nothing real at all," as Marion Gibson writes (see Gibson, "Thinking Witchcraft: Language, Literature, and Intellectual History," in *Witchcraft Historiography*, ed. Jonathan Barry and Owen Davies [New York: Palgrave, 2007], 168).

14. Margaret C. Jacob, "Factoring Mary Poovey's *A History of the Modern Fact*," *History and Theory* 40, no. 2 (May 2001): 280–89. See also Poovey, *A History of the Modern Fact: Problems of Knowledge in the Sciences of Wealth and Society* (Chicago: University of Chicago Press, 1998).

15. Porter, "Witchcraft," 264; E. William Monter, "The Historiography of European Witchcraft: Progress and Prospects," *Journal of Interdisciplinary History* 2, no. 4 (Spring 1972): 435–51. Occasionally, historians have actually assumed that their subjects *were* credulous or necromancers—reading critiques of Mormons or treasure diggers as literal assessments (see Cross, *Burned-Over*, 80–82; Quinn, *Early Mormonism*, 236–39, xxii; and Taylor, "Treasure Seeking").

16. David Holland, *Sacred Borders: Continuing Revelation and Canonical Restraint in Early America* (New York: Oxford University Press, 2011), 94. Holland cites Wallace, *Death*; Juster, *Doomsayers;* and Paul Johnson and Sean Wilentz, *The Kingdom of Matthias* (New York: Oxford University Press, 1994) among the works that exemplify the sociological to the exclusion of the theological.

17. Black, "Poetics," 74. Black alludes to several thinkers in a much larger body of germane scholarship that I avoid in the interest of avoiding a denser theoretical discussion. One example of such scholarship is Dipesh Chakrabarty's argument that the inherently secular construction of Western ideas of historical causation—based on ideas about the autonomous self—by definition prevent the inclusion of supernatural actors and, in so doing, create histories that enormous swaths of religious people could never countenance. Recent work has also focused on the ways in which concepts of the supernatural (and superstition) are dependent on historical context and hence cannot be understood except by letting those who experienced them speak for themselves (see Chakrabarty, *Provincializing Europe: Postcolonial Thought and Historical Difference* [Princeton: Princeton University Press, 2007]).

18. On Tenskwatawa's eclipse, see Jortner, *The Gods*, 3–13; for the exorcism, see Bushman, *Joseph Smith*, 115.

19. Ramsey MacMullen, *Christianizing the Roman Empire* (New Haven: Yale University Press, 1984), 19–20.

20. Economic determinism goes back to Whitney Cross's *The Burned-Over District* and the social control hypothesis. It should be pointed out that virtually all economic determinism suggests that supernaturalism is a response to *bad* economic times, a correlation that in turn suggests only crisis can bring on the supernatural in a modern society. Monica Black has suggested, however, that the uptick in supernatural phenomena in 1950s West Germany was in fact a response to the 1948 currency reform and the beginnings of German recovery (Black, "Miracles in the Shadow of the Economic Miracle: The 'Supernatural 50s' in West Germany," *Journal of Modern History* 84, no. 4 [2012]: 857).

21. Richard Godbeer, *The Devil's Dominion: Magic and Religion in Early New England* (New York: Cambridge University Press, 1992), 227.

22. Butler, *Awash*, 393–94.

23. Ibid., 89, 83. Of course, that is not to say that supernaturalism swelled among the elites but that evidence for the poor believing *more* in such things is largely based on critical reports written in the light of antisupernaturalism rather than an analysis of who believed what. As I point out in chapter 2 (and subsequent chapters), many wealthy donors frequented fortune-tellers or joined new sects.

24. Demos, *Entertaining*, 393. On skepticism versus a culture of skepticism, see Wolfgang Behringer, *Witches and Witch-Hunts: A Global History* (Cambridge: Polity, 2004), chap. 5.

25. I do not mean to suggest that historians who take this approach intend to discredit these groups or are unsympathetic to their claims. My contention is that the particularist approach understands belief as epiphenomenal.

26. For Catholics, see Schultz, *Miracle*, 27–28, 133–34; for Native Americans, see Miller, "1806 Purge," 251; and Wallace, *Death;* for Shakers, see Stein, *Shaker Experience,* 78–79; and Garrett, *Origins,* 138–39; for Mormons, see Bushman, *Stone;* Givens, *Hand of Mormon;* and Fluhman, *Anti-Mormonism,* 13, 19, 39, 40, 56.

27. Winiarski, "Pale Blewish Lights," 501. Edward Pearson's *Designs Against Charleston* features the sort of gaffe Winiarski worried about, when he refers to Pritchard's expertise as typical of "slaves . . . who still placed magic at the center of their world," creating a blanket statement that makes magic an either-or proposition and exoticizes Pritchard and his followers (*Designs,* 124).

28. See P. Morgan, *Slave Counterpoint,* 651; Dennis, *Seneca Possessed,* 65.

29. Bibb, *Narrative,* 26–28.

30. Douglass, *My Bondage and My Freedom,* in Andrews and Gates, *Slave Narratives,* 238–39. The treatment of race in American Enlightenment historiography awaits its historian. Leigh Eric Schmidt, for example, confines his discussion of disenchantment and race to a single paragraph, even though the language of race, civilization, and barbarism saturated the essays and publications of early national debunkers. In this way, he also misses the central political concerns of the case

against superstition and its efforts to define rationality (and citizenship) as the purview of white men (Schmidt, *Hearing Things*, 203).

31. Stroyer, *My Life*, 55–56.

32. Schmidt, *Hearing Things*, 203; Juster and Hartigan-O'Connor, "Angel Delusion," 379–80.

33. Elizabeth Reis has examined some of these (increasingly feminized) angelic visitations in "Immortal Messengers: Angels, Gender, and Power in Early America," in *Mortal Remains: Death in Early America*, ed. Nancy Isenberg and Andrew Burstein (Philadelphia: University of Pennsylvania Press, 2003), 163–75, but asserts that angelic visitations in the nineteenth century occurred against an assumed "traditional Protestantism" (175). As I discuss in chapter 1, the generalized concept of "traditional Protestantism" does not accurately describe the phenomenological outlook of the early United States.

34. *Candid Examiner* 2 (1827): 186–87, 197, 201.

35. Diary of Br. Joseph Mobberly, SJ, 1824, Booth Family Center for Special Collections, Georgetown University Library, Washington, DC.

36. Conference with Handsome Lake, Cornplanter, and Blue Eyes, Speech of Handsome Lake, 3/10/1802, in *The Papers of Thomas Jefferson: Presidential Series*, ed. Barbara Oberg (Princeton: Princeton University Press 2010), 37:33–34, 37.

37. *Testimonies of the Ever Blessed Mother Ann Lee* (hereafter 1816 *Testimonies*), 135–36.

38. Reis, "Immortal Messengers," 170–71; Sarah Alley, *Account of a Trance or Vision* (Philadelphia, 1807); William Babcock Journal, entry for 2/8/1802, American Antiquarian Society; Julia Foote, *A Brand Plucked from the Fire* (Cleveland: Schneider, 1879), 66–68; Russel, *Complete Fortune Teller*, 276.

39. Bell, "Breaking," 115. American historiography routinely lists Thomas as the primary (and often only) source on European magical beliefs. See, for example, Heyrman, *Southern Cross*, 274n1; Hatch, *Democratization*, 291n33; Anderson, *Conjure*, 52–55; and Dennis, *Seneca Possessed*, 11–12, 249–50n2.

40. Alex Owen, *The Place of Enchantment* (Chicago: University of Chicago Press, 1994); Thomas Kselman, *Miracles and Prophecies in Nineteenth-Century France* (New Brunswick, NJ: Rutgers University Press, 1983); David Blackbourn, *Marpingen: Apparitions of the Virgin Mary in Nineteenth-Century Germany* (New York: Knopf, 1994).

41. Klaniczay, *Uses*, 168. Recent studies of eighteenth- and nineteenth-century witchcraft include Owen Davies, *Magic, Witchcraft, and Culture, 1736–1951* (Manchester, UK: Manchester University, 1999); Jacqueline Van Gent, *Magic, Body, and the Self in Eighteenth-Century Sweden* (Boston: Brill, 2009); Krampl, "Witches"; Porter, "Witchcraft"; and Midelfort, *Exorcism*.

42. Coffin, *Memoir*, 70, 100. Recent historiography offers numerous variations on decline. Modernity itself may be enchanted—consumerism and mass entertainment providing a kind of greasepaint supernatural available for purchase (and in some ways, imposed upon the purchaser). Peters Pels suggests the "*supplementarity*

of magic and modernity, that is, the way in which many modern discourses position magic as their antithesis," thereby creating "correspondences and nostalgias by which magic can come to haunt modernity." Sasha Handley writes that reenchantment is unnecessary, given that beliefs in the supernatural never really disappeared in the first place. Owen Davies has demonstrated, in this vein, magic's survival and modern transformations through 1914 or possibly the 1960s (Handley, *Visions of an Unseen World: Ghost Beliefs and Ghost Stories in Eighteenth-Century England* [Brookfield, VT: Pickering and Chatto, 2007], 210–18; see also Peter Pels, "Introduction: Magic and Modernity," in *Magic and Modernity: Interfaces of Revelation and Concealment,* ed. Birgit Meyer and Pels [Stanford: Stanford University Press, 2003], 4–5).

43. Rankin, *Review,* 38–42.

44. Hall, *Worlds of Wonder.*

45. The works considered here are by and large not the great works of American political philosophy, but they are representative texts outlining an understanding of power and the idea of the supernatural that I take as a normative debate for the period—the context, that is, of the "great" works themselves. Quentin Skinner, *Foundations of Modern Political Thought* (Cambridge: Cambridge University Press, 1978), 1:xi–xii.

46. Burns, *Great Debate,* 12. On medieval problems of establishing miracles, see Finucane, *Miracles and Pilgrims*; and Ward, *Miracles and the Medieval Mind.*

47. See Poovey, *A History of the Modern Fact;* Shapiro, *Culture of Fact*; and Steven Shapin, *A Social History of Truth* (Chicago: University of Chicago Press, 1994).

48. Stephen Post Journal, entry for November 1835, box 6, folder 1, L. Tom Perry Special Collections, Harold B. Lee Library, Brigham Young University (hereafter HBLL).

49. John Thayer, *An Account of the Conversion of the Reverend John Thayer, Formerly a Protestant Minister of Boston, Written by Himself* (Hartford, 1832), 12–13, 17.

50. Isaac Post to Joseph and Mary Post, 11/23/48, Post Family Papers, Rare Books Special Collections & Preservation Department, University of Rochester.

51. Testimony of Abigail Crosman, 3/11/42, VI B-16, Shaker Western Reserve Historical Collection.

52. Book of Mormon (1830. Independence, MO: Herald Publishing House, 1973, 39, 477; modern edition 3 Nephi 11:15).

53. Midelfort, *Exorcism,* 57.

54. My terminology of "magic" and "religion" is fairly loose; nor have I specifically defined "modernity." My vagueness is intentional; I do not aim to provide an ironclad theory of religion and democracy but to gesture toward a recurrent theme in the early republic. Moreover, clear definitions fail us in this era when such definitions were being hashed out in the high tide of popular Enlightenment; as I note in chapter 2, Jeffersonian "magic" often relied on the power of Christian prayer for its efficacy.

55. Clark, *Thinking,* 549–59. On the king's touch, see Marc Bloch, *The Royal*

Touch: Sacred Monarchy and Scrofula in England and France, trans. J. E. Anderson (London: Routledge, 1973).

56. Clark, *Thinking*, 610–12.

57. Levack, *Witch-Hunting in Scotland*, 96; see also Clark, *Thinking*, 612n34. Both Bostridge and Sharpe date this politicization of British witchcraft to the Jane Wenham trial of the 1710s. See also Andrew Sneddon, *Witchcraft and Whigs: The Life of Bishop Francis Hutchinson* (Manchester, UK: Manchester University, 2008).

58. F. Hutchinson, *Historical Essay*, 181–82.

59. Manuel, *Confronts*, 47–53.

60. Joseph Lathrop, *Illustrations and Reflections on the Story of Saul's Consulting the Witch of Endor* (Springfield, MA, 1806), 14; Quitman, *Treatise*, 27.

61. Hudson, *Memoir*, 42, 88.

62. *Constitutional Whig*, 9/26/1831; reprinted in *Confessions of Nat Turner and Related Documents*, ed. Kenneth S. Greenberg (New York: St. Martin's, 1997), 81.

63. *Painesville (OH) Telegraph*, 11/18/1831.

64. Quitman, *Treatise*, 39.

65. Bentley, "History of Salem," 268.

66. English versions of Voltaire's *Dictionary* (which contained his comments) appeared in 1765, 1767, 1796, 1807, and 1827 (see Chadwick, *Secularization*, 146).

67. Upham, *Lectures*, vi–vii.

68. See John Fea, *Was America Founded as a Christian Nation?* (Louisville: WJK, 2011) for a thoughtful summary and discussion of both popular and historiographical notions of the "Christian nation" debate.

69. See David Sehat, *The Myth of American Religious Freedom* (New York: Oxford University Press, 2011); Michael I. Myerson, *Endowed by Our Creator: The Birth of Religious Freedom in America* (New Haven: Yale University Press, 2012); and Matthew Stewart, *Nature's God: The Heretical Origins of the American Republic* (New York: Norton, 2014).

70. It is not, therefore, that prophets "signified little" because a public sphere sans divine right kingship addressed only secular political concerns, as Susan Juster claims. War with the Red Sticks was a serious political crisis. John Lardas Modern has also noted the emergence of a secular public sphere in America that supported religion as "the exercise of one's freedom in private that is also beneficial to the public sphere." Other forms of religious practice will be less welcome in the republic. I deviate from Modern's interpretation of secularism existing "at the levels of emotion and mood, underneath the skin," not only because an examination of miracles rather than secularism reveals a host of individuals attributing religious change to ideas but also because Modern's analysis of language as a total system reveals a universe as flat and predictable as that of the social control theorists, with the ominous yet vaguely defined modernity always making decisions for people: "choice being made before it presents itself as such." Given Modern's overwhelming emphasis on elite

white writers, it is also questionable whether he really gets "underneath the skin" of modern secularism (Modern, *Secularism,* 6–7, 298).

71. New Hampshire *Patriot,* 9/1/1818; *Public Laws of the State of Connecticut* (Hartford, 1808), 1:659; *The Town Officer . . . as contained in the laws of the Commonwealth of Massachusetts* (Boston, 1802), 251; *Laws of the State of New Jersey* (1821), 248; *Laws of Maryland . . .* (Annapolis, 1801), 13 (unnumbered); Quinn, *Early Mormonism,* 27, 119. Quinn and Brooke both take Walter to be the man who "trained" Joseph Smith Jr. in rhabdomancy. The sources for this tradition emerged significantly after the fact (see Quinn, *Early Mormonism,* 117–18, 446n150; and Brooke, *Refiner's,* 152).

72. Smith, *Remarkable Occurrences,* 14–15; Stein, *Shaker Experience,* 61.

73. Qtd. in Howe, *Unvailed,* 140. See also Missouri *Intelligencer and Boon's Lick Advertiser,* 8/10/1833, reprinted in *Among the Mormons,* ed. William Mulder and A. Russell Mortensen (1958; Salt Lake City: Western Epics, 1994), 76–80.

74. David Thomas, *The Observer Trying the Great Reformation in This State* (Lexington, KY: Bradford, 1802), 7.

75. Andrew Jackson to Tennessee Troops, 4/2/1814, in *Papers of Andrew Jackson,* 3:57.

76. *Designs,* 280.

77. Smith, *History of the Church,* 3:203–4.

78. Black, "Poetics," 80–81.

79. Alexis de Tocqueville, *Democracy in America,* trans. Arthur Goldhammer (New York: Library of America, 2004), 831.

ONE The Language of the Supernatural

1. Stiles, *Diary,* 3:511.

2. Bushnell, *Nature and the Supernatural,* 438. Much of this chapter draws from Sophia Rosenfeld, *Common Sense: A Political History* (Cambridge: Harvard University Press, 2011).

3. Dwight, *Travels,* 2:135.

4. Acts 8:9–24.

5. Gerard Luttikhuisen, "Simon Magus as Narrative Figure," in *The Apocryphal Acts of Peter: Magic, Miracles and Gnosticism,* ed. Jan N. Bremmer (New York: Oxford University Press, 1998), 39–51.

6. Finucane, *Miracles,* 19–23; Acts 2:15.

7. Finucane, *Miracles,* 20.

8. Augustine, Letter 102:32, in *The Works of Saint Augustine,* 2:2, ed. Roland Teske (New York: New City Press, 2003), 36. See also Ward, *Miracles and the Medieval Mind,* 1–31.

9. Clare Stancliffe, *St. Martin and His Hagiographer: History and Miracle in Sulipicius Severus* (New York: Clarendon, 1983), 257; Finucane, *Miracles,* 50–51.

10. Finucane, *Miracles*, 51.

11. Shaw, *Miracles*, 122, 33–64; Bostridge, *Witchcraft*, 134; Elmer, "Saints or Sorcerers," 147; Walsham, *Providence*, chap. 4.

12. Shaw, *Miracles*, 30–33; Kenneth Silverman, *The Life and Times of Cotton Mather* (New York: Harper and Row, 1984), 127–31; Richardson qtd. in E. Brooks Holifield, *Theology in America* (New Haven: Yale University Press, 2003), 74–75; Hall, *Worlds of Wonder*, chap. 2.

13. Carol F. Karlsen, *The Devil in the Shape of a Woman* (New York: Vintage, 1989), 48–49; Burr, *Narratives*, 81–84; Demos, *Entertaining*, 389.

14. Brian Levack, "The Skeptical Tradition," in *The Witchcraft Sourcebook*, ed. Levack (New York: Routledge, 2004), 275.

15. John Higginson, "An Epistle to the Reader," in John Hale, *A Modest Enquiry into the Nature of Witchcraft* (1702; Boston: Kneeland and Adams, 1756), 3–5. Hale's *Modest Enquiry* (as well as Frances Hutchinson's *Essay*) were hard to come by in the British colonies, which again suggests that any effects they may have had were probably legal rather than popular.

16. See Brian P. Levack, "Crime and the Law," in *Witchcraft Historiography*, ed. Jonathan Barry and Owen Davies (New York: Palgrave, 2007), 146–63, quote at 152; and Levack, *Witch-Hunting*, 94–97, 134. On Salazar, see G. Henningsen, *The Witches' Advocate: Basque Witchcraft and the Spanish Inquisition, 1609–1611* (Reno: University of Nevada Press, 1980).

17. Daston and Park, *Wonders*, 121; Clark, *Thinking*, 251, 255; Elmer, "Saints or Sorcerers," 45.

18. William Turner qtd. in Clark, *Thinking*, 257.

19. Spencer, *Prodigies*, 2–3 (unnumbered).

20. My discussion of the preternatural and the quotes from Aquinas are from Daston and Park, *Wonders*, 121–22, 159–72. See also Clark, *Thinking*, 156–60.

21. Thomas, *Religion and the Decline of Magic*, 104, 89, 79–80.

22. Walsham, *Providence*, 167, 238, 136; Hall, *Worlds of Wonder*, 72.

23. Holifield, *Theology in America*, 73–74.

24. Mather, *Magnalia*, 2:449–51, 401.

25. Increase Mather, *Remarkable Providences*, in Burr, *Narratives*, 23–33.

26. Ibid., 9–10.

27. Spencer, *Prodigies*, 8 (unnumbered).

28. Daston, "Marvelous Facts," 115. Science and demons, however, still had a long history together to come (see Clark, *Thinking*, 264–300).

29. Shapiro, *Culture of Fact*, 169, 183; Daston, "Marvelous Facts," 108, 111, 112.

30. Burns, *Great Debate*, 20, 29, 41.

31. Ibid., chap. 3.

32. John Locke, *A Discourse on Miracles*, ed. I. T. Ramsey (Stanford: Stanford University Press, 1958), 83.

33. Shapiro, *Culture of Fact*, 168–72.

34. Thomas Sherlock, *Tryal of the Witnesses of the Resurrection of Jesus* (London: J. Roberts, 1729), 11, 13, 64.

35. On the use of miracles as a "middle way," see Shaw, *Miracles*, 2–5; Clark, *Thinking*, 255, Burns, *Great Debate*, chap. 1; and Michael Heyd, *Be Sober and Reasonable* (New York: Brill, 1995), 173–74.

36. See Woolston, A *Discourse on the Miracles of Our Saviour*, 2nd printing (London, 1727), 4, 15; see also Herbert Hovenkamp, *Science and Religion*, 10; Burns, *Great Debate*, 76–82; and Shaw, *Miracles*, 161–63. On the Anglophone prelude to Hume, see ibid., chap. 7; Chubb's 1741 *Discourse on Miracles* is discussed on pages 158–60.

37. Porter, "Witchcraft," 213.

38. Shaw, *Miracles*, 63 and conclusion.

39. Thomas Reid, *An Inquiry into the Human Mind*, ed. Derek R. Brookes (1997; University Park: Pennsylvania State University, 2000), 215; Hovenkamp, *Science and Religion*, 7–9.

40. See Bozeman, *Protestants*; Holifield, *Theology in America*, 159–394, esp. 174–96; Hazen, *Village Enlightenment*, 7–12; and Joyce E. Chaplin, *An Anxious Pursuit: Agricultural Innovation and Modernity in the Lower South, 1730–1815* (Chapel Hill: University of North Carolina Press, 1993), 23–55.

41. Bozeman, *Protestants*, 21. Reid and his fellow-thinkers in Edinburgh ("the Wise Club") openly acknowledged their debt to Anthony Ashley Cooper, third earl of Shaftesbury, who in 1709 conceived of common sense as a general agreement as to ethics in a public, political sense (see Rosenfeld, *Common Sense*, chap. 2).

42. Hovenkamp, *Science and Religion*, 10, 19; Bozeman, *Protestants*, 20–23.

43. Hitchcock qtd. in Robert L. Herbert, "The Sublime Landscapes of Western Massachusetts: Edward Hitchcock's Romantic Nationalism," *Massachusetts Historical Review* 12 (2010): 79.

44. Everett qtd in Hazen, *Village Enlightenment*, 9.

45. Dew qtd. in Henry May, *Enlightenment in America* (New York: Oxford University Press, 1976), 334.

46. Dwight, *The Nature and Danger of Infidel Philosophy* (New Haven: Bunce, 1798); *Raleigh (NC) Register*, 6/20/1843.

47. William Perkins Papers, Folio, American Antiquarian Society.

48. Archibald Alexander, *Evidences of the Authenticity, Inspiration and Canonical Authority of the Holy Scriptures* (1836); A. H. Lawrence, *An Examination of Hume's Argument on the Subject of Miracles* (1845); *North American Review* (1846), all reprinted in *Hume's Reception in Early America*, ed. Mark G. Spencer (Bristol, UK, 2002), 1:234–35, 263–64, 271.

49. Hovenkamp, *Science and Religion*, 23.

50. Benjamin Smith Barton, *Memoir Concerning the Fascinating Faculty Which Has Been Ascribed to the Rattle-Snake* (Philadelphia, 1796), 35, 8, vi, 49; Andrew Lewis, *A Democracy of Facts* (Philadelphia: University of Pennsylvania Press, 2011), chap. 1.

51. Noah Webster, *American Dictionary of the English Language* (New York: Con-

verse, 1828), emphasis original. The Baconian emphasis of American evangelicalism and American miracle claims undermines the repeated assertions in American historiography that takes, in Leigh Eric Schmidt's terms, "evangelicals to be the Enlightenment's most vociferous rebuttal." The fact that Christian thinkers and ecclesiarchs took Enlightenment methods in an unusual direction does not make them any less "enlightened" (Schmidt, *Hearing Things*, 8).

52. Hovenkamp, *Science and Religion*, 81; Samuel Stanhope Smith, *Lectures on the Evidences of the Christian Religion* (Philadelphia: Fry and Kammerer for Hopkins and Earle, 1809), 44–45. Smith included the same argument in his *Comprehensive View* (1815). Hume never discussed the king of Siam, but "Of Miracles" does reference a similar problem of a theoretical Indian who refused to believe in frost.

53. John Neal, *Wandering Recollections of a Somewhat Busy Life* (Boston, 1869), 17.

54. "Letter to the Christian Spectator on the Witness of the Spirit," *Methodist Magazine and Quarterly Review*, vol. 19 (New York: T. Mason and G. Lane, 1837), 460.

55. Gallitzin to Anastasia McSherry, 4/11/1839, in Joseph M. Finotti, *The Mystery of Wizard Clip* (Baltimore, 1879), 89. Ghost belief in America often kept the didactic function that Sasha Handley sees waning in British contexts (see Handley, *Visions*, 199–208).

56. James Carnahan, *Christianity Defended* (Utica, NY: Seward and Williams, 1808), 9.

57. John Leland, "A Short Narrative of a Five Hours' Conflict" (ca. 1811), in *The Writings of the Late Elder John Leland*, ed. L. F. Green (New York, 1845), 363.

58. Neal, *Rachel Dyer*, 25, emphasis original.

59. Whittier, *Supernaturalism*, 3, 7.

60. Grimes, *Life*, 61.

61. Pratt, *Dialogue*, 14.

62. John England, "Report to the Archbishop of Baltimore upon the Miraculous Restoration of Mrs. Ann Mattingly," in *The Works of John England* (Baltimore: John Murphy, 1849), 3:394–95, 396, 403, 425.

63. Dewey, *History of the Strange Sounds or Rappings*, ii.

64. Finney, *Lectures*, 5, 37; Carnahan, *Christianity Defended*, 7–8; Tunis Wortman, "A Solemn Address to Christians and Patriots" (New York, 1800), reprinted in *Political Sermons of the American Founding Era, 1730–1805*, ed. Ellis Sandoz, 2:1504; Rankin, *Review*, 27–28.

65. These three and other wonderful events were often referred to as "miracles"; see, for example, the *Columbia Centinel*, 9/15/1790; *Mercury* (Massachusetts) 2/28/1797; and *Utica (NY) Patrol*, 2/2/1815.

66. Allen, *Oracle*, 206, 256.

67. Finney, *Lectures*, 5, 12.

68. *Remarkable Account of Mrs. Rachel Lucas* (Newburyport: Gilmans, 1809), 6–9, 15.

69. Elias Lee, *A Letter to the Rev. James Carnahan* (Utica, NY: Walker, 1808), 4.

70. Bushnell, *Nature,* 438.

71. Barton Warren Stone, *A Short History of the Life of Barton W. Stone,* in James R. Rogers, *The Cane-Ridge Meeting House* (Cincinnati: Standard, 1910), 113–204, quote at 162.

72. McNemar, *Kentucky Revival,* 66–67.

73. Stone, *Short History,* 158.

74. Lyle diary, entry for 6/14/1801, Kentucky Historical Society.

75. *Increase of Piety,* 89; *Signs of the Times,* 4.

76. Carnahan, *Christianity Defended,* 7.

77. Daston, "Marvelous Facts," 114–20; Heyd, *Be Sober,* 173.

78. McLoughlin, *Dissent,* 2:714.

79. Allen, *Oracle,* 244.

80. *Debate Proposed in the Temple Patrick Society,* 3, 10, 12.

81. Chadwick, *Secularization,* 10.

82. Spencer, *Prodigies,* 6–7.

83. Pinchbeck, *Expositor,* 5; Pinchbeck, *Witchcraft,* 12.

TWO The Practice of the Supernatural

1. Davies, *Bewitched;* Peareson to Cooper, *Statutes,* 742–43. Joseph Doddridge also discussed witches transforming people into horses in *Notes,* 126.

2. *Statutes,* 743; *South Carolina Gazette* (Columbia), 11/10/1792.

3. *Charleston (SC) City Gazette,* 11/1/1793.

4. The lawyer was the deist Thomas Cooper (*Statutes,* 743).

5. *Gazette of the United States* (Philadelphia), 9/25/1804; William Powell, *Dictionary of North Carolina Biography* (Chapel Hill: University of North Carolina Press, 1979), 147.

6. Elaine Forman Crane, *Witches, Wife Beaters, and Whores* (Ithaca, NY: Cornell University Press, 2011), chap. 7; Marc Simmons, "History of the Pueblos since 1821," *Handbook of North American Indians* (New York: Smithsonian, 1979), 9:206–23.

7. Hohman, *Long-Lost Friend,* 41. Daniel Harms's critical edition is the most accurate scholarly version of the text.

8. Susan Juster's assertion, for example, that Anglo-American prophets operated in a world "devoid of miracles and other supernatural interventions" cannot be sustained (Juster, *Doomsayers,* 18).

9. On alchemy, see Herbert Leventhal, *In the Shadow of the Enlightenment* (New York: New York University Press, 1976), chap. 4; and Brooke, *Refiner's,* 17–44, 104–16, 257–60. For rattlesnakes, see Lewis, *Democracy,* 38ff; and for vampire exhumation, see Michael E. Bell, *Food for the Dead: On the Trail of New England's Vampires* (New York: Wesleyan University Press, 2001).

10. Richard Weisman, *Witchcraft, Magic, and Religion in Seventeenth Century Massachusetts* (Amherst: University of Massachusetts Press, 1984), 62.

11. Brooke, "Spiritual Seed," 108–9; Butler, *Awash*, 67, 93. Taking a magic-religion dichotomy as standard also shortchanges the religious practice and thinking of non-Europeans in the new republic (see p. 202–3n11).

12. See Dillinger and Davies, *Magic: A Very Short Introduction* (New York: Oxford University Press, 2012).

13. Monod, *Solomon's*, 1–19.

14. Dillinger, *Magical Treasure Hunting*, chap. 2.

15. McAfee Journal, entry for 7/31/1804, Filson Historical Society.

16. Quitman, *Treatise*, 26.

17. Doesticks, *Witches*, 18–21.

18. Quinn, *Early Mormonism*, 19.

19. Davies, *Grimoires*, 1, 189.

20. *Complete Fortune Teller* (1799), 8.

21. Russel, *Complete Fortune Teller*, 274.

22. Hohman, *Long-Lost Friend*, 41.

23. Davies, *Grimoires*, 70, 143, 149; *A Catalogue of the Books Belonging to the Library Company of Philadelphia* (Philadelphia: C. Sherman and Co., 1835) 1:188–92, 1:43; *A Catalogue of the Books Belonging to the Library Company of Philadelphia* (Philadelphia: Bartram and Reynolds, 1807), 4, 239.

24. Russel, *Complete Fortune Teller*, 265, 272, 263.

25. Hafez, *Oneirocritic*, 7–8.

26. Erra Pater, *The Book of Knowledge* (Boston: Folsom and Larkin, 1787).

27. Russel, *Complete Fortune Teller*, 278–79, 281; Hafez, *Oneirocritic*, 16, 51, 72, 74, 76, 103; *New Dream Book or Interpretation of Remarkable Dreams* (Baltimore, 1816), 10, 16, 21–22, 33; Felix Fontaine, *The Golden Wheel Dream-Book* (New York: Dick and Fitzgerald, 1862), 31, 37.

28. *The New Dream Book, or Interpretation of Remarkable Dreams* (Boston: Coverly, 1815), 17, 3; Russel, *Complete Fortune Teller*, 273, 275, 276.

29. Sibly, *New and Complete Illustration*, 1052–54; Monod, *Solomon's*, 275; Quinn, *Early Mormonism*, 11–22.

30. Sibly, *New and Complete Illustration*, 1101.

31. Ibid., 1102–8, 1113.

32. Ibid., 1094, 1118, 1120. The Nal-Gah symbol later appeared among the Smith family's magical implements (Quinn, *Early Mormonism*, 106–8).

33. Hohman, *Long-Lost*, 7–11, 20–22.

34. Ibid., 13, 16–19, 31. Most previous work on the *Friend* has looked at the text in isolation and misattributed its sources to Native Americans, Egyptians, or Druids.

35. Ibid., 71, 249n216, 76, 262n431.

36. Ibid., 51, 53, 58, 67.

37. Ibid., 76, 246n182, 276nn632–33, 84, 271n530. The age of the SATOR

square and its use as a fire extinguisher in German magic is noted at 77, 265n451.

38. Hamilton's 1786 notes are reprinted in Jilson, *Green Leaves from Whitingham*, 119.

39. Joshua Gordon Witchcraft Book, 1784, South Caroliniana Manuscripts, University of South Carolina Library.

40. Ibid.

41. Hohman, *Long-Lost Friend*, 39.

42. Baldwin, *Diary*, 177.

43. Davies, *Grimoires*, 194.

44. Pinchbeck, *Witchcraft*, 18–21. The American Antiquarian Society copy was formerly owned by Andrew Russell.

45. Hohman, *Long-Lost Friend*, 3, 19, 68–69. The attribution of the rabies cure comes from *Niles Weekly Register*, 10/11/17. See also Davies, *Bewitched*, 119–20.

46. Qtd. in Kay Moss, *Southern Folk Medicine, 1750–1820* (Columbia: University of South Carolina Press, 1999), 154.

47. Adelaide Fries, *Records of the Moravians in North Carolina* (Raleigh, NC: Edwards and Broughton, 1922–69), 5:2231.

48. Baldwin, *Diary*, 177–78.

49. Doddridge, *Notes*, 126.

50. Davies, *Bewitched*, 17.

51. Thomas Gooch Papers (d. 1869): Conference for the Logan Circuit . . . in Roberson County, 9/27/1828, Filson Historical Society.

52. *Maryland Gazette* (Annapolis), 7/25/1805; *Wilmington (DE) American Watchman*, 5/26/1810.

53. Philanthropist, *Ransford Rogers*, 7.

54. James Jenkins, *Experience, Labours, and Sufferings of James Jenkins* (n.p., 1842), South Carolina Historical Society, qtd. in Heyrman, *Southern Cross*, 90–91.

55. James Dean Hopkins, *Address to the Members of the Cumberland Bar* (Portland, ME: Charles Day, 1833), 31–32.

56. Davies, *Witchcraft*, 86, discusses the changed relationship in Britain between witch-finders and power: "For nearly two hundred years the victims of witchcraft had had easy access to official means of justice . . . elite authority and popular justice maintained a symbiotic relationship with regard to the threat of witchcraft. Though the witch-accusers were more concerned about getting rid of the particular witches who tormented them, elite authority was far more concerned about the threat of witchcraft to its own grip on power."

57. Webb, *Office and Authority of a Justice of the Peace* (Williamsburg: William Parks, 1736), 361–62; Leventhal, *Shadow*, 86.

58. *Washington Daily National Journal*, 8/18/31; Davies, *Bewitched*, 49–51.

59. *Portsmouth (NH) Journal of Literature and Politics*, 10/2/1824.

60. "Journal and Correspondence of the State Council of Maryland, 2/6/1787," *Archives of Maryland*, 215+ volumes (Baltimore and Annapolis, MD, 1883–), 71:171.

61. *Cahokia Records, 1778–1790* (Springfield: Illinois State Historical Library, 1907), 15.

62. Douglas Egerton, *He Shall Go Out Free: The Lives of Denmark Vesey* (Madison, WI: Madison House, 1999), 118–20; Lois Walker and Susan Silverman, introduction to *A Documented History of Gullah Jack Pritchard and the Denmark Vesey Slave Insurrection of 1822* (Lewiston, ME: Edward Mellen, 2000), v–vii. Egerton has summarized (and dismissed) the recrudescence of the claim that Vesey's conspiracy was the invention of fearful whites (see Egerton, "Forgetting Denmark Vesey, or, Oliver Stone Meets Richard Wade," *William and Mary Quarterly*, 3rd ser., vol. 49, no. 1 [January 2002]:143–52). See *Designs*, 15.

63. "Testimony of Y[orrick Cross?]," in *Designs*, 175–76.

64. "Trial of Gullah Jack," 7/11/1822, in *Designs*, 197.

65. *Providence (RI) Patriot*, 8/3/1822.

66. *Designs*, 197.

67. "Sentence on Jackson," *Designs*, 280. Chireau, *Black Magic*, 67, notes that although Pritchard was never referred to as a Christian, he might have considered himself one anyway.

68. *Philadelphia Independent Gazetteer*, 5/9/1787, 5/17/1787, 7/23/1787.

69. "Witchcraft Accusation against Polly Willey," 1795, New Hampshire Historical Society.

70. *Eastern Herald* (Portland, MA [ME]), 11/17/1796; Coffin, *Memoir*, 70.

71. *Rising Sun* (New Hampshire), 12/13/1796; Davies, *Bewitched*, 76.

72. *Eastern Herald* (Portland, MA [ME]), 11/17/1796.

73. *Baltimore Gazette and Daily Advertiser*, 11/10/1832.

74. *Boston Courier*, 10/21/1830.

75. Davies, *Bewitched*, 106; *National Advocate* (New York), 9/20/1822.

76. *Baltimore Sun*, 10/20/1838. According to the questionable account of W. C. Elam ("Old Times in Virginia and a Few Parallels," *Putnam's Magazine*, August 1869, 209), Yates survived and Marsh was imprisoned.

77. Doddridge, *Notes*, 126; Stroyer, *My Life*, 56; Anderson, *Conjure*, 41; Davies, *Bewitched*, 112.

78. Frederick Douglass, *Narrative of the Life of Frederick Douglass* (1845), in Andrews and Gates, *Slave Narratives*, 329.

79. Bibb, *Narrative*, 25.

80. William Wells Brown, *My Southern Home, or the South and Its People* (Boston: A. G. Brown, 1880), 70. This incident is also discussed in Yvonne P. Chireau, *Black Magic: Religion and the African American Conjuring Tradition* (Berkeley: University of California Press, 2003), 16–17. Conjure as power within slave communities is also discussed in P. Morgan, *Slave Counterpoint*, 610–58. With apologies for academic

quibbling, I take issue only with Morgan's statement that the "religious worldview of early American slaves was primarily magical, not Christian" (631). It is perhaps more accurate to say that early slave religion was predominantly "non-Christian," since magic and Christianity are not mutually exclusive.

81. Brown, *My Southern Home*, 71, 73.

82. William Wells Brown, *Narrative of William W. Brown, A Fugitive Slave, Written by Himself* (1847), in Andrews and Gates, eds., *Slave Narratives*, 414.

83. George Izard, "Diary of a Journey by George Izard, 1815–1816," *South Carolina Historical Magazine* 53, no. 4 (July 1952): 160.

84. Doesticks, *Witches*, 10, 13, 14, 8, 17–26, 57. The 1969 printing (Upper Saddle River, NJ: Gregg: 1969) identifies Doesticks as Thompson.

85. Ibid., 29, 18–21.

86. Richard Parkinson, *A Tour in America in 1798, 1799, and 1800* (London: T. Davison, 1805), 2:467–68.

87. Henry Tufts, *Autobiography of a Criminal* (1807; New York: Duffield, 1930), 148–49.

88. Joseph Pickering, *Inquiries of an Emigrant* (London: E. Wilson, 1832), 32.

89. Whittier to Sarah Josepha Hale, 1/24/1832, in *Letters of Whittier*, 1:71.

90. Lewis, *Lynn*, 208.

91. William Bentley, *Diary*, 4:162.

92. Lewis, *Lynn*, 207. For the correspondence between Whittier and Lewis, see *Letters of Whittier*, 1:66–67.

93. Lewis, *Lynn*, 236, 207–8.

94. Samuel Lorenzo Knapp, *Life of Lord Timothy Dexter* (Newburyport, MA, 1852), 85.

95. Amasa Delano, *A Narrative of Voyages and Travels in the Northern and Southern Hemispheres* (Boston: E. G. House, 1817), 30.

96. *Boston Weekly Magazine*, 2/12/1803; 2/26/1803, 4/2/1803, in *Boston Weekly Magazine* (Boston: Gilbert and Dean, 1803), 1:66, 74, 94. "Rebecca Plainly" later apologized but admonished Pitcher that a "serious, industrious, well informed woman, may find means of support, without having recourse to such mean and despicable artifice" (*Boston Weekly Magazine*, 4/16/1803, 1:102).

97. Taylor, "Supernatural," 26–27.

98. *Leaves*, 115–19; Leventhal, *Shadow*, 107–18. Butler and Taylor, among others, have consulted folkloric accounts collected in the later nineteenth century to detail the extent of treasure digging in the early republic. These works possessed didactic functions and perhaps cannot be relied upon to record the events of treasure hunts accurately. I have attempted here to employ only those histories from 1852 or before, or those that reproduce primary sources. Folklore recorded in the nineteenth century does tend to reproduce the same details as given by eighteenth- and early nineteenth-century sources, so perhaps this caution is unnecessary (see

Richard Dorson's warnings about "fakelore" in *American Folklore and the Historian* [Chicago: University of Chicago Press, 1971], 8–9; and *Jonathan Draws the Long Bow* [Cambridge: Harvard University Press, 1946]).

99. Edward Augustus Kendall, *Travels through the Northern Parts of the United States in the Years 1807 and 1808* (New York: Riley, 1809), 3:84.

100. *The Morristown Ghost, or "Yankee Trick"* (n.p., 1815), 9; Alan Taylor, *Civil War of 1812* (Knopf: New York, 2012), 90–91.

101. *Washington National Intelligencer*, 11–24–51; J. W. Hanson, *History of Gardiner, Pittston, and West Gardiner* (Gardiner, ME: William Palmer, 1852), 169.

102. Philanthropist, *Ransford Rogers*, 11; Jillson, ed., *Leaves*, 122; Merchant of Boston, *Nahant*, 26; *Herald of Freedom*, 12/1/1788.

103. Dillinger, *Magical*, 58.

104. "History of the Divining Rod," 321.

105. *Rochester Gem*, 5/15/1830, in Kirkham, *New Witness*, 2:48.

106. Howe, *History of Mormonism*, 237–38.

107. Philanthropist, *Ransford Rogers*, 14.

108. Dillinger, *Magical*, 61, 56, 121, 72, 62; Hamlet 1:1. A similar reference can be found in Marlowe's *Jew of Malta*, 2:1.

109. Dillinger, *Magical*, 76–78, 174–91.

110. "History of the Divining Rod," 223–24.

111. Howe, *History of Mormonism*, 239.

112. Thurlow Weed, *Life of Thurlow Weed* (Boston: Houghton and Mifflin, 1884), 7.

113. "History of the Divining Rod," 319.

114. Philanthropist, *Ransford Rogers*, 25.

115. Dillinger, *Magical*, 95.

116. Philanthropist, *Ransford Rogers*, 19.

117. Bentley, *Diary*, 3:358.

118. Nathaniel Stacy, *Memoirs of the Life of Nathaniel Stacy* (Columbus, PA: Abner Vedder, 1850), 171–72.

119. Marini, *Radical Sects*, 54–55; Barnes Frisbie, *The History of Middletown, Vermont* (Rutland, VT, 1867), 46–61.

120. "History of the Divining Rod," 321.

121. Merchant of Boston, *Nahant*, 26.

122. John Harriott, *Struggles through Life* (London: C. and W. Galabin, 1807), 217.

123. *Herald of Freedom*, 12/1/1788.

124. Joseph Williamson, "Castine, and the Old Coins Found There," *Collections of the Maine Historical Society*, ser. 1 (Portland: Maine Historical Society, 1859), 6:107–26, 115.

125. Atwater, "Antiquities," 119; Russel, *Complete Fortune Teller*, 272.

126. Josiah Priest, *American Antiquities and Discoveries in the West* (Albany, NY, 1833), 38–39. The remains were, of course, Native American.

127. *Massachusetts Spy*, 2/28/1810.

128. *Haverhill (MA) Gazette*, 8/23/1823.

129. Amory Edwards to George Brent, 8/27/1856, Alderman Library Special Collections, University of Virginia.

130. Russel, *Complete Fortune Teller*, 272. We should not assume that Russel's autobiography was penned by Russel herself, as noted above. If we are considering the supernatural as a debate, however, the referent to this remarkable story of treasure digging yielding freedom is irrelevant. The language of magic in the early republic was the language of freedom—literally, in Russel's case.

131. Hohman, *Long-Lost Friend*, 41.

132. Butler, *Awash*, 83; Whittier, *Supernaturalism*, 57; Baldwin, *Diary*, 176–79.

133. Willem de Blécourt, "On the Continuation of Witchcraft," in *Witchcraft in Early Modern Europe: Studies in Culture and Belief*, ed. Jonathan Barry, Marianne Hester, and Gareth Roberts (New York: Cambridge University Press, 1996), 337; Davies, *Witchcraft*, chap. 2.

134. "Old Whig," *Philadelphia Independent Gazetteer*, 11/1/1787.

THREE The Politics of the Supernatural

1. Andrew Oehler, *The Life, Adventures, and Unparalleled Sufferings of Andrew Oehler* (Trenton, NJ, 1811), 132, 133, 150.

2. Charles J. Pecor, *Magician on the American Stage* (Washington, DC, 1977), 105ff. Further evidence weighs against Oehler's truthfulness. Oehler's descriptions of the viceroy bear no resemblance to the men who actually held that post in 1807–8. Moreover, the colonial legal systems of Latin America were "highly developed and would have surprised any Anglo-American jurist of the period" (Carlos A. Forment, *Democracy in Latin America, 1760–1900* [Chicago: University of Chicago Press, 2003], 1:42).

3. *Debates & Proceedings of the Congress of the United States*, 12th Cong., 1385.

4. Ibid., 1398.

5. Whitman, *Popular Superstitions*, 63.

6. Whittier, *Supernaturalism*, ix.

7. Cook, *Arts of Deception*, 175–76, unequivocally accepts Oehler's story and takes Oehler as evidence that Americans understood magic in a more "rational" way than did Mexicans or Spaniards. As the real reception of Robertson in 1798 suggests, Mexicans were not, in fact, any less rational or rationalizing than Americans; in fact, those terms are problematic when applied to the late eighteenth and early nineteenth centuries.

8. Krampl, "When Witches," 137–54.

9. Klaniczay, quoting Konstantin Franz von Cauz's *De cultibus magicis*, 177.

10. Michael Ostling, *Between the Devil and the Host* (New York: Oxford University Press, 2011), 22, 59–60.

11. Manuel, *Confronts*, 47. Leigh Eric Schmidt extends Manuel's assessment to the English Whig tradition, where, he argues, "unmasked oracles were a token of republicans" (Schmidt, *Hearing Things*, 27). Schmidt neglects the ways in which this "unmasking" was not merely the revelation of information, but a cultural attack, often directed at women and nonwhites.

12. Clark, *Thinking*, 474–75. Superstition was a diabolical problem as well. False or empty ceremonies tempted demons to provoke magical and not miraculous cures, giving Satan a point of entry into the lives of the faithful.

13. Thacher, *Demonology*, 63.

14. Whitman, *Popular Superstitions*, 63.

15. Whittier, *Supernaturalism*, 1–3.

16. Reese, *Humbugs*, 22–23, 266.

17. Whitman, *Popular Superstitions*, 5.

18. Thacher, *Demonology*, 76.

19. Whitman, *Popular Superstitions*, 33.

20. Thacher, *Demonology*, 1.

21. Enoch Lincoln, *The Village* (Portland, MA [ME]: Edward Little, 1816), 50–52. The poem came appended with essays on its themes, including one on "Sketches of the Follies and Cruelties of Superstition."

22. Young, *Wonderful History*, 72, 21, 31. As Owen Davies points out, this conception of witchcraft as imagined was *a* belief at the end of the nineteenth century. Davies further warns that reducing witchcraft beliefs to a single "popular" and a single "elite" viewpoint is not tenable. My comments on "antiwitchcraft" are therefore intended as a broad description of a repeated argument found in multiple cultural contexts in the early republic, not as the sole or even the (exclusively) elite point of view (see Davies, *Witchcraft*, 1–29, 79–100, 120–24).

23. Diarmiad MacCulloch, *The Reformation: A History* (New York: Penguin, 2003), 564.

24. Upham, *Salem Witchcraft*, 90.

25. Pinchbeck, *Expositor*, 12.

26. Whittier, *Supernaturalism*, vii, ix, 13.

27. Upham, *Salem Witchcraft*, vi–vii.

28. *Boston Investigator*, 9/1/1841.

29. Aaron C. Willey, "Observations on Magical Practices," *Medical Repository of Original Essays and Intelligence*, February–April 1812.

30. "An Act Relating to Vagrants in the City of Baltimore," 1804, in *Laws of the State of Maryland*, ed. Virgil Maxcy (Baltimore, Nicklin and Co., 1811), 3:211; *Public Laws of the State of Connecticut* (Hartford: Hudson and Goodwin, 1808), 1:689; New York, *Laws of the State of New-York* (Albany, NY, 1813), 1:114.

31. Clark, *Thinking*, 579–80. See also Davies, *Witchcraft*, 8–11, on Toryism and witchcraft in eighteenth-century Britain.

32. A Connecticut Brick-Layer [Thomas Anderson], *Superstition Detected* (Philadelphia, 1831), 9.

33. Bengt Ankarloo and Stuart Clark, introduction to *Witchcraft and Magic: The Eighteenth and Nineteenth Centuries*, ed. Ankarloo and Clark (Philadelphia: University of Pennsylvania Press, 1999), xii.

34. Jefferson to John Taylor, 6/4/1798, in *The Papers of Thomas Jefferson*, 30:388–89.

35. Gould, "Witch-Hunting," 58–82; Adams, *Specter of Salem*.

36. Sharpe, *Instruments of Darkness*, 42.

37. See Joseph R. Roach, *Cities of the Dead: Circum-Atlantic Performance* (New York: Columbia University Press, 1996); Jason Shaffer, *Performing Patriotism: National Identity in the Colonial and Revolutionary American Theater* (Philadelphia: University of Pennsylvania Press, 2007).

38. James Nelson Barker, *The Tragedy of Superstition* (Philadelphia, 1826), 44, 46.

39. Payne, J. H. *Mahomet* (1809; 2003), 5, 17, 23, American Drama Full-Text Database, Cambridge: ProQuest Information and Learning.

40. Ibid., 10, 17, 19.

41. William Milns, *The Comet, or He Would Be an Astronomer* (Baltimore, 1817) 19. The play was performed first in 1797; there were British, American, five-act, and two-act versions (George Oberkirsh Seilhamer, *History of American Theatre* [New York: Scholarly, 1968], 3:388).

42. Tobias S. Alltruth [Reynaldo de Moscheto], *The Magician and the Holy Alliance* (Philadelphia, 1820), 24. The serpent is probably an allusion to the sea serpent sighted off the coast of New England in the 1810s (see Chandos Michael Brown, "A Natural History of the Gloucester Sea Serpent: Knowledge, Power, and the Culture of Science in Antebellum America," *American Quarterly* 42, no. 3 [September 1990]: 402–36).

43. Thomas Forrest, *The Disappointment, or the Force of Credulity* (Madison: A-R Editions, 1976), 43, 47, 50, 89–90, 105–9.

44. See Jennifer Mason, *Civilized Creatures: Urban Animals, Sentimental Culture, and American Literature, 1850–1900* (Baltimore: Johns Hopkins University Press, 2005), 72.

45. Schmidt, *Hearing Things*, 78–80. Schmidt's history of hearing in the early United States is one of the most recent variations on Weber's disenchantment thesis. Yet far from hearing "loss," Upham wrote in 1867 that "the principal difference in the methods by which communications were believed to be made between mortal and spiritual beings, at the time of the witchcraft delusion and now, is this. Then it was chiefly by the medium of the eye, but at present by the ear" (Upham, *Salem Witchcraft*, 605).

46. *Ghost Stories Collected with a Particular View to Counteract the Vulgar Belief in*

Ghosts and Apparitions and to Promote a Rational Estimate of the Nature or Phenomena Commonly Considered as Supernatural (London, 1823), xvi; U.S. edition 1846.

47. Whittier, *Supernaturalism*, 13–14, 21–22.

48. G. S. C., *Amusement for Good Children* (Baltimore: Warner and Hanna, 1808), 13–16; S. Hays, *Tales for Little Children* (New York: Wood, 1810?), 34.

49. Thacher, *Demonology*, 10–11.

50. Upham, *Lectures*, 147. The Witch of Endor was cited in other period discussions of witchcraft; see, for example, James Newhall, *Lecture on the Occult Sciences, Embracing Some Account of the New England Witchcraft* (Salem, MA, 1845), 8; Whitman, *Popular Superstitions*, 37; Thacher, *Demonology*, 74; *Debate Proposed*, 19.

51. Quitman, *Treatise*, 46.

52. Lathrop, *Illustrations*, 14.

53. Hannah More, "Tawney Rachel," in *Selected Writings of Hannah More*, 60–61, 68; William Godwin, *Lives of the Necromancers* (London: Frederick Mason, 1834), vii, 247, 218, 360–61.

54. Robert Calef, *More Wonders of the Invisible World*, 1700, in Burr, *Narratives*, 304.

55. Gould cites the histories of Salem from 1790 to 1830 as "reflect[ing] the political and social anxieties rampant in the Early Republic." Gretchen Adams traces this political lineage back at least to 1738. I agree with both of them but argue that the important shift is where these political accounts lay the blame—and that this rhetoric was not *merely* metaphor, but an actual fear of "witches" subverting democracy.

56. Hutchinson, *History*, 2:44.

57. Bentley, "History of Salem," 268–70.

58. H. Adams, *History*, 82, 83.

59. Joseph Story, "Discourse Pronounced at the Request of the Essex Historical Society, September 18, 1828," in *The Miscellaneous Writings* (Boston: James Munroe 1835), 80–82.

60. George Barstow, *The History of New Hampshire* (Concord, NH: I. S. Boyd, 1842), 64–70. Barstow went on to serve as a legislator in the new state of California.

61. Upham is far more famous for his later work on the trials, *Salem Witchcraft*, in 1867, from which Paul Boyer and Stephen Nissenbaum drew their map of Salem in *Salem Possessed*. Most of what is in *Lectures* can be found in *Witchcraft*, but the reverse is not true; in the 1867 version, Upham added an extensive section on the social and economic conditions of Salem village, an aside on hallucinatory experience, and an extensive supplement on those who objected to the trials. The 1831 version, by contrast, is much more narrowly focused on the problem of superstition, credulity, and order (see Upham, *Salem Witchcraft*, 1–214, 317–22, 617–82).

62. Upham, *Lectures*, 57, 278.

63. Upham, *Lectures*, 114, 103–10, 89.

64. John C. M'Call, *The Witch of New England* (Philadelphia: Carey and Lea, 1824), 99.

65. Neal, *Rachel Dyer*, 45.

66. Jonathan M. Scott, *The Sorceress, or Salem Delivered* (New York: Charles Baldwin, 1817), viii.

67. Eliza Lee, *Delusion, or the Witch of New England* (Boston: Gray Hilliard, 1840), 124, 150–53.

68. Elam Bliss, *Salem Witchcraft, or Parson Handy of Punkapog Pond* (New York, 1827).

69. William Dunlap, "Tom Bell," *Pensacola (FL) Gazette*, 12/3/36.

70. *European Ventriloquist's Exhibition* (Portsmouth, NH, 1808), 4.

71. For related arguments, see Cook, *Arts of Deception*, 177–80.

72. *The Art of Conjuring Made Easy* (New York, 1822), 5, emphasis added.

73. Day Francis the Great, *Stanislas Outdone: The New Hocus Pocus, or the Whole Art of Legerdemain* (Philadelphia: Nathaniel Hickman, 1818), 18. This description of the gravesite of the prophet Muhammad is wholly fictional. Ricky Jay identifies Day Francis in *Many Mysteries Revealed or, Conjuring Literature in America, 1786–1874* (Worcester, MA: American Antiquarian Society, 1990).

74. *Ventriloquism Explained, and Juggler's Tricks, or Legerdemain Exposed, with Remarks on Vulgar Superstitions* (Amherst, MA, 1834), 40.

75. Chadwick, *Secularization*, 10; Bentley, "History of Salem," 268.

76. *Debate Proposed*, 9. Men were, of course, seized and executed as witches "in earlier times."

77. More, *Selected Writings*, 61, 69.

78. *Boston Liberator*, 3/9/1838.

79. Reese, *Humbug*, vi.

80. Scott, *The Sorceress*, 89–90.

81. Quitman, *Treatise*, 54.

82. *Memoir of Simon Wilhelm . . . with Some Account of the superstitions of West Africa* (New Haven, 1819), 90.

83. Pinchbeck, *Witchcraft*, 14.

84. R. Johnson, *False Alarms* (Philadelphia, 1802), 10–11, 17.

85. Whitman, *Popular Superstitions*, 59.

86. "The Haunted House . . . A Fact," *Indiana Journal*, 11/8/1825.

87. *Ventriloquism Explained* (Amherst, MA, 1834), 14–15.

88. *Brattleboro (VT) Weekly Eagle*, 4/24/1851; *Middletown (CT) Constitution*, 12/31/1851; *Connecticut Courant* (Hartford), 3/14/1846. The story of the frightened slave and master was widely reprinted; see, for example, *Easton (MD) Gazette*, 10/5/1839; and *Hallowell (ME) Gazette*, 2/7/1840.

89. "Legend of Sleepy Hollow," in *Washington Irving: History, Tales, and Sketches*, ed. James W. Tuttleton (New York, 1983), 1061–63.

90. Ibid., 1069.

91. Ibid., 1062–66, 1085.

92. Sharpe, *Instruments of Darkness*, 100.

FOUR Shakers

1. Smith, *Remarkable Occurrences*, 5, 8, 17, 20–22; Benjamin Seth Youngs, "Transactions of the Ohio Mob," 8/31/1810, V:B-235, Shaker Collection of the Western Reserve Historical Society (hereafter OClWHi).

2. Smith, *Remarkable Occurrences*, 14–15.

3. McNemar, "The Heavenly Bridegroom & Bride," in *Millennial Praises: A Shaker Hymnal*, ed. Christian Goodwillie and Carol Medlicott (Amherst: University of Massachusetts Press, 2009), 59.

4. Tyler Parsons, *Mormon Fanaticism Exposed* (Boston, 1841), 5; West, *Scriptural Cautions*, 5; affidavit of Sarah Bean, in Dyer, *Portraiture*, 35.

5. Haskett, *Shakerism Unmasked*, 131.

6. Stiles, *Diary*, 2:510–11.

7. *The Testimony of Christ's Second Appearing*, 1810, xiv (hereafter 1810 *Testimony*).

8. Brown, *An Account*, 4–5, 44–48, 98, 83.

9. The literature of Shakers is vast. See, among many, Stein, *Shaker Experience;* Marini, *Radical Sects*; Diane Sasson, *The Shaker Spiritual Narrative* (Knoxville: University of Tennessee Press, 1983); Priscilla J. Brewer, "'Tho' of the Weaker Sex': A Reassessment of Gender Equality among the Shakers," *Signs* 17, no. 3 (1992); Jean M. Humez, "'Ye Are My Epistles': The Construction of Ann Lee Imagery in Early Shaker Sacred Literature," *Journal of Feminist Studies in Religion* 8 (1992): 83–103. Quotations are from Glendyne Wergland, *Sisters in the Faith: Shaker Women and the Equality of the Sexes* (Amherst: University of Massachusetts Press, 2011), 4.

10. 1816 *Testimonies*, vi, 1–2.

11. Marini, *Radical Sects*, 152; Joseph Meacham, *Concise Statement of the Principles of the Only True Church* (Bennington, VT: Haswell and Russell, 1790), 3.

12. 1816 *Testimonies*, 206.

13. David Meacham et al. to the Kentucky revivalists, 12/30/1804; reprinted in MacLean, *Shakers of Ohio*, 61.

14. Stein, *Shaker Experience*, 4–5. Garrett, *Origins*, and others linked Shaker practices and beliefs to the French Prophets; Stein notes that direct causal evidence is lacking in this case. Anti-Shaker tracts compared Shaker worship to the French Prophets' eccentricities, but the Prophets were routinely mentioned as destabilizing wonder-workers in the antisupernatural formulation. It was a stock comparison, and literal connections between the groups were probably more fancied than real.

15. John Gates Diaries, entry for 5/19/1780, reel 4.6, Pre-Revolutionary War Diaries, Massachusetts Historical Society, Boston.

16. Ibid. *Massachusetts Spy*, 6/15/1780; William McLoughlin, ed., "Olney Winsor's 'Memorandum' of the Phenomenal 'Dark Day' of May 19, 1780," *Rhode Island History* (Winter 1967): 88–90; *Boston Independent Chronicle & Universal Advocate*, 6/8/1780.

17. The historiography on the Dark Day tends toward realist assumptions about natural and supernatural phenomena. One confident assertion that "we now know" the Dark Day was caused by "the common New England practice of burning fields" suggests an easy equation of natural explanations with knowledge and, therefore, of supernatural explanations with error, and from there, to explaining supernaturalism as category mistake (Juster, "Demagogues or Mystagogues? Gender and the Language of Prophecy in the Age of Democratic Revolutions," *American Historical Review* 104, no. 5 [December 1999]: 1560).

18. David Hall diary, entry for 5/20/1780, reel 5, Pre-Revolutionary War Diaries, Massachusetts Historical Society, Boston; William McLoughlin, ed., "Olney Winsor's 'Memorandum' of the Phenomenal 'Dark Day' of May 19, 1780," *Rhode Island History* 7, no. 26 (Winter 1967): 88–90; Issachar Bates, "Sketch of the Life and Experience of Issachar Bates," ed. Theodore E. Johnson, *Shaker Quarterly* 1 (1961): 98–118, 145–63, and 2 (1962): 18–35, quote on 114. On the Dark Day and Bates's conversion, see Carol Medlicott, *Issachar Bates: A Shaker's Journey* (Hanover, NH: University Press of New England, 2013), 38–42, and xvi–xvii on the multiple versions of Bates's narrative.

19. William Plumer, "Plumer's Account of the Shaker Communities in New England," *New England Magazine*, 1900, 304–9; "A Memorandum: Wrote by Isaac Youngs," V:A-3 OClWHi.

20. Marini, *Radical Sects*, 93.

21. *Minutes of the Commissioners for Detecting and Defeating Conspiracies in the State of New York* (Albany, 1910), 2:452–53, 723–24. See also 1816 *Testimonies*, 70–71.

22. Rathbun, *Account*, 5, 10, 12. Rathbone dated his missive 12/5/1780; it was published in 1781.

23. Isaac Youngs, "My Journey Continued," V:A-5, OClWHi.

24. Francois Marquis de Barbé-Marbois, qtd. in Wergland, ed., *Visiting the Shakers*, 14–15.

25. Bates, "Sketch," 1:117, 2:145.

26. 1816 *Testimonies*, 258–59, 254, 52, 255–59, 271 (mislabeled 251).

27. Benjamin Silliman, *A Tour to Quebec* (London: Phillips and Co., 1822), 10.

28. 1816 *Testimonies*, 43, 169; Kendall qtd. in *The Shakers: Two Centuries of Spiritual Reflection*, ed. Robley Edward Whitson (New York, Paulist, 1983), 47; "Incidents Related by Jemima Blanchard of Her Experience and Intercourse with Mother Ann and Our First Parents," written by Roxalana L. Grosvenor, copied by Eliza Rebecca Smith, Item # 1-TB-030, Collection of the United Society of Shakers, Sabbathday Lake, Inc.

29. Brown, *An Account*, 82.

30. Dwight, *Travels*, 3:152.

31. Stein, *Shaker Experience*, 42.

32. On the creation of these works, see ibid., 66–87.

33. *Testimony of Christ's Second Appearing* (Lebanon, OH: McLean, 1808), 468 (hereafter 1808 *Testimony*).

34. Ibid.; 1816 *Testimonies* 33; 1810 *Testimony*, xv.

35. 1810 *Testimony*, 475, 493.

36. Ibid., 476n, 474, 482.

37. 1816 *Testimonies* 255, 51, 258–59.

38. Ibid., 392, 381–87.

39. Stein, *Shaker Experience*, 82, 79; 1816 *Testimonies*, iv and xii.

40. 1816 *Testimonies*, 254, 52, vi; 1810 *Testimony*, xv.

41. Brown, *An Account*, 17–18.

42. William S. Byrd to Williamson, 10/28/1827, in *Letters from a Young Shaker*, 110–11.

43. Autobiography of Abijiah Worster, 1826, VI:A-5, OClWHi.

44. Stephen Stein, "'A Candid Statement of Our Principles': Early Shaker Theology in the West," *Proceedings of the American Philosophical Society* 133, no. 4 (1989): 503–19, quote at 506; *Shakers of Ohio*, 63; "Church Record . . . of the Shaker Community at Pleasant Hill," item 27, Library of Congress Manuscript Shaker Division (hereafter DLCMs).

45. Barton Warren Stone, *Biography of Elder Barton Warren Stone*, ed. John Rogers (Cincinnati, 1847), 38, 61–64; "Extract of a Letter from John Dunlavy to Barton W. Stone, and Other Writings Concerning the 'Kentucky Revival,'" item 29, DLCMs.

46. Bates to Seth Wells, 4/12/1815; Peter Pease to Richard Speir, 12/12/1807, item 245, DLCMs.

47. Byrd, *Letters*, 113.

48. *Report of the Examination of the Shakers at Canterbury and Enfield* (Concord, NH: Ervin Tripp, 1848), 74–75; Eyewitness, *Extract from an Unpublished Manuscript on Shaker History* (Boston: E. K. Allen, 1850), 22.

49. Diary of Rufus Bishop, entry for 10/8/1837, microfilm, New York Public Library; Rufus Bishop to "Much Beloved Ministry" [Union Village?], 1/25/1839, IV:B-36, OClWHi; Testimony of Orren N. Haskins, New Lebanon, 1/27/1842, IV:B-16, OClWHi.

50. Diary of Rufus Bishop, entry for 10/1/1837.

51. Watervliet Church Family Meeting Journal, 1838–1840, reprinted in Jean Humez, *Mother's First Born Daughters: Early Shaker Writings on Women and Religion* (Bloomington: Indiana University Press, 1993), 230–37.

52. C. B., 1841 *Lowell Offering*, reprinted in Wergland, ed., *Visiting*, 285.

53. Ann Mariah Goff's vision, 1/11/1838, IV-B-36, OClWHi.

54. Jefferson White, untitled vision, 12/6/1840, item 6, DLCMs.

55. "A Short Sketch of the Last Sickness of Deacon Nathan Tiffany," February 1840, item 6, DLCMs.

56. Oliver Spencer to South Union, 6/20/1838, IV:B-36, OClWHi.

57. Lamson, *Two Years'*, 79; "A message from our heavenly parents . . . 1842," item 13, DLCMs.

58. Stein, *Shaker Experience*, 165, 183; Louis J. Kern, *An Ordered Love: Sex Roles and Sexuality in Victorian Utopias* (Chapel Hill: University of North Carolina Press, 1991), 105–13.

59. See Humez, *Mother's*, 119–21, 124; and Brewer, *Shaker Communities, Shaker Lives* (Hanover, NH: University Press of New England, 1986), chap. 7, for the argument that the leaders co-opted the revivals for their own purposes. Stein, *Shaker Experience*, 121–22, connects Mother Ann's Work to revitalization.

60. *American Museum or Repository*, 2/1/1787, 149–50.

61. Moses Guest, *Poems on Several Occasions*, reprinted in Wergland, ed., *Visiting*, 25.

62. Ministry at Pleasant Hill to Elders at New Lebanon, 2/23/1820, IV:A-53, OClWHi; Haskett, *Shakerism Unmasked*, 291.

63. Jackson, *Gifts of Power*, 114, 164.

64. Ibid., 178.

65. Hervey Elkins, *Fifteen Years in the Senior Order of the Shakers* (Hanover, NH: Dartmouth Press, 1853), 43.

66. Freegift Wells to Ministry at Pleasant Hill, 3/23/1838, B:IV-36, OClWHi.

67. Testimony of Abigail Crosman, 3/11/42, VI:B-16, OClWHi.

68. Freegift Wells, "A Series of Remarks Showing the Power of the Adversary in Leading Honest Souls Astray," 1/31/1850, VII:B-266, OClWHi.

69. Oliver Spencer to South Union, 6/20/1838, B:IV-36, OClWHi.

70. Dunlavy, *Manifesto* (Pleasant Hill, KY, 1818), 18, 255, 257, 259.

71. Elkins, *Fifteen Years*, 75–76.

72. Garrett, *Origins*, 195, has suggested that Shakers *may* have engaged in nude worship in their earliest American services. This purported activity would explain the perennial charge of nudism against the Shakers, yet the explanation also depends on the realist fallacy that all rumors hide a kernel of truth at their center. Internal Shaker documents do not mention nude dancing.

73. Stiles, *Diary*, 2:510.

74. West, *Scriptural Cautions*, 4, 12–13.

75. John Murray, *Bath-Kol* (Boston: Coverly, 1783), 89–90.

76. Rathbun, *An Account*, 34–35.

77. Murray, *Bath-Kol*, 83; Rathbun, *An Account*, 15.

78. *Theological Magazine* 1 (Sept.–Oct. 1795): 81–87.

79. Wergland, ed., *Visiting*, 27–28.

80. West, *Scriptural Cautions*, 4.

81. Taylor, "Treasure Seeking," 17, 3.

82. Lamson, *Two Years'*, 30, 28.

83. Dwight, *Travels*, 3:153, 169. Dwight derisively noted of the evidences in the *Testimonies*, "The witnesses are all Shakers" (3:160).

84. Backus, *Church History*, 2:410.

85. *Herald of the United States*, 1/23/1796; *Hartford (CT) Gazette*, 3/20/1794; *Spooner's Vermont Journal*, 10/6/1806.

86. Haskett, *Shakerism Unmasked*, 131.

87. *Western Star*, reprinted in the *Norwich (CT) Packet*, 2/11/1796.

88. Rathbun, *An Account*, 34–35; Dyer qtd. in Stein, *Shaker Experience*, 85.

89. *Report of the Examination*, 5–7, 9, 16, 19–24.

90. See Jortner, "The Political Threat of a Female Christ: Ann Lee, Morality, and Religious Freedom in the United States, 1780–1819," *Early American Studies* 7 no. 1 (Spring 2009): 179–204.

91. Smith, *Detected*, 4–5; Eunice Chapman, *No. 2* (Albany: I. W. Clark, 1818), 77.

92. Chapman, *No. 2*, 75.

93. Lamson, *Two Years'*, 27.

94. Green, Benjamin. *The True Believer's Vademecum, or, Shakerism Exposed* (Concord, NH, 1831), 11–12.

95. Smith, *Detected*, 4–5.

96. Wallace qtd. in Youngs, "Transactions of the Ohio Mob," 8/31/1810, V:B-235, OclWHi. On eighteenth-century mobs as engines to enforce community solidary, see Paul Gilje, *Rioting in America* (Bloomington: Indiana University Press, 1999), chap. 2.

97. 1816 *Testimonies*, 93–104.

98. Ibid., 113–27. The Shakers returned to Harvard, where in June 1783 another mob arose to beat and whip them (147–53).

99. Bates, "Sketch," 1:162, 109–10; Letter from Ohio Shakers to Elders at New Lebanon, 12/19/1805, reprinted in *Shaker Quarterly* 12 (1972): 107–16.

100. Lucy Smith to Ruth Landon, 8/12/1825, in Letters and True Copies of Letters Sent to the New Lebanon, NY, Community, 1820–1831, Edward Deming Andrews Memorial Shaker Collection, Winterthur Library; Stein, *Shaker Experience*, 98.

101. "Incidents Related by Jemima Blanchard," 12.

102. 1816 *Testimonies*, 171.

103. Benjamin Youngs to Matthew Houston, 10/20/1806, IV:A-52, OClWHi.

104. "Account of the Persecution at Harvard in the Year 1830," Edward Deming Andrews Memorial Shaker Collection, Winterthur Library. The jury found the Shakers not guilty, but the affair "exposed us to considerable cost & much trouble."

105. Church Record, Pleasant Hill, 1845, item 27, DLCMs.

106. Qtd. in Stein, *Shaker Experience*, 50.

107. McNemar and Calvin Morrell, *An Address to the State of Ohio* (Lebanon, OH: George Smith, 1818).

108. *Shakers of Ohio*, 15–17n; Leander W. Cogswell, *History of the Town of Henniker, Merrimack County, New Hampshire* (Concord: Republican Press, 1880), 90–91; Robert F. W. Meader, "Another Lost Utopia," *Shaker Quarterly* 4:1 (Fall 1964), 123–24.

109. Bentley, *Diary*, 3:426; *Shakers of Ohio*, 286–87, 290.

110. Herman Melville, *Moby-Dick*, chap. 71.

FIVE Native American Prophets

1. Harrison, *Messages and Papers*, 1:183.

2. Draper, 12YY20, Draper Manuscripts.

3. *Washington National Intelligencer*, 9/10/06.

4. Draper, 3YY59, Draper Manuscripts.

5. McNemar, *Kentucky Revival*, 112. McNemar quoted "Bluejacket," who may have been Blue Jacket, the great Shawnee strategist, or his son George Bluejacket.

6. Dunham to Hull, 5/20/07, *Michigan Historical Collections* (Lansing: Michigan Historical Commission, 1929), 40:123 (hereafter MHC); Draper, 1YY38, 12YY8, Draper Manuscripts. The New Madrid quakes as a supernatural event are often attributed to Tecumseh, but the contemporary reports mentioned the Prophet in conjunction with the quakes. See, for example, *Moravian Indian Mission*, 413.

7. Letter of Van Quickenbourne, in Garraghan, *Jesuits*, 1:388.

8. Andrew Jackson to Tennessee Troops, 4/2/1814, in *Papers of Andrew Jackson*, 3:57.

9. Drake, *Tecumseh*, 87.

10. Catlin, *North American Indians*, 364.

11. L. Morgan, *League of the Iroquois*, 220. Morgan's literary efforts regarding the Iroquois are covered in greater detail in Philip Deloria, *Playing Indian* (New Haven: Yale University Press, 1998), chap. 3; and Modern, *Secularism*, chap. 3.

12. Wallace's theory first appeared in "Revitalization Movements," *American Anthropologist*, 8, no. 2 (April 1956): 264–81, and received fuller treatment in *Death and Rebirth*.

13. Hunter, "Delaware Nativist Revival," 40.

14. Cave, *Prophets*, 6.

15. Dowd, *Spirited Resistance*, 18, 129.

16. Hunter, "Delaware Nativist Revival," 47. Revitalization is also realist: new religions emerge *as a response* to social and economic chaos. In other words, ideas emerge in response to societal change rather than vice versa. Wallace applied revitalization to explain the rise of Methodism, Sikhism, Islam, Christianity, and the Egyptian religion of Akhenaton, among others. While I believe prophetic concepts of supernatural proof derived from syncretism with Enlightenment ideas, syncretism is not evidence of revitalization (Wallace, "Revitalization," 264–81). For more recent applications of the theory, see Robert M. Owens, *Mr. Jefferson's Hammer: William*

Henry Harrison and the Origins of American Indian Policy (Norman: University of Oklahoma Press, 2007), 119–27; and Dowd's critique in *Resistance*, 124–31.

17. Cave, *Prophets*, 167.

18. Constantin Volney, *View of the Climate and Soil of the United States of America* (London: J. Johnson, 1804), 477.

19. See Philip Jenkins, *Dream Catchers: How Mainstream America Discovered Native Spirituality* (New York: Oxford University Press, 2004), chaps. 1–2.

20. Anthony Pagden, *The Fall of Natural Man: The American Indian and the Origins of Ethnography* (New York: Cambridge University Press, 1982), 4.

21. For European and colonial conceptualizations of American Indian practices as an inversion or perversion of "true" religion, see Cervantes, *Devil in the New World*.

22. Pagden, *The Fall of Natural Man*, 175–76.

23. R. Po-Chia Hsia, *The World of Catholic Renewal, 1540–1770* (New York: Cambridge University Press, 2005), 167; Cervantes, *Devil in the New World*, 16. For his trouble, de Landa was made a bishop. My brief summary here vastly simplifies complex cultural and intellectual changes and instead presents a general elite view as it developed in Europe in the seventeenth and early eighteenth centuries; but as Cervantes warns, it would "be a mistake to generalize from this evidence and to suggest that the tendency to demonize Indian cultures was so pervasive that it left no room for cultural interaction and assimilation" (ibid., 32–33, 36).

24. Hsia, *The World of Catholic Renewal*, 170.

25. Cervantes, *Devil in the New World*, 39. The long-standing theory that Native Americans were actually Jewish—the Lost Tribes of Israel—may also have contributed to European intellectual and legal parallels between the two groups.

26. Mather, *Magnalia*, 1:55, 2:552; Mather, *Wonders*, 37; Alexander Whitaker, *Good Newes from Virginia*, in *God's New Israel: Religious Interpretations of American Destiny*, ed. Conrad Cherry (Chapel Hill: University of North Carolina Press, 1998), 32. See also Mary Beth Norton, *In the Devil's Snare* (New York: Knopf, 2002).

27. Belknap and Morse, *Report on the Oneida*, 9; Dowd, *Spirited Resistance*, 1–22; Jortner, *The Gods*, 28–29.

28. L. Morgan, *League of the Iroquois*, 154.

29. Volney, *View of the Climate*, 477–78.

30. Cave, *Prophets*, 3.

31. Harrison, *Messages and Papers*, 1:299–300.

32. This version of Neolin's message is drawn from Schoolcraft, *Algic Researches*, 119.

33. McNemar, *Kentucky Revival*, 114; Speech of the Trout, May 4, 1807, MHC 40:123.

34. Schoolcraft, *Algic Researches*, 120.

35. Kirkland, *Journals*, 418.

36. Forsyth to Clark, 12/23/1812, in Emma Helen Blair, *The Indian Tribes of the Upper Mississippi* (Cleveland: Arthur H. Clark, 1912), 2:274.

37. Hubbard, "A Kickapoo Sermon," 473.

38. For Handsome Lake, see the Code of Handsome Lake, 22; and Parker, "The Religion of Handsome Lake," in *The Life of General Ely S. Parker* (Buffalo: Buffalo Historical Society, 1919), 252; for Tenskwatawa, see Benjamin Youngs, "A Journey to the Indians March 1807," Winterthur, Andrews Collection; and McNemar, *Kentucky Revival*, 111ff.

39. Schoolcraft, *Algic Researches*, 117.

40. Charles Beatty, "Journal of Beatty's Trip to the Ohio Country in 1766," *Journals of Charles Beatty*, ed. Guy Soulliard Klett (University Park: Pennsylvania State University Press, 1962), 65.

41. Kenekuk to Clark, in Mooney, *Ghost Dance*, 695.

42. Code of Handsome Lake, 62.

43. McNemar, *Kentucky Revival*, 113–14.

44. Card-players and the "immoral woman" from Code of Handsome Lake, 73–74. Parker tactfully left out critical words in the original Haudenosaunee in the story of the "immoral woman," but the phrase "he lifted up an object from a pile and thrust it within her" leaves little doubt as to the nature of her punishment.

45. Hubbard, "A Kickapoo Sermon," 474.

46. Code of Handsome Lake, 73–74.

47. McNemar, *Kentucky Revival*, 113–14.

48. Heckewelder, *Account*, 293–94.

49. Dowd, *Spirited Resistance*, xvii, 29–30.

50. P. Verhaegen to the editor of the *Annales*, 6/20/1838, *Annales de la Propagation de la Foi* (Lyon: Pelagaud et Lesne, 1838), 471. Thanks to Emily Jortner for the translation.

51. L. Morgan, *League of the Iroquois*, 231, 240.

52. Blair, *Indian Tribes*, 2:277; John Tanner, *The Falcon: A Narrative of the Captivity and Adventures of John Tanner* (1830; New York: Penguin, 2000), 145.

53. Dowd, *Spirited Resistance*, 169–73; Cave, *Prophets*, 158.

54. Code of Handsome Lake, 28–30.

55. Schoolcraft, *Algic Researches*, 116–21.

56. L. Morgan, *League of the Iroquois*, 229.

57. Code of Handsome Lake, 68; Parker, *Life*, 260.

58. Cited in Mooney, *Ghost Dance*, 695.

59. Qtd. in Garraghan, *Jesuits*, 1:388.

60. Conference with Handsome Lake, Cornplanter, and Blue Eyes, 3/10/1802, in *Papers of Thomas Jefferson*, 37:29–42.

61. Stiggins, *Creek Indian History*, 88.

62. Andrew Jackson to Rachel Jackson, 12/19/1813, in *Papers of Andrew Jackson*, 2:494.

63. Black Hawk, *Life of Black Hawk*, ed. J. Gerald Kennedy (New York: Penguin, 2008), 45.

64. L. Morgan, *League of the Iroquois*, 154.

65. Heckewelder, *Account*, 238.

66. Addendum of Cornells, 6/23/1813, in *American State Papers: Indian Affairs* (Washington: Gales and Seaton, 1832), 1:846. See also Claudio Saunt, *A New Order of Things* (New York: Cambridge University Press, 1999), 253.

67. John Keating, *Narrative of an Expedition to the Source of St. Peter's River* (Philadelphia: Carey, 1824), 1:230–31. Cave makes the point that Tenskwatawa therefore "made few Sac converts," but Keating's comment suggested just the opposite—though according to Keating, many such converts regretted their choice in the wake of the War of 1812 (*Prophets*, 114).

68. Schoolcraft, *Algic Researches*, 119–20.

69. Wallace, *Death*, 259, 260–61, 285–94; Dennis, *Seneca Possessed*, 96–100, 257n31.

70. Youngs, "Journey," 33.

71. Each of these explanations carries its own difficulties. There is no comparative data on the gender breakdown of witch accusations before European contact; certainly prophets in the early republic accused both men and women. Nevertheless, Tenskwatawa and Handsome Lake curtailed female power, so a rethinking of gender roles is a likely contributor to these outbreaks. On cultural reintegration, see Miller, "1806 Purge"; and Jortner, *The Gods*, 118, 259n50. The case that land sales and redistribution fomented the trials is suggested by Alison Games, *Witchcraft in Early North America* (New York: Rowman and Littlefield, 2010), 81–83; by implication, it forms part of Dennis's argument in *Seneca Possessed*.

72. Robin Briggs, *Witches and Neighbors* (New York: Penguin, 1996), 6–7.

73. Clark, *Thinking*, 550.

74. Wallace, Dowd, Cave, and Dennis all begin their analyses of Native American prophets and/or witchcraft with an extensive examination of the cultural dislocation and disintegration among Eastern Woodlands communities, 1763–1800. Such a method presupposes that the witch trials are social in origin—the "real" problems of Native America "produced" witchcraft trials. This argument depends on realist explanations of the supernatural. An intellectual and political reading of nativist emergence in the early republic better assesses the religious content and contours of this movement.

75. Frank W. Porter III, "Strategies for Survival: The Nanticoke Indians in a Hostile World," *Ethnohistory* 26, no. 4 (1979), 325–45, 329–30. It is somewhat inaccurate to speak of a Delaware "nation" in the early to mid-eighteenth century; Delaware social organization functioned more on village lines. However, the dislocations of the eighteenth century sent numerous Delawares to new polyglot settlements in central Pennsylvania. The "Delaware" nation emerged from this exodus—perhaps explaining why they might be open to a new religious ideals that taught Indians to ignore their differences and become one people.

76. Zeisberger, *History*, 126.

77. "Journal of James Kenny, 1761–1763," *Pennsylvania Magazine of History & Biography* 21, no. 1 (1913): 34–35.

78. White, *Middle Ground*, 271, 281; Jortner, *The Gods*, 29–35.

79. Zeisberger, *Moravian Mission Diaries of David Zeisberger*, 275, 159; Heckewelder, *Account*, 290–92.

80. Halliday Jackson, "Journal," 145; Henry Simmons, "Henry Simmons' Version of the Visions," in H. Jackson, "Journal," 345–49, quote at 345; Dennis, *Seneca Possessed*, 96; Merle H. Deardorff and George S. Snyderman, "A Nineteenth-Century Visit to the Indians of New York," *Proceedings of the American Philosophical Society* 100, no. 6 (December 1956): 582–612.

81. Parker, *Life*, 357.

82. Code of Handsome Lake, 39–40.

83. H. Jackson, *Civilization*, 343.

84. Wallace, *Death*, 256; H. Jackson, *Civilization*, 42–43.

85. David Swatzler, *A Friend among the Seneca: The Quaker Mission to Cornplanter's People* (Mechanicsburg, PA: Stackpole, 2000), 205.

86. Wallace, *Death*, 259.

87. Christopher Densmore, *Red Jacket: Diplomat and Orator* (Syracuse, NY: Syracuse University Press, 1999), 57.

88. "From the Journal—Opening Military Road, 1801," entry for June 8–10, 1801, Joseph Ellicott's Letter Books, *Publications of the Buffalo Historical Society* 26 (1922): 122–23; Wallace, *Death*, 258–60.

89. Taylor and the Committee qtd. in Dennis, *Seneca Possessed*, 256n28.

90. Kirkland, *Journals*, 418.

91. Wallace, *Death*, 261, 265–80.

92. Code of Handsome Lake, 46. Alternative Iroquois punishments are described in L. Morgan, *League of the Iroquois*, 321–22; and Mary Jemison, *A Narrative of the Life of Mrs. Mary Jemison*, ed. June Namias (Norman: University of Oklahoma Press, 1992), 174. See also Dennis, *Seneca Possessed*, 95–114.

93. Code of Handsome Lake, 29.

94. Wallace, *Death*, 292–93. Deardorff and Snyderman, "Nineteenth-Century Visit," 598n18, and Dennis, *Seneca Possessed*, 105, give the date as 1808.

95. Jemison, *Narrative of the Life*, 97, 143; Lemuel Covell, *Memoir of the Late Reverend Lemuel Covell, Missionary to the Indians* (Brandon, VT, 1839), 135–37, tells the story of the Tuscarora witchcraft outbreak, wherein the mere arrival of the Christian ends the ignorance and superstition of the Indians. It is questionable whether Covell's story is a genuine reflection of his missionary experience or a rose-colored interpretation embellished by Covell's editor, Deidamia Covell Brown (his daughter).

96. Wallace, *Death*, 286–88.

97. Catlin, *North American Indians*, 34.

98. Keating, *Narrative*, 1:235–36.

99. C. C. Trowbridge, *Shawnese Traditions*, ed. Vernon Kinietz and Erminie W. Voegelin (New York: AMS, 1980), 45; Cave, *Prophets*, 79.

100. Hubbard, "Kickapoo Sermon," 476.

101. *Moravian Indian Mission*, 401–2. Dowd suggests Beata was an independent prophet (see Jortner, *The Gods*, 111, 257n3).

102. *Moravian Indian Mission*, entry for 2/13/1805–2/16/1805.

103. Ibid., 413.

104. Ibid., entries for 2/21/1806 and 2/22/1806, 408–9.

105. Jortner, *The Gods*, 116–18.

106. The five victims were Joshua, Tetapatchsit, Billy Patterson, Ann Charity, and at least one other (*Moravian Indian Mission*, 415, 418).

107. Cave, *Prophets*, 85.

108. See Jortner, *The Gods*, 119–20.

109. Wallace, *Death*, 260; Address of Blue Eyes, 3/15/02, in *Papers of Thomas Jefferson*, 37:37. Jackson, *Civilization*, 42, confirms this angelic warrant, although whether he speaks of 1801 or is merely paraphrasing is not clear.

110. Address of Handsome Lake, 3/15/1802; reply of Henry Dearborn, 3/17/02, both in *Papers of Thomas Jefferson*, 37:36–42.

111. Prophet to WHH, 8/1/1808, in Harrison, *Messages and Papers*, 1:299–300.

112. Speech of Trout, MHC, 40:132.

113. Intelligence report of Kenton et al., Draper, 7BB46, Draper Manuscripts.

114. William Wells to Secy of War, 7/14/07, in *Territorial Papers of the United States* (Washington: National Archives, 1934–), 7:465

115. Herring, *Kenekuk*, 20–23.

116. Graham to Clark, 1827, in Mooney, *Ghost Dance Religion*, 694.

117. Herring, *Kenekuk*, 46–66; Cave, *Prophets*, 236–37.

118. Wallace, *Death*, 286–88; Karim Tiro, *The People of the Standing Stone: The Oneida Nation from the Revolution through the Era of Removal* (Amherst: University of Massachusetts Press, 2011), 124.

119. WHH Annual Message, 10/17/1809, in Harrison, *Messages and Papers*, 1:383.

120. WHH Annual Message, 11/12/1810, in Harrison, *Messages and Papers*, 1:492–93.

121. Jortner, *The Gods*, 180–85.

122. WHH to Eustis, 11/26/1811, in Harrison, *Messages and Papers*, 1:651.

123. WHH to Clark, 12/13/11, in Harrison, *Messages and Papers*, 1:670.

124. *Sketch of the Life of Major General William Henry Harrison* (n.p., 1836), 11; Drake 82. This *Sketch* should not be confused with Isaac Rand Jackson's *Sketch of the Life and Public Services of William Henry Harrison*, also published in 1836, and which contains similar language. Similar portrayals can be found in S. J. Burr, *Life and Times of William Henry Harrison* (New York, 1840); and Richard Hildreth, *The People's Presidential Candidate* (Boston, 1839).

125. *Sketch of the Life of Major General William Henry Harrison,* 14, 17, 18.

126. Stiggins, *Creek Indian History,* 83–84.

127. John Sugden, "Tecumseh's Travels Revisited," *Indiana Magazine of History* 96, no. 2 (June 2000): 150–68; Cave, *Prophets,* 143–47.

128. Kathryn Braund, *Deerskins and Duffels: The Creek Indian Trade with Anglo-America, 1675–1815* (1993; Lincoln: University of Nebraska Press, 2008), 186–88.

129. Jackson to Creek Chiefs, 9/4/1815, in *Papers of Andrew Jackson,* 3:382.

130. Addendum of Cornells, 6/23/1813, ASPIA 1:846. Identification of Cornells is found in Dowd, *Spirited Resistance,* 157.

131. McAfee, *History of the Late War,* 497.

132. "Extract of a Journal Written in the Creek Nation of Indians," *Boston Intelligencer,* 10/24/1818.

133. McAfee, *Late War,* 27, 19.

134. *Richmond (VA) Enquirer,* 4/13/1814, quoting the *Milledgeville (GA) Journal,* 3/20/1814.

135. Stiggins, *Creek Indian History,* 87, 93.

136. Schoolcraft, *Algic Researches,* 116.

137. L. Morgan, *League of the Iroquois,* 221–22.

138. Verhaegen, *Foi,* 470–71.

139. *Washington Daily National Intelligencer,* 8/3/1821.

140. William Allinson, "Journal, describing a visit to Indians in New York state in 1809," vol. 2, Allinson Family Papers, Haverford College; see also Wallace, *Death,* 293.

141. Swatzler, *A Friend,* 205.

142. Dennis, *Seneca Possessed,* 65.

143. Jordan Paper, *Native North American Religious Traditions: Dancing for Life* (Westport, CT: Praeger, 2007), 91.

SIX Latter-day Saints

1. John Pulsipher, *A Short Sketch of the History of John Pulsipher,* Marriott Library Special Collections, University of Utah, n.d., ca. 1871.

2. *Essex (MA) Gazette,* 9/1/32; James McChesney, *An Antidote to Mormonism* (1839), in Kirkham, *New Witness,* 2:162; *Painesville (OH) Telegraph,* quoting the affidavit signed by a committee at Geauga County, Ohio, 1/31/34; Origen Bachelor, *Mormonism Exposed* (1838), in Kirkham, *New Witness,* 2:159, 161.

3. Pulsipher, *Short Sketch.*

4. Whitmer, *Historian to Dissident,* 56–57.

5. See Harper, "Infallible Proofs," 99–118.

6. Rigdon, *Oration,* 9.

7. Jan Shipps, *Mormonism: The Story of a New Religious Tradition* (Urbana: University of Illinois Press, 1985), 7. Shipps insists on the centrality of the gold bible

for understanding Mormonism, as opposed to an emphasis on Smith himself or his completed theological and cosmological teachings (32–33).

8. *Rochester (NY) Gem* 5/15/30, in Kirkham, *New Witness*, 2:46–49

9. *Rochester (NY) Daily Advertiser*, 4/2/1830, in Kirkham, *New Witness*, 2:40; *Palmyra (NY) Freeman*, reprinted in *Rochester (NY) Advertiser & Telegraph*, 8/31/29; James McChesney, *Supplement to an Antidote to Mormonism* (1839), 1, Digital Collections, Harold B. Lee Library (hereafter HBLL), http://contentdm.lib.byu.edu/cdm /ref/collection/BOMP/id/2053.

10. *Messenger & Advocate*, 2/21/1835, in Kirkham, *New Witness*, 1:97. On anti-Mormonism and its relationship to other "antis," see Fluhman, *Anti-Mormonism*, 19.

11. Howe, *Unvailed*, 265–66.

12. Ibid., 85. The attacks on Brodie are of long standing (beginning with Hugh W. Nibley's *No Ma'am, That's Not History*) but perhaps unfair. Her argument—that Joseph Smith more or less deliberately deceived his followers based on an imagined set of plates and invented revelations—presents something of an easy target. For example, Brodie claims that Smith could not work miracles yet was somehow able "to make other people see visions." Nevertheless, both her work and her argument remain foundational to modern LDS historiography.

13. Quinn, *Early Mormonism*, 236, 239, xxii. See also Hill, *Quest*, chap. 1. Stephen Harper notes that historiography of early Mormons often assumes this kind of "disorientation" from reports *about* the Mormons; the classification of Mormon converts as somehow "other," writes Harper, is not established by social analysis, but by anti-Mormon critics (Harper, "Dictated by Christ," 275). Jan Shipps provides a detailed account of Mormon historiography and the "new Mormon history" in "Richard Lyman Bushman, the Story of Joseph Smith and Mormonism, and the New Mormon History," *JAH* 94, no. 2 (September 2007): 498–516.

14. Quinn, *Early Mormonism*, 9; Harper in *Opening the Heavens: Accounts of Divine Manifestations, 1820–1844*, ed. Jack Welch and Erick Carlson (Provo, UT: Brigham Young University, 2005), 329; "Infallible," 106–7; Givens, *Hand of Mormon*, 12, 209–18; Harper, "Politics," 284; Bushman, *Mormonism: A Very Short Introduction* (New York: Oxford University Press, 2008), 14; Bushman, *Stone*, 127, 147–52.

15. Pratt, *Dialogue*, 14–15.

16. *Palmyra (NY) Reflector*, 1/22/1830, 12/22/1829.

17. Ibid., 6/12/1830.

18. See Grant Underwood, *The Millenarian World of Early Mormonism* (Urbana: University of Illinois Press, 1993); and Givens, *Hand of Mormon*, 62–72.

19. *Millennial Star* 1, no. 75 (August 1840), qtd. in Underwood, *Millenarian World*, 91. Underwood demonstrates that not all parts of the Book of Mormon had equal weight among the early Saints. References by the early Saints to the Book itself and its miracles suggest that its message about miracles was one of the central components of early Mormon missions.

20. See Hill, *Quest*, 23; Kirkham, *New Witness*, 1:428; William McLellin, *The*

Journals of William McLellin, ed. Shipps and John Welch (Provo: BYU Studies, Brigham Young University, and the University of Illinois Press, 1994), 29, 103; and *Messenger & Advocate* 1:1 (October 1834).

21. Book of Mormon, 1830, 39 (hereafter 1830 ed.); modern edition (1982, hereafter given as chapter and verse [not present in the original translation]), 1 Ne 16.

22. 1830 ed., 41, 48–49, 330; 1 Ne 16, 18:12 & 21; Alma 37:40.

23. 1830 ed., 330; Alma 37:38–41.

24. 1830 ed., 140, 213, 249, 447; Jacob 7:5, Mosiah 27:18; Alma 10:9; Helaman 14:28.

25. 1830 ed., 17, 421; 1 Ne 7:10; Helaman 5:50. Emphasis added.

26. 1830 ed., 455. In this aspect, too, the Book of Mormon is distinct from the New Testament, whose miracles are often misunderstood, confusing, or ambiguous. In his New World ministry, Christ explains this distinction to the Nephites and Lamanites: "So great faith I have not seen among all the Jews; therefore I could not shew unto them so great miracles, because of their unbelief" (1830 ed., 498; 3 Ne 19:35).

27. 1830 ed., 474, 477; 3 Ne 10:1, 11:13–15.

28. 1830 ed., 489–90, 510, 513; 3 Ne 17:9, 24–25, 29:7.

29. 1830 ed., 516, 519, 520; 4 Ne 1:29; Morm 1:13–19.

30. 1830 ed., 535–6; Morm 9:7–11.

31. McLellin, *Journals*, 107, 125n28. Moronihah was likely a misspelling of Ammonihah, thus making the passage Alma 9–16.

32. Ibid., 107; 1830 ed., 249; Alma 10:12.

33. Underwood, *Millenarian World*, 79, 87.

34. Givens, *Hand of Mormon*, 84.

35. *Messenger & Advocate*, December 1835.

36. 1830 ed., 589–90; Givens, *Hand of Mormon*, 40. Scholars have often divided these testimonies into "supernatural" (Three Witnesses) versus "natural" (Eight Witnesses), at least in part based on later writings and commentaries by the witnesses about their experiences. The presence of the testimonies as affidavits, however, was the key evidentiary point for a Mormon church seeking converts in the 1830s (Dan Vogel, "The Validity of the Witnesses' Testimonies," *American Apocrypha: Essays on the Book of Mormon*, ed. Vogel and Brent Metcalfe, [Salt Lake City: Signature, 2002], 88–89).

37. Campbell, *Delusions*, 94.

38. Atwater, "Antiquities," 120–25.

39. *View of the Hebrews* is usually cited as an example of the currency that notions of ancient Americans had in the early United States; its irrepressibility as a citation may also derive from the fact that Brodie and others have accused Smith of plagiarizing and sacralizing its text to create the Book of Mormon. The research of Dale Broadhurst, however, identified at least fourteen printed discourses on this topic through 1839, including Benjamin Smith Barton, *New Views on the Origin of*

the Tribes and Nations of America (1798), Constantin Volney, *Ruins* (1811), and Moses Fisk, *Conjectures Respecting the Ancient Inhabitants of North America* (1820) (Dale Broadhurst Papers, University of Utah Special Collections).

40. Lorenzo Dow, *Lorenzo Dow's Thoughts on Various Religious Opinions* (Baltimore: Samuel Magill, 1807), 14.

41. Josiah Priest, *American Antiquities and Discoveries in the West* (Albany: Hoffman and White, 1833), 115; Quinn, *Early Mormonism*, 495n77.

42. Journal of Edward Partridge, entry for February 1835, 6, LDS Church History Archives, Salt Lake City.

43. *Evening & Morning Star*, February 1833, qtd. in Givens, *Hand of Mormonism*, 97-98.

44. George Burket journal, entry for 12/2/1825, LDS Church History Archives.

45. Orson Hyde, *Prophetic Warning to All the Churches* (Toronto, 1836); L. Tom Perry Special Collections, HBLL.

46. Jared Carter Journal 14, 10, 21, LDS Church History Archives.

47. David W. Patten Journal, n.d., LDS Church History Archives.

48. *The Orson Pratt Journals*, ed. Elden J. Watson (Salt Lake City: E. J. Watson, 1975), 18, entry for 6/23/1833.

49. See Zebedee Coltrin diary 1832, 30, 43, LDS Church Archives; "Oliver Cowdery's Kirtland Ohio 'Sketch Book,'" ed. Leonard J. Arrington, *BYU Studies* 12, no. 4 (Summer 1972): 425; and Whitmer, *Historian to Dissident*, chaps. 6 and 9.

50. *Palmyra (NY) Reflector*, 6/30/30.

51. Joseph Smith Jr., *History of the Church*, 1:82.

52. Doctrine & Covenants 129:8.

53. Carter Journal, 5.

54. Theodore Turley Mission Journal, 1839–40, 65, L. Tom Perry Special Collections, HBLL.

55. *Elders' Journal*, Oct 1837, qtd. in Stanley B. Kimball, *Heber C. Kimball: Mormon Patriarch and Pioneer* (Urbana: University of Illinois Press, 1981), 47.

56. "Journal of Orson Hyde, While Absent on a Mission in Company with Samuel H. Smith, Feb 1/1832 to 12/22/1832," bound with *Miscellaneous Mormon Diaries*, vol. 11, entry for 3/20/32, L. Tom Perry Special Collections, HBLL.

57. McLellin, *Journals*, 106–12.

58. Smoot to Joseph Fielding Smith, 1894, reprinted in Lycurgus Wilson, *The Life of David W. Patten, the First Apostolic Martyr* (1900; Peoria, AZ: Eborn, 1992). An undated reminiscence about Nauvoo in 1847 reports another sighting of Cain, which refers as well to Patten's having told the story of meeting Cain (see Horace Strong Rawson Reminiscence, [n.d.], microfilm, LDS Archives; see also Matthew Bowman, "A Mormon Bigfoot: David Patten's Cain and the Concept of Evil in LDS Folklore," *Journal of Mormon History* 33, no. 3 [2007]: 62–82).

59. Campbell, *Delusions*, 85, 90, 94.

60. Ibid., 94.

61. The introduction to Howe, *Unvailed* (viii–ix), repeats page 85 of *Delusions* almost verbatim.

62. Howe, *Unvailed*, 12, 43, 30, 17, 94, 15, 16, 100, 43, 115, 130.

63. Ibid., 32, 22–23, 71, 84, 135, 28.

64. Ibid., 196, quoting Ezra Booth.

65. Harper, "Infallible," 99–103.

66. Journal of Lorenzo Barnes, 1835, 72, L. Tom Perry Special Collections, HBLL.

67. Howe, *Unvailed*, 112, 17, 145, emphasis original. Howe alternately describes the Mormons as wealthy or poor throughout the work, suggesting either that Howe could not be bothered with the details or that economic status probably did not correlate with attraction to the Mormon message.

68. Qtd. in Hill, *Quest*, 29.

69. *Newport (RI) Mercury*, 6/18/31.

70. *New Bedford (MA) Mercury*, 1/3/1833.

71. *Star* (Ohio), reprinted in *Painesville (OH) Telegraph*, 8/25/31.

72. *Painesville (OH) Telegraph*, 11/18/31.

73. Qtd. in Howe, *Unvailed*, 140. See also *Missouri Intelligencer and Boon's Lick Advertiser*, 8/10/1833, reprinted in *Among the Mormons*, ed. William Mulder and A. Russell Mortensen (1958; Salt Lake City: Western Epics, 1994), 76–80.

74. Harris qtd. in Howe, *Unvailed*, 14.

75. *Times & Seasons*, 4/13/1844, qtd. in Bushman, *Stone*, 522.

76. Winn, *Exiles*, 109.

77. "Sketch Book," 414; Winn, "'Such Republicanism as This': John Corrill's Rejection of Prophetic Rule," in Launius and Thatcher, eds., *Differing Visions*, 63; Quinn, *Early Mormonism*, 287.

78. Qtd. in Brodie, *No Man Knows*, 427–29; see also Klaus Hansen, *Mormonism and the American Experience* (Chicago: University of Chicago Press, 1981), 4.

79. Newel Knight, "Newel Knight's Journal," *Classic Experiences and Adventures* (Salt Lake City: Bookcraft, 1969), 65.

80. Book of Commandments (1833; Independence, MO: Herald Publishing House, 1972), 67–68. In 1856, Emer Harris testified that afterward, Page's stone was destroyed and his pages burned (Quinn, *Early Mormonism*, 248, 542n84).

81. Joseph Smith, *History*, 2:144.

82. *Far West Record: Minutes of the Church of Jesus Christ of Latter-day Saints*, 1830–1844, ed. Donald Q. Cannon and Lyndon W. Cook (Salt Lake City: Deseret, 1983), 85–91.

83. Vogel, "James Colin Brewster: The Boy Prophet Who Challenged Mormon Authority," in Launius and Thatcher, eds., *Differing Visions*, 120–39, 121. In 1843, Brewster denied using a seer stone.

84. Lucy Mack Smith, *Biographical Sketches of Joseph Smith the Prophet* (1853; New York: Arno, 1969), 211–12.

85. Ronal E. Romig, "David Whitmer: Faithful Dissenter, Witness Apart," in Launius and Thatcher, eds., *Differing Visions*, 34–36; Journal of Edward Partridge, entry for 12/27/1835.

86. Winn, "Corrill," 49–50.

87. Ibid., 69.

88. Joseph Smith, *History of the Church*, 2:499; Winn, "Corrill," 120; Hill, *Quest*, 71.

89. Davis Britton, "The Waning of Mormon Kirtland," *BYU Studies* 12, no. 4 (Summer 1972): 456–57.

90. Mary Fielding, letter of 6/15/1837, qtd. in Hill, *Quest*, 59, 61, 220n34, 37.

91. Compare, for example, Hill, *Quest*, 75–98; Quinn, *The Mormon Hierarchy: Origins of Power* (Salt Lake: Signature, 1994), 93–102; and Bushman, *Stone*, 349–52.

92. See Reed C. Durham Jr., "The Election Day Battle in Gallatin," *BYU Studies* 13, no. 1 (Autumn 1972), 36–61; and Bushman, *Stone*, 350–51.

93. "Note of Warning," reprinted in Durham, "Election Day Battle," 53–54.

94. Rigdon, *Oration*, 4–5.

95. Ibid., 6.

96. Ibid., 12, emphasis added.

97. Corrill qtd. in Winn, *Exiles*, 133.

98. Rigdon, *Oration*, 12.

99. Bushman, *Stone*, 355.

100. Doctrine & Covenants, 115. Note that the "house" mentioned here refers to the LDS temple the Saints were commanded to build and should probably not be read metaphorically.

101. Qtd. in Bushman, *Stone*, 355.

102. *Argus* (Missouri), 9/27/1838, qtd. in Hill, *Quest*, 79.

103. *Quincy (IL) Whig*, 9/8/1838.

104. *Daily Commercial Advertiser*, 9/19/1838. Note that this use of the term "extermination" came a month before Boggs's extermination order and therefore referenced Rigdon, not Boggs.

105. Lee, *Mormonism Unveiled*, 60.

106. Douglas Miln to William Beckett, 2/16/1840, Filson Historical Society.

107. Quoted Hill, *Quest*, 91.

108. *Quincy (IL) Whig*, 9/8/1838, emphasis added.

109. *New York Spectator*, 11/22/1838.

110. *Republican* (Missouri), 11/9/1838, in Hill, *Quest*, 91.

111. Lilburn W. Boggs to John B. Clark, 27 October 1838, Mormon War Papers, 1837–1841, Missouri State Archives, Jefferson City.

112. Joseph Smith, *History*, 3:203–4.

113. Winn, *Exiles*, 144.

SEVEN The Sects That Weren't

1. Stewart, *Freewill Baptists*, 276, gives fifty as the largest number of Babcockists. Their 1810 Declaration of Faith had sixteen signatures ("Declaration of the Faith of the Church of Christ of Springfield, VT," 1/13/1810, William Smyth Babcock Miscellaneous Papers, American Antiquarian Society [hereafter WSB]).

2. WSB 8/31/1809; 9/5/1809; 9/6/1809; "Declaration of the Faith," WSB 1/13/1810.

3. WSB 5/29/1803; 8/23/1801.

4. WSB, undated entry (1/1/1804); 6/14/1801; 1/3/03; 3/29/1809; 5/11/1803.

5. WSB 7/18/1805; 1/9/1805.

6. WSB 8/12/1805; 7/13/1810; 7/17/1805; 7/8/1810; 4/4/1810; 7/22/1810; 3/27/1810.

7. WSB 7/30/1809; 10/27/1808; 4/10/1809; 9/12/1810.

8. Among several references to shared manifestations and the death of the child, see WSB 4/14–15/1809; 5/4/1811; and 10/9/1811.

9. See Kenneth Scott, "The Osgoodites of New Hampshire," *New England Quarterly* 16, no. 1 (March 1943): 20–40.

10. James Bradley Finley, *Pioneer Life in the West* (New York: Hunt and Eaton, 1853), 257–58, 373; Peter Cartwright, *Autobiography of Peter Cartwright* (Nashville: Abingdon, 1984), 76–77. Finley alternately referred to Sargent's disciples as "mostly women" and "all women"; Cartwright describes Sargent authorizing "men preachers and women preachers." Sargent's name was variously spelled Sarjent and Sarjeant.

11. Stewart, *Freewill Baptists*, 275.

12. Juster and Hartigan-O'Connor, "Angel Delusion," 402, 375–76.

13. WSB 5/6/1802. Juster and Hartigan-O'Connor refer to the "rumors of sexual impropriety" but explain Babcock's response by quoting his purported excuse, which was part of the rumor itself: "Despite his excuses ('I told them the woman desired it & I felt it duty to gratify her'), listeners stayed away." As Juster and Hartigan-O'Connor have it, the excuse was that Babcock felt the woman *wanted* to be kissed. Babcock's actual excuse was that the whole story was untrue (Juster and Hartigan-O'Connor, "Angel Delusion," 376–77).

14. Babcock engaged in premarital sex, as noted, but "arrested emotional and sexual development" seems a bit much to diagnose on the basis of an evening of premarital sex. The historians similarly ascribe the decline of the movement to increasing skepticism in those final months, but there is no such suggestion in the diary. (Moreover, the suggestion that "skepticism" undoes belief in the "supernatural" is problematic.) Juster and Hartigan-O'Connor also suggest that the angel was circumscribed by the female sphere—childbirth, family relations, personal piety. Therefore, the angelic messages represented women's efforts to obtain greater autonomy and control over their family and religious lives. Yet the angel did not limit himself to the presumed "female" sphere; he gave instructions

about theology, communion, justice, and finances (Juster and Hartigan-O'Connor, "Angel Delusion," 389–90, 399–404).

15. Ibid., 401–2. On the "unsexing" of female preachers, see Brekus, *Strangers and Pilgrims*, 15–16.

16. WSB 4/16/1810. On dialogic revelation, see Givens, *Hand of Mormon*, chap. 8.

17. Sterling Delano, *Brook Farm: The Dark Side of Utopia* (Cambridge: Belknap Press of Harvard University Press, 2004), xii.

18. Juster, *Doomsayers*, chap. 6; Brekus, *Strangers and Pilgrims*, 82–105; Larson, "Indescribable Being."

19. Wisbey, *Pioneer Prophetess*, 7–8; "A Memorandum of the introduction of that fatal fever, call'd in the Year 1776, the Columbus Fever," n.d., Jemima Wilkinson Papers (hereafter JWP).

20. "A Memorandum"; Brownell, *Enthusiastical Errors*, 14, 4.

21. Last Will and Testament, JWP.

22. *Travels in the Years 1791 and 1792 in Pennsylvania, New York and Vermont: Journals of John Lincklaen*, ed. Helen Lincklaen Fairchild (New York: Putnam, 1897), 62.

23. *The American Magazine* (bound volume), vol. 1, no. 2 (Philadelphia, PA: Carey, Stewart, and Co., 1790), 302; Stiles, *Diary*, 3:334.

24. Ruth Spencer to P.U.F., 9/23/1818, JWP.

25. Brownell, *Enthusiastical Errors*, 5, 15.

26. Windsor, VT, *Spooner's Vermont Journal*, 3/22/1791; *Massachusetts Spy*, 6/19/1788.

27. Brownell, *Enthusiastical Errors*, 8.

28. Jackson, "Journal," 135.

29. Rachel Malin's Book, entry for 11/6/1819, JWP; Brownell, *Enthusiastical Errors*, 13.

30. Stiles, *Diary*, 2:381.

31. Brownell, *Enthusiastical Errors*, 11, 16.

32. Ibid., 9–10.

33. Lydia Meirich to P.U.F.?, May 1784, JWP.

34. Hudson, *Memoir*, 122.

35. Sarah Niles to P.U.F., undated, JWP.

36. *American Museum*, vol. 1, no. 2, 150, 152.

37. "Extract from a Journal of a Tour to Niagara Falls," 6/9/1812, *The Christian Disciple* (Boston: Joseph T. Buckingham), 5:278.

38. "Lang Syne," qtd. in Wisbey, *Pioneer Prophetess*, 26.

39. Brekus, *Strangers and Pilgrims*, 95. Larson, "Indescribable Being," argues by contrast that the P.U.F. transcended gender and that genderlessness was a serious religious category for early republicans.

40. Manuscript Diary of the Rev. John Pitman, Rhode Island Historical Society, qtd. in Wisbey, *Pioneer Prophetess*, 54.

41. "A Ride to Niagara," *The Port Folio* (Philadelphia) 4, no. 3 (September 1810):

236–37. The ex-Friend was a Mr. Brown; a large number of the Brown family joined Wilkinson's church early in her preaching career (Wisbey, *Pioneer Prophetess*, 61).

42. *Freeman's Journal*, 2/14/1787.

43. *Chillicothe (OH) Supporter*, 10/6/1819.

44. *New-Jersey Journal* (Elizabethtown), 5/28/88.

45. Hudson, *Memoir*, viii.

46. Ibid., 12, 19, 21, 26.

47. Ibid., 42, 44.

48. Ibid., 147–50.

49. *Eastern Argus* (Portland, ME), 7/2/1830.

50. *Western Palladium*, 9/5/1829; Stanley J. Thayne, "Walking on Water: Nineteenth-Century Prophets and a Legend of Religious Imposture," *Journal of Mormon History* 36, no. 2 (Spring 2010): 170–71.

51. Hudson, *Memoir*, 137.

52. Ibid., 27, 134.

53. Ibid., 13, 14.

54. Wisbey notes the prevalence of this particular statement of Hudson's in anti-Wilkinsonian writings; he also notes that followers vigorously denied she had ever said such a thing (see Wisbey, *Pioneer Prophetess*, 64 and 165–66).

55. Brownell, *Enthusiastical Errors*, 8.

56. Ibid., 14, 11.

57. Juster, *Doomsayers*, 223; Brekus, *Strangers and Pilgrims*, 91–93; Wisbey, *Pioneer Prophetess*, 21, 27, 33–34. Stephen Marini classifies Wilkinson's doctrine as Arminian, and therefore tending to the New Light rather than the Old Light denominations in the wake of the Great Awakening. Though a strict classification of this sort is difficult to maintain given the vagueness of Wilkinson's theology, Marini's reading is probably correct. But by the 1780s, the New Lights had established themselves in New England, and so Brekus's contention that Wilkinson offered no challenge to the standing Protestant order also stands (Marini, *Radical Sects*, 49).

58. JW to John & Orpha Rose, qtd. in Wisbey, *Pioneer Prophetess*, 29.

59. Jemima Wilkinson, *The Universal Friend's Advice, to Those of the Same Religious Society*, in Wisbey, *Pioneer Prophetess*, 197–204. On Wilkinson's plagiarism, see ibid., 33; and Brekus, *Strangers and Pilgrims*, 92.

60. Jacob Osgood to Thomas Osgood, 10/15/1831, New Hampshire Historical Society.

61. "Ride to Niagara," 236.

62. Stiles, *Diary*, 3:289.

63. "Extract from a Journal," 278.

64. Savery, *Journal*, 59.

65. Wisbey, *Pioneer Prophetess*, 62–63, 88; Stiles, *Diary*, 2:380–81, Savery, *Journal*, 59; *Freeman's Journal*, 2/14/1787.

66. Qtd. in Wisbey, *Pioneer Prophetess*, 97.

67. Ibid., 93–95.

68. Ibid., 100–116.

69. Parker to JW, n.d., JWP.

70. Wisbey, *Pioneer Prophetess*, 115–23. There is some indication that the town at the Gore was *also* referred to as "Jerusalem"; see Sarah Richard's Book, entry for 6/1/1791, JWP. I here use "the Gore" to refer to the first settlement and "Jerusalem" for the second.

71. Wisbey, *Pioneer Prophetess*, 142–47.

72. Savery, *Journal*, 58–59.

73. "Extract from a Journal," 277–78.

74. Jonathan Botsford to John Lansing, 2/17/1802, JWP; *Second Census of the United States, Population Schedules—New York*, reel 28 (of 52), 1944, National Archives, Washington; *Population Schedules of the Third Census of the United States*, reel 33 (of 71), 1944, National Archives, Washington.

75. Max H. Parkin, "Independence, Missouri," in *Historical Atlas of Mormonism*, ed. S. Kent Brown, Donald Q. Cannon, and Richard H. Jackson (New York: Simon and Schuster, 1994), 40, finds about 1,200 residents around Independence, Missouri, in 1833; the *Encyclopedia of Mormonism* gives the LDS population of Kirtland as 2,000 in 1838 (with 1,000 Gentiles resident as well) (Milton Backman, "Kirtland, Ohio," in *Encyclopedia of Mormonism*, ed. Daniel Ludlow [New York: Macmillan, 1992], 2:793–798). Larson, "Indescribable Being," 578; R. Jackson, *Gifts of Power*, 135.

76. Savery, *Journal*, 58–59.

77. Wisbey, *Pioneer Prophetess*, 142–51.

78. Ibid., 144.

79. Depositions of Witnesses, 10/20/1813, JWP.

80. Carter to P.U.F., 10/1/1808, JWP.

81. "D. B. W.", qtd. in Wisbey, *Pioneer Prophetess*, 182; and Brekus, *Strangers and Pilgrims*, 84.

82. "A Neighbor," *Washington Daily National Intelligencer*, 9/11/1819. The veracity of the Neighbor's comments were questioned in the 10/11/1819 issue of the *Intelligencer*; the Neighbor defended his position in the 11/22/1819 issue.

83. *New York Columbian* (Penn Yan), 7/14/1819; "A Neighbor"; Wisbey, *Pioneer Prophetess*, 162–64.

84. Wisbey, *Pioneer Prophetess*, 166–69; Stafford Canning Cleveland, *History and Directory of Yates County* (Penn Yan, NY: S. C. Cleveland, 1873), 1:110; *American Masonick Record and Albany Saturday Magazine*, 9/5/1829.

85. Among others, see *New-England Galaxy*, 9/10/1819; *Rhode Island American*, (Providence), 8/10/1819; and *Christian Watchman*, 7/24/1819.

86. *Painesville (OH) Telegraph*, 7/12/1831.

87. Young, *Wonderful History*, 74; Quitman, *Treatise*, 25; *Rochester (NY) Gem* 5/15/30, in Kirkham, *New Witness*, 2:46–49.

88. Joyce Butler, "Cochranism Delineated," 151.

89. Ridlon, *Saco Valley*, 1:269–85; Joyce Butler, "Cochranism Delineated," 159–60.

90. Joyce Butler, "Cochranism Delineated," 149.

91. D. M. Graham, *Life of Clement Phinney* (Dover, NH: Burr, 1851), 81; Ridlon, *Saco Valley*, 152–53; Stinchfield, *Cochranism*, 3.

92. *Boston Recorder*, 7/14/1818; Stinchfield, *Cochranism*, 7.

93. *Portland (MA [ME]) Gazette*, 6/1/1819.

94. Joyce Butler, "Cochranism Delineated," 161n12; Stinchfield, *Cochranism*, 1.

95. Stinchfield, *Cochranism*, 5, 3, 4; Graham, *Phinney*, 82; Joyce Butler, "Cochranism Delineated," 155; G. Smith, *Report of the Trial of Jacob Cochrane*, 6, 16. Cochran's name is variously spelled "Cochrane" and "Cochran" in the sources; Joyce Butler suggests Cochran himself left off the "e" (see Butler, "Cochranism Delineated," 160n1). The *Report* published by Smith is not an official transcript but rather Smith's own reconstruction of the testimony given.

96. G. Smith, *Report of the Trial of Jacob Cochrane*, 29, 13; Stinchfield, *Cochranism*, 9, 14.

97. Stinchfield, *Cochranism*, 8–9.

98. Ibid., 4, 5, 10–11; "The Cochranism Fanaticism in York County," *Maine Historical Society Quarterly* 20, no. 1 (Summer 1980): 20–39.

99. G. Smith, *Report of the Trial of Jacob Cochrane*, 12–14.

100. Stinchfield, *Cochranism*, 6, 14.

101. *Portland (MA [ME]) Gazette*, 6/1/1819; *Keene (NH) Sentinel*, 10/16/1819; for similar articles, see *Kennebec American Advocate and Kennebec Advertiser*, 10/16/1819; and *Concord (NH) Observer*, 7/5/1819.

102. *Massachusetts Spy*, 6/9/1819.

103. G. Smith, *Report of the Trial of Jacob Cochrane*, 16.

104. *Keene (NH) Sentinel*, 10/16/1819; *Boston Recorder*, 6/19/1819; *Newburyport (MA) Herald*, 6/4/1819.

105. Stinchfield, *Cochranism*, 8, 3.

106. G. Smith, *Report of the Trial of Jacob Cochrane*, 21.

107. Stinchfield, *Cochranism*, 10; G. Smith, *Report of the Trial of Jacob Cochrane*, 21.

108. G. Smith, *Report of the Trial of Jacob Cochrane*, 9–16, 37.

109. Ibid., 16, 19.

110. *Portland (MA [ME]) Gazette*, 6/1/1819.

111. *New England Galaxy & Masonic Magazine* (Boston), 6/4/1819.

112. Graham, *Phinney*, 89.

113. Ridlon, *Saco Valley*, 1:282.

114. Joyce Butler, "Cochranism Delineated," 159; Richard Van Wagoner, *Mormon Polygamy* (1986; Salt Lake City: Signature, 1989), 8; George D. Smith, "The Nauvoo Roots of Mormon Polygamy, 1841–1846," *Dialogue* 34, no. 2 (Spring/Summer 2001): 126.

115. Ridlon, *Saco Valley*, 1:281.

116. Journal of Orson Hyde, entry for 10/24/1832, "While Absent on a Mission in Company with Samuel H. Smith, Feb 1/1832 to 12/22/1832," bound with *Miscellaneous Mormon Diaries,* vol. 11, HBLL.

117. Thomas Campbell to Sidney Rigdon, 2/4/1831, reprinted in James H. Hunt, *Mormonism: Embracing the Origin, Rise, and Progress of the Sect* (St. Louis: Usick and Davies, 1844), 110; Leonard Woolsey Bacon, *History of American Christianity* (New York: Scribner, 1898), 335.

Conclusion

1. Joseph Smith Jr. qtd. in Bushman, *Stone,* 366; *Quincy (MA) Whig,* 9/8/1838; *New York Spectator,* 11/22/1838; Nathaniel Philbrick, *Bunker Hill: A City, a Siege, a Revolution* (New York: Viking, 2013), 128; Arthur Bernon Tourtellot, *Lexington and Concord* (New York: Norton, 1963), chap. 7.

2. Winn, *Exiles,* 144.

3. In a sense, however, Haun's Mill never left the Mormon consciousness, and it certainly was on their minds in the trek to Utah and de facto independence, 1846–66.

4. John Adams, "Defense of American Constitutions," *The Works of John Adams,* ed. Charles Francis Adams (Boston: Little, Brown, 1850), 4:293.

5. Winnifred Sullivan, *The Impossibility of Religious Freedom* (Princeton: Princeton University Press, 2005), 4, 10.

6. Sehat, *Myth of American Religious Freedom,* vii. See also Fea, preface to *Was America Founded as a Christian Nation?*

7. "South Carolina's New Senator Has a 'Team' of Prayer 'Warriors' on His Side," *Observer.com,* 12/17/2012, http://observer.com/2012/12/south-carolinas-new -senator-has-a-team-of-prayer-warriors-on-his-side/.

8. Whittier, *Supernaturalism,* 43, 58.

Selected Bibliography

Adams, Gretchen A. *The Specter of Salem: Remembering the Witch Trials in Nineteenth-Century America*. Chicago: University of Chicago Press, 2008.

Adams, Hannah. *An Abridgement of the History of New-England: For the Use of Young Persons*. London, 1806.

Allen, Ethan. *Reason the Only Oracle of Man*. Bennington, VT: Haswell and Russell, 1784.

Anderson, Jeffrey E. *Conjure in African American Society*. Baton Rouge: Louisiana State University Press, 2005.

Andrews, William L., and Henry Louis Gates, eds. *Slave Narratives*. New York: Library of America, 2002.

Atwater, Caleb. "Description of the Antiquities Discovered in the State of Ohio." *Archaeologia Americana: Transactions & Collections of the American Antiquarian Society* 1 (1820): 105–312.

Babcock, William Smyth. Miscellaneous Papers. American Antiquarian Society.

Backus, Isaac. *A Church History of New England*. London, 1793.

Baldwin, Christopher C. *Diary of Christopher Columbus Baldwin*. Worcester, MA: American Antiquarian Society, 1901.

Barry, Jonathan, and Owen Davies, eds. *Witchcraft Historiography*. New York: Palgrave, 2007.

Bayley, Solomon. *A Narrative of Some Remarkable Incidents in the Life of Solomon Bayley*. London: Harvey and Darnton, 1825.

Belknap, Jeremy, and Jedidiah Morse. *Report on the Oneida, Stockbridge, and Brotherton Indians, 1796*. New York: Museum of the American Indian, 1955.

Bell, Karl. "Breaking Modernity's Spell: Magic and Modern History." *Cultural and Social History* 4.1 (March 2007): 115–22.

Bentley, William. "A Description and History of Salem." *Collections of the Massachusetts Historical Society for the year 1799* (Boston: Samuel Hall, 1800), 212–88.

———. *Diary of William Bentley*. Salem, MA: Essex Institute, 1911.

Bibb, Henry. *Narrative of the Life of Henry Bibb.* http://docsouth.unc.edu/neh/bibb /bibb.html.

Black, Monica. "The Supernatural and the Poetics of History." *Hedgehog Review* 13, no. 3 (Fall 2011): 72–81.

Book of Commandments. 1833. Independence, MO: Herald Publishing House, 1972.

Book of Mormon. 1830. Independence, MO: Herald Publishing House, 1973.

Bostridge, Ian. *Witchcraft and Its Transformations, 1650–1750.* New York: Oxford University Press, 1997.

Bozeman, Theodore Dwight. *Protestants in an Age of Science: The Baconian Ideal and Antebellum American Religious Thought.* Chapel Hill: University of North Carolina Press, 1977.

Brekus, Catherine A. *Strangers and Pilgrims: Female Preaching in America, 1740–1845.* Chapel Hill: University of North Carolina Press, 1998.

Brooke, John L. *The Refiner's Fire: The Making of Mormon Cosmology, 1644–1844.* New York: Cambridge University Press, 1994.

———. "'The True Spiritual Seed': Sectarian Religion and the Persistence of the Occult in Eighteenth-Century New England." In *Wonders of the Invisible World: 1600–1900,* edited by Peter Benes, 107–26. Boston: Boston University Press, 1995.

Brown, Thomas. *An Account of the People Called Shakers.* Troy, NY: Parker and Bliss, 1812.

Brownell, Abner. *Enthusiastical Errors, Transpired and Detected.* New London, CT: Timothy Green, 1783.

Burns, R. M. *The Great Debate on Miracles from Joseph Glanvill to David Hume.* Lewisburg, PA: Bucknell University Press, 1981.

Burr, George Lincoln. *Narratives of New England Witchcraft Cases.* 1914. Mineola, NY: Dover, 2002.

Bushman, Richard. *Joseph Smith: Rough Stone Rolling.* New York: Vintage, 2007.

Bushnell, Horace. *Nature and the Supernatural.* 1858. New York: Scribner, 1886.

Butler, Jon. *Awash in a Sea of Faith.* Cambridge: Harvard University Press, 1990.

Butler, Joyce. "Cochranism Delineated: A Twentieth-Century Study." In *Maine in the Early Republic: From Revolution to Statehood,* edited by Charles E. Clark, James S. Leamon, and Karen Bowden, 146–64. Hanover, NH: University Press of New England, 1988.

Byrd, William S. *Letters from a Young Shaker: William S. Byrd at Pleasant Hill.* Edited by Stephen Stein. Lexington: University Press of Kentucky, 1985.

Campbell, Alexander. *Delusions: An Analysis of the Book of Mormon.* Boston: Benjamin Greene, 1832.

Carnahan, James. *Christianity Defended.* Utica, NY: Seward and Williams, 1808.

Catlin, George. *North American Indians.* Edited by Peter Matthiessen. New York: Penguin, 1989.

Cave, Alfred A. *Prophets of the Great Spirit: Native American Revitalization Movements in Eastern North America*. Lincoln: University of Nebraska Press, 2006.

Cervantes, Fernando. *The Devil in the New World*. New Haven: Yale University Press, 1994.

Chadwick, Owen. *The Secularization of the European Mind in the 19th Century*. New York: Cambridge University Press, 1975.

Chireau, Yvonne P. *Black Magic: Religion and the African American Conjuring Tradition*. Berkeley: University of California Press, 2003.

Clark, Stuart. *Thinking with Demons: The Idea of Witchcraft in Early Modern Europe*. New York: Oxford University Press, 1997.

Code of Handsome Lake. In Arthur C. Parker, *Parker on the Iroquois*, edited by William N. Fenton, 16–80. Syracuse, NY: Syracuse University Press, 1968.

Coffin, Paul. *Memoir and Journals*. Portland, ME: Thurston, 1855.

Complete Fortune Teller. New York, 1799.

Cook, James W. *The Arts of Deception: Playing with Fraud in the Age of Barnum*. Cambridge: Harvard University Press, 2001.

Cross, Whitney. *The Burned-Over District*. Ithaca, NY: Cornell University Press, 1950.

Daston, Lorraine. "Marvelous Facts and Miraculous Evidence in Early Modern Europe." In *Superstition and Magic in Early Modern Europe: A Reader*, edited by Helen Parish, 108–31. New York: Bloomsbury, 2015.

Daston, Lorraine, and Katherine Park, *Wonders and the Order of Nature, 1150–1750*. New York: Zone, 1998.

Davies, Owen. *America Bewitched: The Story of Witchcraft after Salem*. New York: Oxford University Press, 2013.

———. *Grimoires: A History of Magic Books*. New York: Oxford University Press, 2009.

———. *Magic, Witchcraft, and Culture, 1736–1951*. Manchester, UK: Manchester University Press, 1999.

Debate Proposed in the Temple Patrick Society: Whether Witches Had Supernatural Power. Philadelphia: Young, 1788.

Demos, John. *Entertaining Satan*. New York: Oxford University Press, 1982.

Dennis, Matthew. *Seneca Possessed: Indians, Witchcraft, and Power in the Early American Republic*. Philadelphia: University of Pennsylvania Press, 2010.

Designs Against Charleston: The Trial Record of the Denmark Vesey Conspiracy of 1822. Edited by Edward A. Pearson. Chapel Hill: University of North Carolina Press, 1999.

Dillinger, Johannes. *Magical Treasure Hunting in Europe and North America: A History*. New York: Palgrave, 2012.

Doctrine & Covenants. 1835. Independence, MO: Herald Publishing House, 1971.

Doddridge, Joseph. *Notes on the Settlement and Indian Wars of the Western Parts of Virginia and Pennsylvania*. 1912. Parsons, WV: McClain 1960.

Doesticks, Q. K. Philander. *The Witches of New York*. New York: Rudd and Carlton, 1859.

Dowd, Gregory Evans. *A Spirited Resistance: The North American Indian Struggle for Unity, 1745–1815*. Baltimore: Johns Hopkins University Press, 1992.

Drake, Benjamin. *The Life of Tecumseh and of His Brother the Prophet*. 1841. Charleston, SC: BiblioBazaar, 2006.

Draper, Lyman. Draper Manuscripts. State Historical Society of Wisconsin, Madison.

Dwight, Timothy. *Theology Explained and Defended*. New York: Carvill, 1829.

———. *Travels in New-England and New-York*. London: Baynes, 1823.

Finney, Charles G. *Lectures on the Revivals of Religion*. 1835. Edited by Richard M. Friedrich. Fenwick, MI: Alethea in Heart, 2005.

Finucane, Ronald C. *Miracles and Pilgrims: Popular Beliefs in Medieval England*. Totowa, NJ: Rowman and Littlefield, 1977.

Fluhman, Spencer. *"A Peculiar People": Anti-Mormonism and the Making of Religion in Nineteenth-Century America*. Chapel Hill: University of North Carolina Press, 2012.

Fontaine, Felix. *The Golden Wheel Dream-Book*. New York: Dick and Fitzgerald, 1862.

Garraghan, Gilbert. *The Jesuits of the Middle United States*. New York: America Press, 1938.

Garrett, Clarke. *Origins of the Shakers: From the Old World to the New World*. Baltimore: Johns Hopkins University Press, 1998.

Givens, Terryl. *By the Hand of Mormon: The American Scripture that Launched a New World Religion*. New York: Oxford University Press, 2002.

Godbeer, Richard. *The Devil's Dominion: Magic and Religion in Early New England*. New York: Cambridge University Press, 1992.

Gordon, Joshua. Witchcraft Book, 1784. South Caroliniana Manuscripts. University of South Carolina Library.

Gould, Philip. "New England Witch-Hunting and the Politics of Reason in the Early Republic." *New England Quarterly* 68, no. 1 (March 1995): 58–82.

Grimes, William. *The Life of William Grimes*. Edited by William L. Andrews and Regina E. Mason. New York: Oxford University Press, 2008.

Hafez, Ibrahim Ali Mahomed. *The Oneirocritic*. New York, 1790[?].

Hall, David D. *Worlds of Wonder, Days of Judgment: Popular Religious Belief in Early New England*. New York: Knopf, 1989.

Harper, Stephen C. "'Dictated by Christ': Joseph Smith and the Politics of Revelation." *Journal of the Early Republic* 26, no. 2 (Summer 2006): 275–304.

———. "Infallible Proofs, Both Human and Divine: The Persuasiveness of Mormonism for Early Converts." *Religion and American Culture* 10, no. 1 (Winter 2000): 99–118.

Harrison, William Henry. *Messages and Papers of William Henry Harrison*. Edited by Logan Esarey. Indianapolis: Indiana Historical Society, 1922.

Haskett, William. *Shakerism Unmasked*. Pittsfield: B. H. Walldey, 1828.

Hatch, Nathan O. *The Democratization of American Christianity*. New Haven: Yale University Press, 1989.

Hazen, Craig James. *The Village Enlightenment in America*. Urbana: University of Illinois Press, 2000.

Heckewelder, John. *Account of the History, Manners, and Customs of the Indian Nations*. Philadelphia: Committee of History, Moral Science, and General Literature, 1819.

Herring, Joseph B. *Kenekuk, the Kickapoo Prophet*. Lawrence: University Press of Kansas, 1988.

Heyrman, Christine. *Southern Cross: The Beginnings of the Bible Belt*. New York: Knopf, 1997.

Hubbard, Gurdan S. "A Kickapoo Sermon." *Illinois Monthly Magazine* 1 (1831): 473–76.

Hill, Marvin S. *Quest for Refuge: The Mormon Flight from American Pluralism*. Salt Lake City: Signature, 1989.

"History of the Divining Rod: With the Adventures of an Old Rodsman." *United States Magazine and Democratic Review* 26 (1850): 218–25, 317–27.

Hohman, Johann George. *The Long-Lost Friend: A 19th Century Grimoire*. Edited by Daniel Harms. Woodbury, MN: Llewellyn, 2012.

Hovenkamp, Herbert. *Science and Religion in America, 1800–1860*. Philadelphia: University of Pennsylvania Press, 1978.

Howe, E. D. *History of Mormonism*. Painesville, OH: 1840.

———. *Mormonism Unvailed*. Painesville, OH, 1834.

Hudson, David. *Memoir of Jemima Wilkinson*. 1821. New York: AMS, 1972.

Hunter, Charles. "The Delaware Nativist Revival of the Mid-Eighteenth Century." *Ethnohistory* 18, no. 1 (1971): 39–49.

Hutchinson, Francis. *Historical Essay Concerning Witchcraft*. London, 1718.

Hutchinson, Thomas. *History of the Colony and Province of Massachusetts-Bay*. 1797. Edited by Lawrence Shaw Mayo. Cambridge: Harvard University Press, 1936.

Jackson, Andrew. *Papers of Andrew Jackson*. Edited by Harold D. Moser et al. Knoxville: University of Tennessee Press, 1991.

Jackson, Halliday. *Civilization of the Indian Natives*. Philadelphia: Marcus Gould, 1830.

———. "Halliday Jackson's Journal, to the Seneca Indians, 1798–1800." Edited by Anthony F. C. Wallace. *Pennsylvania History* 19, no. 2 (April 1952): 117–47, and no. 3, 325–49.

Jackson, Rebecca. *Gifts of Power: The Writings of Rebecca Jackson, Black Visionary, Shaker Eldress*. Edited by Jean Humez. Amherst: University of Massachusetts Press, 1981.

Jefferson, Thomas. *Papers of Thomas Jefferson*. Edited by Barbara Oberg. Princeton: Princeton University Press, 2003.

Jillson, Clark, ed. *Green Leaves from Whitingham, Vermont*. Worcester, MA, 1894.

Jortner, Adam. *The Gods of Prophetstown.* New York: Oxford University Press, 2012.

Juster, Susan. *Doomsayers: Anglo-American Prophecy in the Age of Revolution.* Philadelphia: University of Pennsylvania Press, 2003.

Juster, Susan, and Ellen Hartigan-O'Connor. "The 'Angel Delusion' of 1806–1811: Frustration and Fantasy in Northern New England." *Journal of the Early Republic* 22, no. 3 (Autumn 2002): 375–404.

Kirkham, Francis, W., ed. *New Witness for Christ in America.* Independence, MO: Zion's, 1951.

Kirkland, Samuel. *The Journals of Samuel Kirkland.* Edited by Walter Pilkington. Clinton, NY: Hamilton, 1980.

Klaniczay, Gábor. *The Uses of Supernatural Power: The Transformation of Popular Religion in Medieval and Early Modern Europe.* Princeton: Princeton University Press, 1990.

Krampl, Ulrike. "When Witches Became False: *Séducteurs* and *Crédules* Confront the Paris Police at the Beginning of the Eighteenth Century." In *Werewolves, Witches, and Wandering Spirits: Traditional Belief & Folklore in Early Modern Europe,* edited by Kathryn A. Edwards, 137–54. Kirksville, MO: Truman State University Press, 2002.

Lamson, David. *Two Years' Experience among the Shakers.* West Boylston, MA, 1848.

Larson, Scott. "'Indescribable Being': Theological Performances of Genderlessness in the Society of the Publick Universal Friend, 1776–1819." *Early American Studies* 12, no. 3 (Fall 2014): 576–600.

Lathrop, Joseph. *Illustrations and Reflections on the Story of Saul's Consulting the Witch of Endor.* Springfield, MA: Henry Brewer, 1806.

Launius, Roger D., and Linda Thatcher, eds. *Differing Visions: Dissenters in Mormon History.* Urbana: University of Illinois Press, 1994.

Lee, John D. *Mormonism Unveiled.* 1891. Albuquerque: University of New Mexico Press, 2008.

Levack, Brian. *Witch-Hunting in Scotland: Law, Politics, and Religion.* New York: Routledge, 2008.

Leventhal, Herbert. *In the Shadow of the Enlightenment.* New York: New York University Press, 1976.

Lewis, Alonzo. *History of Lynn.* Boston: J. H. Eastburn, 1829.

Lewis, Andrew. *A Democracy of Facts.* Philadelphia: University of Pennsylvania Press, 2011.

Library of Congress Shaker Collection of Records.

Lincoln, Enoch. *The Village.* Portland, MA [ME]: Edward Little, 1816.

MacLean, J. P. *The Shakers of Ohio.* Philadelphia: Porcupine, 1975.

Manuel, Frank. *The Eighteenth Century Confronts the Gods.* Cambridge: Harvard University Press, 1959.

Marini, Stephen A. *Radical Sects of Revolutionary New England.* Cambridge: Harvard University Press, 1982.

Mather, Cotton. *Magnalia Christi Americana*. New York: Russell and Russell, 1967.

———. *Wonders of the Invisible World*. Boston, 1693.

McAfee, Robert Breckinridge. *History of the Late War in the Western Country*. 1816. Bowling Green, OH: Historical Publications Company, 1919.

———. *Journal, 1803–7*. Filson Historical Society, Louisville, KY.

McLellin, William. *The Journals of William McLellin*. Edited by Jan Shipps and John Welch. Provo, UT: BYU Studies, 1994.

McLoughlin, William. *New England Dissent, 1630–1833*. Cambridge: Harvard University Press, 1971.

McNemar, Richard. *The Kentucky Revival*. Albany, NY: Hosford, 1808.

Merchant of Boston. *Nahant, and Other Places on the North-Shore*. Boston: William Chadwick, 1848.

Midelfort, H. C. Erik. *Exorcism and Enlightenment: Johann Joseph Gassner and the Demons of Eighteenth-Century Germany*. New Haven: Yale University Press, 2005.

Miller, Jay. "The 1806 Purge among the Indiana Delaware: Sorcery, Gender, Boundaries, and Legitimacy." *Ethnohistory* 41, no. 2 (Spring 1994): 245–66.

Modern, John Lardas. *Secularism in Antebellum America*. Chicago: University of Chicago Press, 2011.

Monod, Paul. *Solomon's Secret Arts*. New York: Oxford University Press, 2013.

Mooney, James. *The Ghost Dance Religion and the Sioux Outbreak of 1890*. Washington: Government Printing Office, 1896.

Moravian Indian Mission on White River: Diaries and Letters. Translated by Lawrence Henry Gipson. Edited by Harry T. Stocker, Herman T. Frueaff, and Samuel C. Zeller. Indianapolis: Indiana Historical Bureau, 1938.

More, Hannah. *The Selected Writings of Hannah More*. Edited by Robert Hole. London: Pickering, 1996.

Morgan, Lewis. *The League of the Iroquois*. 1851. New York: Corinth, 1962.

Morgan, Philip D. *Slave Counterpoint: Black Culture in the Eighteenth-Century Chesapeake & Lowcountry*. Chapel Hill: University of North Carolina Press, 1998.

Neal, John. *Rachel Dyer*. Portland, ME: Shirley and Hyde, 1828.

New Dream Book, or Interpretation of Remarkable Dreams. Boston: Coverly, 1815.

New Dream Book or Interpretation of Remarkable Dreams. Baltimore, 1816.

Oehler, Andrew. *The Life, Adventures, and Unparalleled Sufferings of Andrew Oehler*. Trenton, NJ: D. Fenton, 1811.

Pater, Erra. *The Book of Knowledge*. Boston: Folsom and Larkin, 1787.

Peter Elmer, "Saints or Sorcerers? Quakerism, Demonology, and the Decline of Witchcraft in Seventeenth-Century England." In *Witchcraft in Early Modern Europe: Studies in Culture and Belief*, edited by Jonathan Barry, Marianne Hester, and Gareth Roberts, 145–79. New York: Cambridge University Press, 1996.

Philanthropist. *An Account of the Beginnings, Transactions, and Discovery, of Ransford Rogers*. Newark, NJ: John Woods, 1792.

Pinchbeck, William. *The Expositor, or Many Mysteries Unraveled*. Boston, 1805.

————. *Witchcraft, or the Art of Fortune-Telling Unveiled*. Boston, 1805.

Porter, Roy. "Witchcraft and Magic in Enlightenment, Romantic, and Liberal Thought." In *Witchcraft and Magic: The Eighteenth and Nineteenth Centuries*, edited by Bengt Ankarloo and Stuart Clark, 191–282. Philadelphia: University of Pennsylvania Press, 1999.

Pratt, Parley P. *A Dialogue between Josh. Smith and the Devil*. N.p., 1844.

Quinn, D. Michael. *Early Mormonism and the Magic World View*. Salt Lake City: Signature, 1998.

Quitman, Frederick. *A Treatise on Magic*. Albany, NY: Balance, 1810.

Rankin, Adam. *Review of the Noted Revival in Kentucky*. Pittsburgh: John Israel, 1802.

Rathbun, Valentine. *An Account of the Matter, Form, and Manner of a New and Strange Religion*. Providence: Bennett Wheeler, 1781.

Reese, David. *Humbugs of New-York*. New York: John Taylor, 1838.

Ridlon, G. T. *Saco Valley Settlements and Families*. Rutland, VT: Tuttle, 1895.

Rigdon, Sidney. *Oration Delivered by Mr. S. Rigdon on the 4th of July, 1838*. Far West, MO, 1838.

Rosenfeld, Sophia. *Common Sense: A Political History*. Cambridge: Harvard University Press, 2011.

Russel, Chloe. *The Complete Fortune Teller and Dream Book*. In "'The Complete Fortune Teller and Dream Book': An Antebellum Text 'By Chloe Russel, a Woman of Colour,'" by Eric Gardner. *New England Quarterly* 78, no. 2 (June 2005): 259–88.

Savery, William. *Journal of the Life, Travels, and Religious Labors of William Savery*. Compiled by Jonathan Evans. London: Charles Gilpin, 1844.

Schmidt, Leigh Eric. *Hearing Things: Religion, Illusion, and the American Enlightenment*. Cambridge: Harvard University Press, 2000.

Schoolcraft, Henry Rowe. *Algic Researches*. 1839. Mineola, NY: Dover, 1999.

Schultz, Nancy Lusignan. *Mrs. Mattingly's Miracle*. New Haven: Yale University Press, 2011.

Shaker Collection of the Western Reserve Historical Society. Glen Rock, NJ.

Shapiro, Barbara. *A Culture of Fact: England 1550–1720*. Ithaca, NY: Cornell University Press, 2000.

Sharpe, James. *Instruments of Darkness: Witchcraft in Early Modern England*. Philadelphia: University of Pennsylvania Press, 1996.

Shaw, Jane. *Miracles in Enlightenment England*. New Haven: Yale University Press, 2006.

Sibly, Ebenezer. *A New and Complete Illustration of the Occult Sciences*. London: C. Stalker, 1795.

Smith, Gamaliel. *Report of the Trial of Jacob Cochrane*. Kennebunk, MA [ME]: James K. Remich, 1819.

Smith, James. *Remarkable Occurrences Lately Discovered among the People Called Shakers*. Carthage, TN: William Moore, 1810.

————. *Shakerism Detected*. Paris, KY: Joel Lyle, 1810.

Smith, Joseph, Jr. *History of the Church of Jesus Christ of Latter-day Saints*. 1839. Edited by B. H. Roberts. Salt Lake City: Deseret, 1971.

Sneddon, Andrew. *Witchcraft and Whigs: The Life of Bishop Francis Hutchinson*. Manchester, UK: Manchester University Press, 2008.

Spencer, John. *A Discourse Concerning Prodigies*. Cambridge: John Field, 1663.

Statutes at Large of South Carolina. Edited by Thomas Cooper. Columbia: A. S. Johnston, 1837.

Stein, Stephen. *The Shaker Experience in America*. New Haven: Yale University Press, 1992.

Stewart, I. D. *History of the Freewill Baptists*. Dover, NH: William Burr, 1862.

Stiggins, George. *Creek Indian History*. Edited by Virginia Pounds Brown. Birmingham, AL: Birmingham Public Library Press, 1989.

Stiles, Ezra. *Literary Diary*. New York: Scribner, 1901.

Stinchfield, Ephraim. *Cochranism Delineated*. Boston: Hews and Goss, 1819.

Stroyer, Jacob. *My Life in the South*. Salem: Salem Observer, 1885.

Taylor, Alan. "The Early Republic's Supernatural Economy: Treasure Seeking in the American Northeast, 1780–1830." *American Quarterly* 38, no. 1 (Spring 1986): 6–34.

Testimonies of the Ever Blessed Mother Ann Lee. Hancock, MA: Talcott and Deming, 1816.

Testimony of Christ's Second Appearing. Lebanon, OH: McLean, 1808.

Testimony of Christ's Second Appearing. Albany: Hosford, 1810.

Thacher, James. *An Essay on Demonology, Ghosts, and Apparitions*. Boston: Carter and Hendee, 1831.

Thomas, Keith. *Religion and the Decline of Magic*. 1971. New York: Scribner, 1999.

Upham, Charles. *Lectures on Witchcraft Comprising a History of the Delusion at Salem in 1692*. Boston: Carter, Hendee, and Babcock, 1832.

———. *Salem Witchcraft*. 1867. Mineola, NY: Dover, 2000.

Wallace, Anthony F. C. *The Death and Rebirth of the Seneca*. New York: Vintage, 1969.

Walsham, Alexandra. *Providence in Early Modern England*. New York: Oxford University Press, 1999.

Ward, Benedicta. *Miracles and the Medieval Mind*. Philadelphia: University of Pennsylvania Press, 1982.

Webster, Noah. *American Dictionary of the English Language*. New York: Converse, 1828.

Wergland, Glendyne R., ed. *Visiting the Shakers, 1778–1849*. Clinton, NY: Richard Couper, 2007.

West, Benjamin. *Scriptural Cautions*. Hartford, CT: Webster, 1783.

White, Richard. *The Middle Ground: Indians, Empires, and Republics in the Great Lakes Region, 1650–1815*. New York: Cambridge University Press, 1991.

Whitman, Bernard. *Lecture on Popular Superstitions*. Boston: Bowles and Dearborn, 1829.

Whitmer, John. *From Historian to Dissident: The Book of John Whitmer*. Edited by Bruce Westergren. Salt Lake City: Signature, 1995.

Whittier, John Greenleaf. *Letters of John Greenleaf Whittier*. Edited by John B. Pickard. Cambridge: Belknap Press of Harvard University Press, 1975.

———. *The Supernaturalism of New England*. 1847. Baltimore: Clearfield, 1997.

Wilkinson, Jemima. Papers, 1771–1849. Cornell University Regional History and University Archives.

Winiarski, Douglas. "'Pale Blewish Lights' and a Dead Man's Groan: Tales of the Supernatural from Eighteenth-Century Plymouth, Massachusetts." *William and Mary Quarterly*, 3rd ser., vol. 55, no. 4 (October 1998): 497–530.

Winn, Kenneth H. *Exiles in a Land of Liberty: Mormons in America 1830–1846*. Chapel Hill: University of North Carolina Press, 1990.

Wisbey, Herbert A. *Pioneer Prophetess: Jemima Wilkinson, the Publick Universal Friend*. Ithaca, NY: Cornell University Press, 1964.

Young, David. *The Wonderful History of the Morristown Ghost: Thoroughly and Carefully Revised*. Newark, NJ: Benjamin Olds, 1826.

Zeisberger, David. *History of the Northern American Indians*. Columbus: Heer, 1910.

———. *Moravian Mission Diaries of David Zeisberger*. Edited by Hermann Wellenreuther and Carola Wessel. Translated by Julie T. Weber. University Park: Pennsylvania State University Press, 2005.

Index

Recent Books in the Jeffersonian America Series

Maurizio Valsania
Nature's Man: Thomas Jefferson's Philosophical Anthropology

John Ragosta
Religious Freedom: Jefferson's Legacy, America's Creed

Robert M. S. McDonald, editor
Sons of the Father: George Washington and His Protégés

Simon P. Newman and Peter S. Onuf, editors
Paine and Jefferson in the Age of Revolutions

Daniel Peart
Era of Experimentation: American Political Practices in the Early Republic

Margaret Sumner
Collegiate Republic: Cultivating an Ideal Society in Early America

Christa Dierksheide
Amelioration and Empire: Progress and Slavery in the Plantation Americas

John A. Ruddiman
Becoming Men of Some Consequence: Youth and Military Service in the Revolutionary War

Jonathan J. Den Hartog
Patriotism and Piety: Federalist Politics and Religious Struggle in the New American Nation

Patrick Griffin, Robert G. Ingram, Peter S. Onuf, and Brian Schoen, editors
Between Sovereignty and Anarchy: The Politics of Violence in the American Revolutionary Era

Armin Mattes
Citizens of a Common Intellectual Homeland: The Transatlantic Origins of American Democracy and Nationhood

Julia Gaffield, editor
The Haitian Declaration of Independence: Creation, Context, and Legacy

Robert M. S. McDonald
Confounding Father: Thomas Jefferson's Image in His Own Time

Adam Jortner
Blood from the Sky: Miracles and Politics in the Early American Republic